Beyond the Veil

Beyond the Veil
Reflexive Studies of Death and Dying

Edited by
Aubrey Thamann and Kalliopi M Christodoulaki

berghahn
NEW YORK • OXFORD
www.berghahnbooks.com

First published in 2021 by
Berghahn Books
www.berghahnbooks.com

© 2021, 2024 Aubrey Thamann and Kalliopi M Christodoulaki
First paperback edition published in 2024

All rights reserved. Except for the quotation of short passages for the purposes of criticism and review, no part of this book may be reproduced in any form or by any means, electronic or mechanical, including photocopying, recording, or any information storage and retrieval system now known or to be invented, without written permission of the publisher.

Library of Congress Cataloging-in-Publication Data

Names: Thamann, Aubrey, editor. | Christodoulaki, Kalliopi M, editor.
Title: Beyond the Veil: Reflexive Studies of Death and Dying / edited by Aubrey Thamann and Kalliopi M Christodoulaki.
Description: New York: Berghahn Books, 2021. | Includes bibliographical references and index.
Identifiers: LCCN 2021010650 (print) | LCCN 2021010651 (ebook) | ISBN 9781800730649 (hardback) | ISBN 9781800730656 (ebook)
Subjects: LCSH: Death. | Bereavement—Psychological aspects.
Classification: LCC HQ1073 .B49 2021 (print) | LCC HQ1073 (ebook) | DDC 306.9—dc23
LC record available at https://lccn.loc.gov/2021010650
LC ebook record available at https://lccn.loc.gov/2021010651

British Library Cataloguing in Publication Data

A catalogue record for this book is available from the British Library

ISBN 978-1-80073-064-9 hardback
ISBN 978-1-80539-322-1 paperback
ISBN 978-1-80539-435-8 epub
ISBN 978-1-80073-065-6 web pdf

https://doi.org/10.3167/9781800730649

Contents

List of Figures vii

Introduction 1
    Aubrey Thamann and Kalliopi M Christodoulaki

PART I. Delaying Death

1. An Absent Presence: The Co-constitution of Loss 13
   Alison Witchard

2. Immortality and Existential Terror: Learning the Language of Living Forever 29
   Jeremy Cohen

PART II. Caregiving

3. Living, Caring, and Dying: Music and the House of Endless Losses 53
   Carina Nandlal

4. Death and Fulfillment: Mortuary Performance and the Impact on Self 69
   Kalliopi M Christodoulaki

PART III. Confronting Death

5. Crossroads: Life and Death in Indiana 89
   Aubrey Thamann

6. "What Has the Field Done to You?" Researching Death, Dying, and Bereavement between Closeness and Distance 109
   Ekkehard Coenen

7. The Historical Study of Death and Dying:
   The Intersection of Familial Stories and Catholic Rituals   125
   Sarah Nytroe

PART IV. Memorialization

8. Touch 'Em All: Memorializing Harmon Killebrew   151
   Debbie A. Hanson

9. After Life: Laying Flower Memes on My Mother's Grave
   and the Recollective Realm of Life after Death   167
   Olivia Guntarik and Claudia Bellote

10. A Monumental Problem: Memorializing the
    Jonestown Dead   187
    Rebecca Moore

11. Long Live Chill: Exploring Grief, Memorial, and Ritual
    within African American R.I.P. T-shirt Culture   209
    Kami Fletcher

Conclusion   235
   Kalliopi M Christodoulaki and Aubrey Thamann

Index   243

Figures

9.1 A shrine for the author's deceased mother. Photo by Olivia Guntarik. 168
9.2 Photographs and a postcard written by the author to her mother. Photo by Olivia Guntarik. 171
10.1 Monument placed at Evergreen Cemetery by the Emergency Relief Committee in 1979. Photo by Laura Johnston Kohl, courtesy The Jonestown Institute. 191
10.2 The four plaques comprising the monument devoted to those who died 18 November 1978, dedicated at Evergreen Cemetery in May 2011. Photo by Mercurywoodrose, courtesy Wikimedia Creative Commons. 196
10.3 Flowers laid upon the new plaque, 2011. Photo by Laura Johnston Kohl, courtesy The Jonestown Institute. 197
10.4 The monument at Evergreen Cemetery was completely refurbished for the fortieth anniversary of Jonestown, 2018. Photo by Laura Johnston Kohl, courtesy The Jonestown Institute. 201
10.5 A pillow monument commemorating the 2011 dedication of the new monument was installed for the fortieth anniversary observance, 2018. Photo by Laura Johnston Kohl, courtesy The Jonestown Institute. 202
11.1 *Left*: Author wears Willie's official R.I.P. t-shirt and symbolically takes him with her to Hangzhou, China. *Right*: Willie's official R.I.P. t-shirt. Photos by Kami Fletcher and Valeria Brunson. 208
11.2 Willie's family, by blood or bond, wearing the official R.I.P. t-shirt. *Left to right*: close friend Jarren; cousin Candice; cousin Valeria. Photos by Jarren Jefferson, Candice Taylor, and Valeria Brunson. 213

11.3	Examples of unofficial R.I.P. t-shirts for Willie. *Clockwise from left*: Snooky, Willie's mother, at her place of work. Cousin Jonathan pictured before going out for weekend fun. Cousin Arianna, during the days before the funeral, wearing the hooded sweatshirt that she had commissioned as an unofficial R.I.P. t-shirt. An unofficial R.I.P. t-shirt with heaven's golden streets, lots of money cascading in the background, and an altered picture of Willie with angel wings alongside the woman who commissioned the shirt. Photos by Aleta "Snooky" Fletcher, Jonathan Thompson, and Arianna Winters.	214
11.4	Wearing an R.I.P. t-shirt dedicated to his friend Neech, Yorrel Hughes poses with his daughter. Photo by Yorrel Hughes.	217
11.5	The Shorter family memorializing the passing and celebrating the life of Jason Shorter. The top picture is at the repast—Jason Shorter's mother (in the middle), father (in the white baseball cap), and Jason's cousins. The bottom picture is Jason's first postmortem birthday celebration, complete with birthday cake (as pictured). Photos by Cozetta Phillips.	220
11.6	Posing for a picture after bowling, Willie's family celebrates his first postmortem birthday. The day included a balloon release at the cemetery, bowling, and a celebration at a dance hall with a DJ and live music. Family members are shown presenting a hand sign to signal the letter "L," meaning "Long Live Chill." This is an expression used to invoke Willie's memory and never forget his life. Photo by Aleta "Snooky" Fletcher.	221
11.7	Cousin Jakihia clutches the R.I.P. hoodie for her little brother E. J., who passed away in 2007 at only four months old. Cousin Shanicqua (third from the left, wearing ripped, knee-less denim blue jeans) dons an unofficial R.I.P t-shirt for Willie. Her R.I.P. t-shirt features the two of them FaceTiming. The high-resolution picture resulted in the shirt costing fifty dollars. This picture was taken in 2017 at Jakihia's aunt Caroll's (in the middle wearing the white long-sleeved blouse) fiftieth birthday party. Photo by Shanicqua Wise.	222

Introduction

Aubrey Thamann and Kalliopi M Christodoulaki

> Death is our constant companion, and it is
> death that gives each person's life its true meaning.
> —Paulo Coelho, *The Diary of a Magus*[1]

The editors of this collection met in 2003 while working on their doctoral studies at Purdue University. Death was a topic we both gravitated toward as graduate students, and mortuary practices became an important part of both of our graduate work. We stayed in touch after completing our degrees and talked about working together in the future. We reconnected in 2012 at the memorial celebration held for O. M. Watson, a beloved emeritus professor in our anthropology department, who was also my mentor and one of the reasons Kalliopi became an anthropologist. In 2017, I was asked by the sociology department at Wittenberg University in Ohio to present my research at their biannual colloquium. In preparing for this talk, I revisited the funeral directors I had spent so much time with and the family members and friends I had lost during my studies. I knew it was time to collaborate. Kalliopi and I both found this topic to be so beautiful and meaningful in its simplicity, yet no one had done this kind of study. Our work within our respective disciplines had exposed us to reflexivity and studying mortuary practices as participant observers, but we had not come across a study that connected the two. I reached out to Kalliopi and we put together a call for papers. The response took us by surprise; people from a variety of disciplines contacted us about their work. From these, we selected those who understood what we wanted to explore. The resultant collection is a collaboration of like-minded scholars whose experiences with death profoundly shaped their scholarly work.

This interdisciplinary collection of essays utilizes reflexive scholarly inquiry to interrogate cultural responses to dying and death. The essays analyze various aspects of death while acknowledging that death affects us all, including researchers who study death. Any analysis of the topic cannot be decontextualized; yet, almost all academic studies of death ignore the scholar's relationship to death and mortality. This is short-sighted, as we must all inevitably grapple with loss and mortality as we examine cultural responses to death. In this work we try to rectify this omission by highlighting how the contributors have both critically viewed mortuary practices as observers/researchers while also being emotionally invested participants.

In his essay "Death in the Ethnographic Present," Renato Rosaldo questions the traditional ways of analyzing death and bereavement in ethnographic work. He writes:

> Ethnographic writing concentrates, in short, on routine expressions of grief and programmed ways of handling the corpse immediately after death. Thus the central subjects become the least involved and the deceased rather than the chief mourners. In all cases, the ethnographer stands as spectator, witnessing events from the outside and not asking people about their subjective experiences. Most ethnographic accounts see grief in partial and mechanistic ways and even remain sceptical about the emotional experience of grieving. They (implausibly) maintain that the work of mourning occurs only in connection with formal rituals.[2]

Rosaldo then includes excerpts from a journal he kept in the months following his wife's death, as well as those from several other authors, as examples of how grief could be portrayed in U.S. culture. His focus is on bereavement, on the emotions felt. The funeral rituals were important but not central. In conducting cultural analysis, then, why do we largely ignore bereavement?

Rosaldo argues that "the problem with ethnographic writing on death resides … in an excessive reliance on a metaphoric rather than a metonymic analysis of culture in general and ritual in particular … rituals are regarded as coherent arenas within which cultural wisdom can be explored."[3] The examples of this are easy to find. Rosaldo offers some in this essay. We often forget (or ignore) that even we as cultural analysts are still subject to the pull and sway of our own cultures. In suffering a loss, we grieve; others merely follow ritual.

Émile Durkheim wrote of the significance of rituals in this metaphoric way. In discussing mourning rituals, examples of what he called "piacular rites," or those rites that require or are equivalent to atonement, he wrote of both negative and positive rites—taboos and performative acts.[4] Positive rites exist, for Durkheim, to create and maintain social solidarity; this is primarily the result of a force arising from participation in a shared system of beliefs and values, which molds and controls individual behavior. In this functionalist approach, mourning does not represent feelings but instead exists as the rituals performed to sustain social connections and one's role in society. Specific mourners perform specific acts based on relation to the deceased. These roles are usually divided by gender and lineal relation, such as maternal male kin, wives, sons, or daughters. Mourning ritual acts are performed not out of any real feeling of loss but because these acts serve to reify social connections and roles.

Durkheim argued further that once mourning is performed to completion, it is over. For Durkheim, mourning is not a spontaneous, emotionally based reaction to a death but rather a demonstration that the loss has actually had an effect. Any way we might physically demonstrate grief—whether through crying, wailing, self-harm, or other ways—merely fulfills a social obligation.[5] Durkheim did not see mourning and the rituals performed surrounding the death of a family or community member in relation to emotions expressed but as means to cement social ties.

Durkheim also argued that mourning rituals are obligatory, both from a societal point of view and from that of the individual. He wrote, "For a family to tolerate that one of its members should die without being mourned would give witness thereby that it lacks moral unity and cohesiveness."[6] A society, according to Durkheim, functions the same way—it needs to demonstrate that the individual plays an important role in social cohesion in order for the individual to work toward that same social cohesion.

The authors in this collection do not believe that mourning rituals are performed solely to maintain social ties; rather, this is merely a result of performing them instead of the sole reason. It makes sense to provide a funeral for a deceased person. After all, we want to know that we matter. Funerals show that the deceased mattered in life, and we want funerals for ourselves for the same reason. Social cohesion can be maintained by demonstrating that individuals are important and that their absence has a collective effect. However, most of the authors herein have lost people and know that feelings accompanying loss are very real—anger, sorrow, guilt, and even happiness.

Further, the mourning process is hardly over once the rituals are completed. Rosaldo continued to write about his wife's death and its effect on his research for years after she died. In chapter 5, Aubrey Thamann discusses a cousin taking her wedding ring back thirteen years after the suicide of her husband. Rebecca Moore is still working on how to properly memorialize her family members and others who died at Jonestown. Grief is not over once the funeral ritual has concluded. Durkheim saw the actions performed as being the only (or at least most important) aspect of the funeral process, and as having one sole function—that is, the maintenance of social structure. Yet the authors in this collection demonstrate that the rituals can be a vehicle through which we can express those feelings and that people do not always mourn according to custom, or even at all.

Durkheim is not alone in his assessment of the important role funeral rites play in creating social solidarity and how relationships can be demonstrated through mourning ritual. David Mandelbaum, in his chapter in Feifel's interdisciplinary collection on death, writes:

> Participation in the ceremony has yet another effect on the participants. It gives them a renewed sense of belonging to a social whole, to the entire community. ... The villagers and visitors go in procession, led by music, to clear the cremation ground, build the pyre, prepare the feast, and do other work in preparation for the ceremony. These group activities and the dancing which follows not only bring general enjoyment but enhance feelings of social unison.[7]

Later he argues that "rites performed for the dead generally have important effects for the living. A funeral ceremony is personal in its focus and is societal in its consequences."[8] Much like Durkheim, Mandelbaum sees the essential nature of mourning ritual for social cohesion, but is this the only point? The authors in this collection demonstrate that it is not.

Vicki Lensing tells us that funerals have several goals, including those that are physical, social, psychological, and sometimes religious. She writes:

> The social goal is to provide group support for the mourners by the community recognizing the change in relationships brought about by the death. The psychological goals are to assist the mourners in accepting the reality of the death and provide a starting point to process the feelings associated with grief.[9]

Lensing, a funeral director, wrote this article to speak directly to her colleagues in the funeral industry, but it is relevant here. She recognizes the significance to social solidarity, here discussed as "relationships," but notes with the deeper analysis Rosaldo argues for that the emotions connected to loss are equally important. This collection is meant to continue the discussion started by Rosaldo.</FL>

One impetus for the undertaking of this project was to bring together individuals who would add to the conversation begun by Renato Rosaldo's influential essay "Grief and a Headhunter's Rage," in which he questions the privileged position of the researchers along with the problems that arise when you try to apply a Western scientific model to studying culture. In this essay, Rosaldo discusses his initial objective analysis of why the Ilongot people practiced headhunting. He laments his inability to really connect to the practice, which his consultants explained by saying that "rage, born of grief, impels [them] to kill [their] fellow human beings."[10] Rosaldo goes on to say that he did not understand the practice largely because he did not understand the connection of grief to rage. Up to that point, he had not experienced a loss that filled him with both emotions. He writes, "The *emotional force* of a death, for example, derives less from an abstract brute fact than from a particular intimate relation's permanent rupture."[11] Rosaldo then explains that following the death of his brother in 1970, he began to understand the connection the Ilongot felt between grief and rage, but it was not until the sudden death of his wife shortly after beginning fieldwork with the Ifugaos, also of the Philippines, that he truly understood. He writes, "Immediately on finding her body I became enraged. How could she abandon me? How could she have been so stupid as to fall? I tried to cry. I sobbed, but rage blocked the tears."[12] It is in this moment that Rosaldo finally internalized the reason the Ilongot practiced headhunting.

Connected to our collection is Rosaldo's use of this reflexivity—this placement of his own experiences in tandem with those of the people whose cultures he studied. Rosaldo tells us that his "use of personal experience serves as a vehicle for making the quality and intensity of the rage in Ilongot grief more readily accessible to readers than certain more detached modes of composition."[13] This is what we've done here—the authors in this collection have used their personal experiences to make their research more relatable to our readers. We have all utilized reflexivity to bolster our work.

Our collection shows the universality of death as a topic of study across disciplines while adding a seldom-heard voice to the conversation: that of the researcher. The scholars herein are able to conduct a much deeper analysis of their subject matter by connecting their own experiences with bereavement. The results thus contribute both as additions to the scholarly conversation of each author's specific field and as an overall collection.

The move toward a more reflexive study of culture began in anthropology in the 1970s, although the concept had been around for several decades by that time.[14] Rosaldo illuminated how an objective, scientific approach when dealing with death and grief did not allow one to truly understand those experiencing loss. By bringing our awareness to ourselves, we do not deny that we are impacted by these events. In some instances, we had to confront our own impending death, even when, as Freud wrote, "our own death is indeed unimaginable, and whenever we make the attempt to imagine it we can perceive that we really survive as spectators."[15] We are all spectators to the world around us, including when we contemplate our death or the death of a loved one. The importance of reflexivity is that in our postmodern world, one that questions science and objectivity, we can with this study show continuities between the researchers. For as Philip Carl Salzman argued, "The way to improve ethnographic research is, thus, not for the solitary researcher to delve within him- or herself, or to make him- or herself the subject of the account, but to replace solitary research with collaborative, team research, in which the perspective and insights of each researcher can be challenged and tested by the others."[16] That is what we have tried to do with this research. We wanted to examine how death, a normal biological process, impacts all of us, not just those we have chosen to study.

Each author selected has a unique perspective on an observance relating to the dead, death, or dying. Some have had close ties to either the terminally ill or the deceased; others have extrapolated from what they have observed as bystanders to an expansion or modification of the researcher's own philosophy or emotional state relating to dying and/or death. These accounts each include both a critical analysis of the practices witnessed and an understanding of the emotional component that all aspects of death provoke in humans, whether it is disgust, fear, awe, sadness, anger, or even joy. As Jean L. Briggs showed so clearly in her ethnography *Never in Anger: Portrait of an Eskimo Family*,[17] the thoughts and emotions of the researcher and of those being researched can be incorporated in a meaningful way into the study and subsequent analysis of the topic being investigated. The outcome is a better understanding of cultural practices and the various perspectives and feelings individuals have about a particular topic. We found that all the contributors helped to illuminate both their thoughts and feelings along with those of their research subjects.

The contributors in part 1 of this collection consider what it means to fear death and how their study subjects might put death off for as long as they can. For the first chapter, "An Absent Presence: The Co-constitution of Loss," Alison Witchard interviewed women who are genetically predisposed to develop breast and ovarian cancer, many of whom elected to have preventative mastectomies and risk-reducing bilateral salpingo-oophorectomy. Alongside this, Witchard contemplates how the loss of her own grandmother, her first major loss, affected how she as a researcher came to understand the choices made by her consultants, whether that meant preventative surgery or not. In chapter 2, "Immortality and Existential Terror: Learning the Language of Living Forever," Jeremy Cohen writes about the time he spent at RAADfest—an annual conference "dedicated to radical longevity and life-extension." As Cohen discusses his fieldwork with people who believe they have unlocked the secret to immortality, he reflects on his own near-death experiences as well as the death of his great-uncle, ultimately questioning the various ways people try to mitigate their fears of death and dying.

In part 2 we move closer to death, as the authors in this section address caregiving at the end of life while grappling with the potential of death. In chapter 3, "Living, Caring, and Dying: Music and the House of Endless Losses," Carina Nandlal, an art historian and music scholar, examines what it means to be a caregiver to a person with dementia and how music has helped her and her family cope. Nandlal also more broadly explores the connections of music and empathy to cultural understandings of eldercare in present-day Australia. Kalliopi M Christodoulaki considers the consequences of the illness, care, and subsequent death of her grandmother in chapter 4, "Death and Fulfillment: Mortuary Performance and the Impact on Self." Christodoulaki examines the effect this loss has had on her own identity, not only as a granddaughter and member of the community but also as a researcher studying the connections between loss, grief, and identity.

The authors in part 3 confront death, exploring the ritual processes we use as we come to terms and cope with death. Aubrey Thamann discusses the cultural importance of funeral work, weaving in her own experiences with loss and grief in chapter 5, "Crossroads: Life and Death in Indiana." She works to emotionally and theoretically reconcile the losses in her life and comes to understand how funeral directors help bring together people in mourning to help them with the grieving process. In his desire to understand his own research into death work more thoroughly, Ekkehard Coenen became a funeral director while conducting his research in chapter 6, "'What Has the Field Done to You?' Researching Death, Dying, and Bereavement between Closeness and Distance." Coenen focuses specifically on the balance funeral directors must strike between emotional connection and professional distance while working with grieving families and explores how the feelings of disconnection he had from funeral workers changed so that he was able to shape his perspective of the profession and thus impact his writing about the subject. The final chapter in this section, chapter 7, is Sarah Nytroe's "The Historical Study of Death and Dying: The Intersection of Familial Stories and Catholic Rituals," which explores the intersection of the personal and professional realms in her historical research of a "good death" in the Catholic experience. Wanting to connect more deeply to her work, Nytroe began interviewing family members regarding their changing experiences with death before and after Vatican II. She also came to learn how Catholic rituals helped her grandparents deal with the death of their child.

Finally, in part 4, we move beyond the event of death to memorialization. Debbie A. Hanson discusses memorializing Harmon Killebrew, a former Minnesota Twins baseball player, in chapter 8, "Touch 'Em All: Memorializing Harmon Killebrew." Hanson offers us a case study in performative commemoration, including spontaneous shrines, cybershrines, and news articles to show how the death of a popular figure creates a community while highlighting his best attributes. In chapter 9, Olivia Guntarik and Claudia Bellote intersperse their discussion of cybershrines and digital cemeteries, "After Life: Laying Flower Memes on

My Mother's Grave and the Recollective Realm of Life after Death," with pieces of Guntarik's own cybermemorialization of her mother. Guntarik and Bellote look at what it means to enshrine someone online while navigating through the visits from grief tourists and negative responses from online trolls. The best way to grieve is also discussed in chapter 10. A dispute over the "proper" way to memorialize the dead is at the center of Rebecca Moore's "A Monumental Problem: Memorializing the Jonestown Dead." Moore, who lost three family members at Jonestown, argues that the act of remembering is neither simple nor straightforward, especially in instances of stigmatized death. In the final chapter of this collection, "Long Live Chill: Exploring Grief, Memorial, and Ritual within African American R.I.P. T-shirt Culture," Kami Fletcher analyzes African American death and mourning customs. Her cultural analysis runs parallel to her personal experiences wearing the shirts. Fletcher situates these shirts within the broader history of the American Black experience and connects to her own place in that history. By wearing the t-shirts, mourners take control of how the deceased is remembered. It connects them to those who have passed and is a way to foster ties within the community and in the family.

Through all these accounts we have a view of death as being an impactful event that people address in various ways. Whether trying to prevent it, coming to terms with it alone, or searching for the support of others, we as authors have learned from death, but maybe not enough to understand it. Richard A. Kalish may be correct in saying the following: "Yet, I believe the truth remains that death is one event that our scientists know no more about than the sorcerers in New Guinea. We may know more about how dying occurs, at least the biological aspects, but none of us knows what death is."[18]

What follows is an attempt, as St. Augustine instructed, to "let death be thy teacher."

Aubrey Thamann is an American studies scholar and anthropologist. She received her doctorate from Purdue University in 2016. Her dissertation was an ethnographic study of funeral directors in Indiana, focusing on the social role they play in offering us the much-needed shared experience of collective grief in the funeral. An interdisciplinary scholar at heart, Thamann has begun research into the fields of fat studies and food studies, specifically exploring where these fields intersect.

Kalliopi M Christodoulaki is a cultural anthropologist and independent researcher currently working as a limited term lecturer at Purdue University. She received her doctorate in anthropology from Purdue University in 2010, and her dissertation research focused on gender roles, community identity, and value systems on the island of Karpathos in Greece. Her research interests include religious practices, social identity, and cultural change.

Notes

1. Paulo Coelho, *The Diary of a Magus: The Road to Santiago*, trans. Alan Clarke (San Francisco: HarperCollins, 1992), 123.
2. Renato Rosaldo, "Death in the Ethnographic Present," *Poetics Today* 9, no. 2 (1988): 429.
3. Ibid., 431.
4. Renato Rosaldo, "Grief and a Headhunter's Rage," in *Culture and Truth: The Remaking of Social Analysis* (Boston: Beacon Press, 1993), 1–21.
5. Émile Durkheim, *The Elementary Forms of Religious Life*, trans. Karen E. Fields (New York: The Free Press, 2001), 392–93.
6. Ibid., 400.
7. David G. Mandelbaum, "Social Uses of Funeral Rites," in *The Meaning of Death*, ed. Herman Feifel (New York: McGraw-Hill Book Company, 1959), 196.
8. Ibid., 189.
9. Vicki Lensing, "Grief Support: The Role of Funeral Service," *Journal of Loss and Trauma* 6 (2001): 49.
10. Rosaldo, "Grief and a Headhunter's Rage," 1.
11. Ibid., 2, italics in original.
12. Ibid., 9.
13. Ibid., 11.
14. See Philip Carl Salzman, "On Reflexivity," *American Anthropologist* 104, no. 3 (2002): 805–13.
15. Sigmund Freud, "Thoughts for the Times on War and Death," *In Civilization, War and Death*, Psycho-Analytical Epitomes 4, ed. John Rickman (London: Hogarth Press and The Institute of Psycho-Analysis, 1953), 92.
16. Salzman, "On Reflexivity," 812.
17. Jean L. Briggs, *Never in Anger: Portrait of an Eskimo Family* (Cambridge, MA: Harvard University Press, 1970).
18. Richard A. Kalish, *Death and Dying: Views from Many Cultures* (Farmingdale, NY: Baywood Publishing, 1977), 2.

Bibliography

Briggs, Jean L. *Never in Anger: Portrait of an Eskimo Family*. Cambridge, MA: Harvard University Press, 1970.
Durkheim, Émile. *The Elementary Forms of Religious Life*. Translated by Karen E. Fields. New York: The Free Press, 2001.
Freud, Sigmund. "Thoughts for the Times on War and Death." In *Civilization, War and Death*, Psycho-analytical Epitomes 4, edited by John Rickman. London: Hogarth Press and The Institute of Psycho-Analysis, 1953.
Kalish, Richard A. *Death and Dying: Views from Many Cultures*. Farmingdale, NY: Baywood Publishing, 1977.
Lensing, Vicki. "Grief Support: The Role of Funeral Service." *Journal of Loss and Trauma* 6 (2001): 45–63.

Mandelbaum, David G. "Social Uses of Funeral Rites." In *The Meaning of Death*, edited by Herman Feifel. New York: McGraw-Hill Book Company, 1959.

Rosaldo, Renato. "Death in the Ethnographic Present." *Poetics Today* 9, no. 2 (1988): 425–34.

———. *Culture and Truth: The Remaking of Social Analysis*. Boston: Beacon Press, 1993.

Salzman, Philip Carl. "On Reflexivity." *American Anthropologist* 104, no. 3 (2002): 805–13.

Part I

Delaying Death

CHAPTER 1

An Absent Presence

The Co-constitution of Loss

Alison Witchard

A package arrived on my doorstep a few months ago. It was addressed from my cousin. She and I had always been close growing up, and I was interested to see what she had sent. As I opened the box, I lifted out a mug, packed carefully in bubble wrap. I knew immediately what it was, the color, pattern, and shape engrained in my mind over decades of use—one of my grandmother's mugs. Nan had passed away close to two years before, after a steady decline from bowel cancer. Nan was an anchoring presence in my life—having her around, even though not physically close, instilled me with a sense of calm and purpose. I wanted to make her proud and live by her example. Despite being in the midst of a research project that held death at its core, I had not yet personally experienced the loss of a loved one. While I listened to my informants explain the longing they felt for their mothers, grandmothers, and sisters who had been lost to cancer, I tried my best to understand how it would feel if I also lost someone close. But it was not until I lost Nan that I came to appreciate what they were describing.

When Nan passed away, I felt unmoored from the world. I thought of her constantly, when I was awake and then in dreams. I relived again and again her last few months of suffering. I cried as I thought of all the things I could no longer share or experience with her. After two years, and I still think about Nan most days, about what she would do and say and how she would react to the things happening in the world. As I held this mug, sent as a loving reminder from my cousin, I was immediately back at her kitchen table, sitting with her, my mother, and sisters and cousins as she offered slices of fruitcake and pointed out the native birds in her garden. Losing Nan was like losing a part of myself, a part of this shared world of possibilities and potential—something I had previously never fully appreciated in my conversations with my informants. Experiencing the loss of Nan and feeling the profound impact of her absence in our family clarified how I came to conceptualize the ways in which women explain their decision to undergo risk-reducing surgeries—that is, removing their breasts and ovaries—before cancer can develop.

Methods

In this chapter I consider the experiences of women at risk of hereditary cancer in dealing with death and draw upon my own position in witnessing the death of a loved one from cancer. Between 2013 and 2016 I conducted multisited ethnographic fieldwork among women at risk of hereditary breast and ovarian cancer and their families in Australia and the United States. During this time, I interviewed thirty-five Australian women who identified as at risk of hereditary cancer. I also undertook participant observation within the wider hereditary breast and ovarian cancer community, attending fundraisers, public outreach events, and ambassador weekends as well as medical research conferences and information days held across the country. I also conducted two focus groups with at-risk women and men in Australia. I primarily undertook participant observation within a cancer prevention and genetics clinic in Boston during my time in the United States. Over a period of six months, I observed over fifty genetic counseling appointments, spanning between thirty minutes and an hour. While based in the United States, I also attended conferences and fundraisers organized by the leading US support group for hereditary breast and ovarian cancer. I conducted a further twelve interviews with women at risk of hereditary breast and ovarian cancer.

My informants had a strong family history of cancer and had tested positive or were awaiting testing for a gene mutation linked to hereditary breast and ovarian cancer syndrome. Women carrying a Breast Cancer 1 (BRCA1) mutation have a 46–87 percent lifetime chance of developing breast cancer and a 39–63 percent lifetime chance of developing ovarian cancer, while women carrying a Breast Cancer 2 (BRCA2) mutation have a 38–84 percent chance of developing breast cancer and a 16.5–27 percent chance of ovarian cancer.[1] Although the presence of a mutation in either of these genes does *not* necessarily result in cancer, the prevalence of cancer among women with mutated BRCA genes is up to five times higher than those women who do not carry these mutations.

The United States and Australia, where my fieldwork was carried out, like many countries around the world, offer clinical recommendations or guidelines on risk reduction. These aim to give the patient the information required to make choices regarding regimes of risk reduction. Some of the current recommendations for managing the risks conferred by a BRCA1/BRCA2 gene mutation involve breast awareness, clinical breast exams every six to twelve months, breast magnetic resonance imaging (MRI) screening, and annual mammograms. There is also the option of a risk-reducing mastectomy, with or without reconstruction, alongside counseling to outline effectiveness, potential risks, and options for reconstruction. A risk-reducing salpingo-oophorectomy (the removal of the ovaries and fallopian tubes) is recommended for women with a BRCA1/BRCA2 mutation, ideally between the ages of thirty-five and forty, or on the completion of childbearing. For women not electing to undergo this procedure, concurrent transvaginal ultrasounds and a CA-125 (cancer antigen 125) test are recommended every six months, although the effectiveness of these technologies remains subject to debate.[2] By removing the ovaries, women enter into surgically induced menopause. Women may choose to have these menopausal symptoms mitigated by hormone replacement therapy depending on their family history and the possible risks of these drugs.

Parts and Wholes

To approach notions of the body, family, and death through the experience of hereditary cancer, I will focus on what I call "one's presence" rather than "the individual," because the use of the latter term suggests a whole and discrete body that relates to other bodies as such. The presence I will explore is sometimes not a "whole" body, characterized as it is by the absence of ovaries and breasts, in favor of one that is able to "be around" as a *part* of the family. In this notion of the family, we see parts of bodies connecting and caring in habitual relation to and with one another to form fleshy collectivities. These fleshy collectives make bodies, at times, blurred.

It has long been recognized within anthropology that certain body parts carry particular symbolic weight within Western culture. This importance is often linked with the biological function of the part or organ in question but also its role in fostering an embodied sociality between persons.[3] Some parts of the body, for example breasts and ovaries, are more important than others are in creating and maintaining the family. However, it is also the case that these body parts and movements are replaceable and replicable using other actions and even stand-in parts, such as implants, to ensure the sociality of the family can continue, especially in the face of possible death. What is not replaceable, however, is the multiplicity of partial relations the person conducts as a member of the family. The continued affective presence of the person, their ability to "be around," is assured when the parts that threaten to eliminate them—that is, potentially cancerous breasts and ovaries—are removed. Because these parts are replaceable and replicable, the affective presence of the person remains, and so too does the family. The at-risk woman remains a part of the family rather than a w/hole, that is, an absence.

Remembering Present Body Parts

As genes and gene mutations are passed down, so too are the embodied experiences of living with illness and caring for those who suffer most acutely. These shared memories are rendered upon the flesh of the diagnosed but also those loved ones that are intimately enfolded in such familial skin. The pain associated with cancer leaves an indelible mark upon those at risk regardless of their diagnosis or lack thereof. They may not be fully "healthy" or yet "diseased," but their bodies are nevertheless heavy with the memories of caring for their dying loved ones. They remember raising spoons to the mouths of their loved ones, carrying limp bodies from the bed to the couch and back again, and placing ice on blistering tongues. These embodied memories are just as pertinent as those of embracing during times of joy and laughter, commensality, and camaraderie.

Let us consider the experiences of Mia, a thirty-one-year-old woman from northern Australia. Following the recommendations of their doctors, Mia and her twin sister decided to undergo a regime of heightened surveillance for a few years after they tested positive for a BRCA gene mutation. Mia's mother was diagnosed with breast cancer when she was forty-three and had a total of three different primary breast tumors in the span of five years. Mia remembers vividly how, while still in her teens, she would go and sit with her mother during her radiation treatments. She saw firsthand the immense pain her mother was in and the "blisters on her tongue." Mia said that she would have undergone risk-reducing surgery much sooner if it had not been for her mother's insistence to wait until she had children to undergo surgery. Mia explained that she and her partner were planning to have a third child within the next eighteen months. Six weeks after the birth of her second daughter however, Mia spoke of having an overwhelming feeling in her body, something "indescribable." "Something in my body" she noted "was overwhelmingly telling me to have surgery, so that I would definitely be here for them." She continued, "If it wasn't for this gut feeling I would keep them [her breasts] so I can breastfeed my next baby. But I just had this gut feeling that it was time for them to go."

"I adored breastfeeding my girls," Mia said. "I will miss the feeling of breastfeeding, of being with my baby, and I am scared the next baby is not going to want to snuggle in, [but] I have to do what is right for me and for my children at the time." Mia decided to undergo a risk-reducing mastectomy with direct implant reconstruction. Although she had considered undergoing flap surgery, in which a part of the tissue is removed and reconstructed to form breasts, Mia worried about the recovery time for this procedure. "My two babies love to be cuddled; I can't take that away from them. Six weeks without being able to pick them up will be horrible enough, I couldn't cope with the three-month flap recovery." With direct implants, she informed me, the recovery would be much shorter, so she could pick up her girls: "At least with implants, my kids can snuggle me."

In this example, we see that Mia does not want her breasts to be a source of suffering and pain like they were for her mother, nor does she want her own daughters to remember her breasts or see their own in the same fearful light. Mia's concern that her breasts may become too present, as sources of pain and suffering, does not, however, equate with her seeing them as separate from herself, as a Cartesian reading would suggest. It is not the case that her breasts are excised from her bodily bounds to protect her mind. Mia's decision to undergo her surgery was initiated by what she described as a profoundly embodied and somewhat indescribable bodily sense that it was time for her to remove them. It was not, for Mia, a minded, rational calculation of risk versus benefits.

Mia was astutely aware of forms of relationality that have been created and nurtured by her breasts as they nourished her daughters and created a place for them to snuggle into for comfort. It is with this in mind that she chose a reconstruction method that will allow her most rapidly to once again cuddle and pick up her children. Breasts and ovaries, for many of my informants like Mia, carried more than one meaning. Mia's breasts were important in creating relationships with her daughters, to the degree that she worried that her next child would not want to snuggle into her, to be comforted by her breasts. Yet they were also parts that were present in another sense, as sources of suffering, of pain, and of disease. These parts could become so present that they would in fact destroy the relationships that they had helped create. They could impede Mia's ability to "be around" long into the future. Mia had to make her breasts absent so that they could not come to assume a presence like her mother's had.

From Absent Body to Present Body, to Body Who Is an Absent Presence

What Mia's experiences illustrate are the ways in which parts of the body become present or become known to be present when the risk of hereditary breast and ovarian cancer is made apparent. What many of my informants reported was the emergence of a present body, or bits of it, and the relations in which it is entailed as the women were made aware of their cancerous potential. This awareness or presence of body part does not necessitate a separation of mind and body, a splitting along Cartesian lines as would be expected if we were to read their experiences along the lines paved out by Kavanagh and Broom.[4] In their view, parts of the body come to be understood and talked about as objects able to be excised from the bodily whole. At-risk women, they conclude, come to experience their own body as "potentially dangerous—as liable to destroy [them]."[5] This fear, they suggest, creates an ambivalent, even disassociated relationship between the body and mind/self. As such, they ascertain, the at-risk woman clearly "separated her self from her body. Her body could be dissected, hazardous parts identified and removed, while the self remained—no longer under threat from the body."[6]

Instead of experiencing a fundamental separation of themselves from their bodies, I suggest that women at risk of hereditary cancer want to return to the absent body, where things run along habitually beyond their conscious attention. In what is a cruel irony, the means of achieving this habitual, absent body primarily entails removing the problematic body parts—that is, cutting off the breasts and recreating them or cutting out the ovaries and replicating their hormonal regulation through chemical alternatives. There is no denying that body parts such as breasts and ovaries are important in ways that are inherently gendered. They cannot, however, come to be nor remain too present if the family is to continue on in syncopated habituality. This is the rub of hereditary cancer syndromes—that one needs to cut off the very parts that play a crucial role in relations so that they can continue as a presence and, more importantly, an absent presence.

As Bille et al. argue in their work on loss and bereavement, the relationship between presence and absence is more complex than merely a relationship between two antonymic categories.[7] They note that a paradox "exists in the properties of presence and absence showing that they inherently depend on one another for their significance to be fully realized and conceptualized."[8] By holding absence and presence in concert, they take on meanings that "are local, complex, and not necessarily consistent."[9] This seeming contradiction takes particular form among my informants, all of whom are striving for a particular type of existence. They want to be *absent*, as in habitual, as in "I don't think about my breasts as ticking time bombs anymore." And yet they want a *presence*, as in "I'm still here." This woman is still here, still in the family, but not haunted by the relentless anxiety her breasts might otherwise bring. A present presence is undesirable; imagine worrying each and every day that cancer will develop. And absence, in the form of death, is, of course, the worst of all the scenarios. An absent presence—that is what my informants wanted.

Being Around

Women at risk of hereditary cancer experience the parts of their bodies that threaten to develop cancer as increasingly looming in their lives, preventing them from operating in habitual terms. This presence of, say, the breast, or the ovary, has the effect of making women realize just how important those parts are to creating and continuing in social relations. One of the primary ways in which my informants returned things to normal, made present breasts and ovaries habitually absent, was, in fact, to make them physically absent—by cutting them off. But often cutting them off or out was not sufficient to make them absent in the way Leder speaks of, not sufficient to make them habitual.[10] Women in my study had to find ways of replicating what those parts had done and been involved in. Had they not, then the absence of those parts would, ironically, have made them continually present. It is only when the relations between bodies can safely ignore the absence of a part that absence, in the true sense in which Leder means it, can return to familial relations.[11] What these women I interviewed and spent time with want the most is to be present—present without cancer and for the long haul—in their families, but they want this presence to be characterized by habituality and an absent body. It is the absent body, fully present and alive in the family, unencumbered by cancer or cancerous potentiality, that the women in my study spoke of.

After undergoing her risk-reducing mastectomy, Laura, a twenty-eight-year-old woman from Sydney, Australia, felt that she was finally almost an absent presence. She explained how she was, for the moment, an absent presence, something she never thought she would experience after testing positive for a BRCA mutation:

> It used to consume me, the breast cancer risk. My nan died of bowel cancer, or it could have been ovarian. It was a while ago, so they didn't know. But it used to consume me, I always knew I was going to die of cancer, I have always known that. But ever since the surgeries I haven't thought about it at all. I am so glad [about my decision], the relief I felt straightaway, the first three days are killers, but it was so worth it. I was the first grandchild for my grandmother and she died a month before I was born and the same with my daughter, she would have been my mum's first grandchild, but she died a year before she was born, so I never expected to see my grandchildren, or they never saw their daughters get married, so I thought I would never get to see my children get married, but now I am kinda excited for it. Because I think now I actually have a chance to see it, to see them grow up. I have broken this curse by doing this stuff. So it does get me a bit excited because I never thought I would see this day. I have that hope that I will make it there now instead of just expecting not to make it.

The deceased, Scheper-Hughes writes, are uncanny: "They inhabit rooms, closets, attics and clothing."[12] They also inhabit body parts in ways that challenge understandings of bodies as "indivisible, inalienable, integral containers and signifiers of human existence."[13] As Laura felt most acutely, her body parts were haunted by her deceased mother's and grandmother's body parts—their cancerous breasts and ovaries. Their parts came to consume her. Her breasts, as reincarnations of theirs, became too present. It was only by removing and replacing them did Laura feel that they would recede into absence, breaking the "curse" and allowing her to become an absent presence—one that would be around to see her own children marry and have children.

Thirty-six-year-old Ashley was on her way to being an absent presence for herself and her family. After being tormented by cancer lying in wait, many parts of her body had been almost unbearably present. But now they were becoming increasingly absent, as was her sense that she might remain alive and be present in her family for the long haul:

> I do [think about my risk] more now that I am contemplating the next surgery [a risk-reducing salpingo-oophorectomy], but I go through [periods] not thinking about it too much until something pops up or I have a decision to make, like at the moment. But generally, I go through life not thinking about it and not thinking about breast cancer much anymore. I am trying to enjoy life and plan lots of holidays with the family and our time ahead. ... I guess when I first [found out about the mutation] I was a bit scared about looking forward to the future as I didn't know what was going to happen, but now there is a bit of space. ... There were times when it was really tough to think [positively], but in the end I was sick of worrying. ... I think we will travel and have holidays, and I really love working, the last few weeks have been great. And my husband wants to get into the police force. He quit his business and sold the equipment. So it is all happening. We have allocated a holiday fund so we can do holidays. We definitely now have that mindset that family time is so important and that we need to have good memories and doing things with the kids. And that is another reason my husband sold the business, as he didn't get much time at all with the boys, and now he is a house husband, and he is loving being at home with Tylor and dropping Ben at school. So I think, through all the hard times, we now have a really good balance. We have family time, time with the kids instead of always working. And onwards from there every year [we will travel], it's all about having good times together.

Now that her breasts and soon-to-be-removed ovaries have receded into absence, Ashley finally feels that she can begin to once again plan her life and her family around shared times and activities. She makes plans around being together and enjoying the syncopated family life of going on holidays and taking the kids to school. Now that her body is slowly returning to absent presence, she feels able to appreciate the time they have together as once again unrestrained or limited.

Indeed, the feeling of an all-too-present body was something that my nan experienced as she was diagnosed with cancer. She spoke of her frustration in not being able to do the things she once loved—walking her dog, gardening, reading. As the cancer spread throughout her bowel, even the daily rituals of eating and drinking became increasingly difficult. Sharing a meal with her family became a challenge, despite my resourceful mother's dedication to pureeing the Sunday roast for her, so we could all eat together. Despite my nan's steely optimism, her increasingly present body made her participation in the usual rhythms of the family almost impossible. It was this inability to partake in the most fundamental acts of daily life that influenced Nan to undergo surgery to remove the tumor in her bowel. She was aware of the risks of the operation given her advanced age, but, as she said, the risks were worth taking if it meant that she could get back to life as an absent presence.

Death and Absence

Sophie was diagnosed with inflammatory breast cancer, a rare and aggressive form of cancer, when she was thirty-five years old and pregnant with her first child Matthew. Despite undergoing chemotherapy while pregnant and continuing extensive treatment following the birth of her son, Sophie's cancer returned after five and half years of remission. Sophie was then diagnosed with metastatic breast cancer. While her physicians suspected there might be a genetic cause behind her diagnosis, they had not yet identified which genes carried a pathogenic mutation. A creative writer by trade, Sophie wrote extensively in her work of the legacy that she wants to leave for and through her son. She spoke of the gift of stories, memories, language, and creativity that she has, through creating and giving care, inscribed into his very being. These gifts, Sophie envisaged, will live on in her child long after she is gone. They too will manifest into the tree that she plans to have her ashes buried beneath. She wrote of how she will become part of the root ball that will be taken up by the tree, becoming the nutrients that will help the tree to fruit, leaf, and nut, just as she hopes that the skills, the stories, and the love she planted in her son will continue to sprout long after her death.

When is it, Derrida asks, that we are most aware of our own mortality?[14] It is when facing the likelihood of death, he concludes, and, more importantly, the death of those social relations that are inextricably tied to our fleshy existence: both in the sense of death's embodied and biological existence as Sophie so poignantly expresses. Thanatophobia, the fear of death, of one's own mortality, is often drawn upon as symptomatic of modernity, as more people look to medical technologies as a way of overcoming their own mortality.[15] The fear of death was certainly spoken about in my informants' explanations of their decision to undertake risk-reducing surgery or regimes of surveillance. If we look beyond the death of the person, however, we can consider what such a fleshy demise might mean for the social relations in which the body is inherently entwined and how this is directive toward particular forms of action. The significance of this approach is in the insights it yields for understanding how women make sense of the impending loss of the potentiality of shared flesh, this being instrumental in creating relations of the family. It is at this point that Derrida's theorizing of death is pertinent. Facing death and absence, Derrida writes, is a situation in which one's entanglements with others is most deeply felt.[16] The surrendering of one's own life is not enough to ensure another's immortality. However, Derrida suggests, one's very being in the world, as a social body created and maintained through fleshy interactions with others, inculcates a certain type of relationality.[17] In quoting Levinas, Derrida writes, "I am responsible for the death of the other to the extent of including myself in that death. That can be shown in a more acceptable proposition: 'I am responsible for the other inasmuch as the other is mortal.' It is the other's death that is the foremost death."[18] Here, we are not only talking about a physical death but also a death of the bodily relations of sociality that are crucial to creating and maintaining people in familial configurations. As the examples I have detailed above suggest, this recognition of the fleshy, partial collective of the family produces a situation in which women at risk of hereditary cancer remove certain, and significant, body parts to ensure continuance of the family and their absent presence within it.

Drawing on Heidegger's phenomenological insights into death and being-toward-death, Peters submits that fear of death exposes the inherent sociality or collectivity of fear.[19] The fear of death itself is surpassed by a fear of the fear experienced by loved ones who will live on in your absence. He writes, "But what if the fear of fear was not a fear of one's own fear in the face of death but the fear of the other's fear?"[20] Fear, Jain asserts, is a "central, understudied aspect of cancer ... that sticky, primal emotion cements so many unspoken elements of the cancer conglomerate."[21] Peters details the existence of a dire need felt by those dying to attend to other's fears and one's own fear of this fear, it being

> a genuinely intersubjective solicitude concerned, primarily at least, not with the demise of the self, but, rather, the fear the other has in the face of that demise. It is the other's loss, their suffering, their pain that opens such fear out. ... The thought of (let us say) my own death is fearful to me to the degree that I am able to empathize with the fear of my child whose fear is not for my fear (the necessary dissymmetry that both interrupts and enlivens all empathic ambitions) but for my absence. Not my absence as a body, as a father/mother figure, but my absence as a particular weave within my child's internal time consciousness, my absence from the future and futurity of their identity—their own partial death. It is this fear that

might compel me, when death is certain and definite, to intensify my engagement with the future in an effort to *keep alive* for the other.[22]

We see this intensification of engagement with the future and one's future absence in Sophie's attempts to instill her presence in and through her son in the form of words, stories, embodied memories, and bodily acts of care. For her, these seemingly mundane but crucial acts represent a means of writing herself into her child's future identity, of "being around" for him despite her physical absence. Sophie sought to prevent what Peters calls the "partial death" of elements of her child that may accompany her own passing. She endeavors to live on in some tangible form, as a tree, a nut, a fruit that can communicate with her son and her partner when her "speaking human voice [is] gone."

As Peters asserts, the family as a social unit is likely to continue onward after the death of a family member such as the mother or father.[23] However, it will be fundamentally different to what it was, and what it could have been, had the person lived on. He continues:

> The futurity of death is not conceived of instantaneously as absolute discontinuity, but, rather, as a *fearful hollowing out of continuity as one among many futures comes to an end*. ... Thus my child's fear in the face of my death is not only the fear of my absence but of an *absence that exceeds me, that opens out onto a plurality of past futures that I carry within me*. ... These are "part of me" as that which I never was or will be, a pluralization of my absence.[24]

In this pluralization of absence, the death of a loved one issues forth a partial death in one's familial others that is not only of the "now" but extends into futures, curtailing certain possibilities and trajectories. As a loved one passes away, so too do the physical, material, and embodied connections that created and maintained the family as a site of partial engagements, whatever form it takes. Loss is thus co-constituted and shared not unlike the body. The recognition of this death of key, partial relations may prompt the dying person to make efforts to protect these relations and the ways they will be remembered and memorialized: As Peters notes, "The dying man or woman [may] compress a 'life' into a discourse of memory that significantly heightens the sense of loss. To 'die well' in this sense ... [is] providing the other with a life that is capable of being lost, it is to provide the other with the material necessary for their own suffering."[25]

The death of the person becomes the death of a certain configuration, experience, and embodiment of the family. After death, this configuration transforms into embodied memory, a point that Peters makes when he suggests that "my absence" is an "absence that exceeds me, that opens out" onto others. One's physical death does not necessitate the destruction of all connections with the living, as Peters, Desjarlais, and others remind us.[26] Indeed, we need, as Bille et al. argue, to pay closer attention to the "ability of such absences," of a person or thing, "to imply and direct attention towards presence."[27] Losses are able to have a "powerful presence in people's lives precisely because of their absence." Losses change and alter the family in profound ways. Marilyn Strathern, in her work on kinship in England, observes these ways in which the presence of an absence fundamentally alters possibilities for ongoing relationality in the family.[28] At death, Strathern asserts, "the deceased [is] colloquially "cut off" from a stream of existence that was more than him or her, as he or she was cut off from an active part in social relationships. Death terminated the enjoyment of relations, such as marriage, that remained thereafter frozen in the record."[29]

Death forecloses particular temporal horizons and modes of relationality. Taking note of phenomenological understandings of temporality, Geertz put forth the notion of social time as an awareness of the passing of time that is marked by the disappearance of concrete persons.[30] This notion of time as experienced by the passing of significant others has particular relevance for those belonging to a family affected by hereditary cancer, as they often come to face mortality at an early age. Witnessing this "disappearance of concrete individuals," of grandmothers, mothers, aunts, sisters, fathers, in prolonged and painful ways and living with the enduring emotional weight of such embodied absences has a profound effect on at-risk women.[31] To curtail the chaos and suffering, the enduring presence of multiple absences that may accompany generations of cancer diagnosis, at-risk women work to ensure that the endings foreshadowed by hereditary cancer syndromes do not eventuate. As I detailed in this chapter, this endeavor often entails the decision to forego parts of one's body, those that are so crucial to making the familial unit. Felt memories and bodily archives of the breasts', ovaries', and womb's (partial) role in the enfolding of familial others are set to be removed, surgically, from the body, bringing to the fore feelings of loss, grief, and uncertainty. However, attempts to secure an absent presence sees that the removal of such parts may in turn prevent a breast or an ovary from becoming its opposite, a destroyer of the social body and familial relations by allowing its fatal cancerous potential to be realized.

Let us return to Sophie. She spoke directly to the notion of presence, as she worried that she might not be present for her son's progression from childhood to adulthood. She told me,

> I definitely feel that with my son … I have to give him a foundation and certain value system now and I can't wait to instill certain things in him because I have to put him on this path now in case I die, you know. There is this constant feeling like I am performing. The way I feel in life is that I'm always performing for other

people's memories, and I feel that especially with my son. I want to do things and behave in certain ways so that he'll remember me in a certain way when I die. So it's like I'm outside of my life looking in on this performance of my life, this performance for other people. ... And that is the problem with death, because you become intangible. And even if you're a religious person, you're still intangible, and I think, like last night, he said to me, "Can you kiss my pillow so that I have a kiss on my pillow forever" ...There is a sense in death that you want to hold on to something and give your child something to hold on to, and that's why I want be buried in a tree [*chuckles*]. I want there to be this tree he can go to and say, "My mum is in this tree, this tree is my mum." I want there to be something living.

Sophie wanted desperately to be present in her son's life. She wanted to "be around" for him for as long as she could. But the treed presence she told to me, material and tangible as it was, could not be the absent presence that all my informants wanted to obtain. This absent presence is not only one we can describe as "habitual" and "behind present attention" but one characterized equally by the relations that absence enables. The absent breasts, cut off and yet still present as they had been replaced by implants in women such as Ashley and Laura, were now presently absent, for their lovers and their kids, entailed fully in a sociality of the family. A sense of belonging arises from joint experiences of real parts or, indeed, replacement parts that stand in for the relations that were once issued from and received by real breast flesh. Reconstructed breasts do not just replicate the swelling one needs to wear a sweater, so that the ravages of pre-cancer are conspicuously absent to the casual observer. They also collect up the enfleshed relations that breasts once did, sufficient enough for an absent body, sufficient enough to be a continuing presence.

Reflecting on Loss

Despite initial hopes for recovery, the operation to remove Nan's tumor proved too much for her, and she passed away in hospital a week later. But she did not regret her decision to undergo the operation, nor did we. Her body had become too present; she could no longer partake in the rhythms of the life she cherished, and, as such, she felt ready to take on the risks of removing the tumor. Following her death, our family has continued on as a social unit, though different to what it was when Nan as alive. With Nan's death, we lost an anchoring presence within our family, someone who bought us together, mediated tensions and misunderstandings, and bought joy to each and every one of us. Her absence is felt to our core, and yet we hold on to and nurture the remaining embodied connections we have to her—her magnificent garden, her well-worn mugs, her open-mindedness, and her passion for justice.

In this chapter I have argued that, rather than causing a Cartesian divide between mind and body, being at risk of hereditary breast and ovarian cancer makes women aware of how integral their bodies are to the making and caring of the family. At-risk women feel bodily parts becoming increasingly present in a way that interferes with the habitual interactions of the family.[32] While the "present" breast or ovary draws attention to their role in certain socialities, it impedes these operations in the everyday—it threatens one's ability to "be around" for their loved ones. One of the key ways that my informants sought to make these body parts absent, to achieve an "absent presence," was to remove them from their bodies. Removing the part, however, was alone sometimes not enough to make them absent. These parts were replaced and replicated, so that their absence would not infer a presence. What my informants really wanted was to be present in their families unencumbered by cancer or death. These women wanted to be an absent presence, to be part of the habituality of the family borne in and of the fleshy interactions of everyday life. To be fully present and alive in the family was what the at-risk women I met wanted most.

Alison Witchard completed her PhD in medical anthropology at the Australian National University. Following her research on women with hereditary breast and ovarian cancer, Dr. Witchard took on senior research and policy roles within a number of government organizations, including the Royal Commission into Institutional Responses to Child Sexual Abuse. Dr. Witchard currently holds the role of lead, performance reports, at a government health performance agency in Sydney, Australia.

Notes

1. Fergus Couch, Katherine Nathanson, and Kenneth Offit, "Two Decades after BRCA: Setting Paradigms in Personalized Cancer Care and Prevention," *Science* 28, no. 348 (2014): 1466. Mary-Claire King, Joan Marks and Jessica Mandell, "Breast and Ovarian Cancer Risks Due to Inherited Mutations in BRCA1 and BRCA2," *Science* 24, no. 302 (2003): 643.
2. Mary Daly et al., *NCCN Clinical Practice Guidelines in Oncology: Genetic/Familial High-Risk Assessment; Breast and Ovarian* (Fort Washington, PA: National Comprehensive Cancer Network Incorporated, 2016), 1–2.
3. Lesley Sharp, "Organ Transplantation as a Transformative Experience: Anthropological Insights into the Restructuring of the Self," *Medical Anthropology Quarterly* 9, no. 3 (1995): 357–89. Lenore Manderson, *Surface Tensions: Surgery, Bodily Boundaries, and the Social Self* (Oxon: Routledge, 2011).
4. Anne Kavanagh and Dorothy Broom, "Embodied Risk: My Body, Myself?" *Social Science and Medicine* 46, no. 3 (1998): 437–44.
5. Ibid., 442.
6. Ibid.

7. Mikkel Bille, Frida Hastrup, and Tim Sorensen, *An Anthropology of Absence: Materializations of Transcendence and Loss* (New York: Springer, 2010), 3–22.
8. Ibid., 9.
9. Ibid.
10. Drew Leder, *The Absent Body* (Chicago: University of Chicago Press, 1990), 4–5.
11. Ibid.
12. Nancy Scheper-Hughes, "Dissection: The Body in Tatters; Dismemberment, Dissection, and the Return of the Repressed," in *A Companion to the Anthropology of the Body and Embodiment*, ed. Fran Mascia-Lees (West Sussex: Wiley-Blackwell, 2011), 184.
13. Ibid.
14. Jacques Derrida, *The Gift of Death* (Chicago: University of Chicago Press, 1995), 56.
15. Ulrich Beck, *Risk Society: Towards a New Modernity* (London: Sage Publications, 1992), 204–10.
16. Derrida, *Gift of Death*, 56.
17. Martin McQuillan, "'Another Death' Jacques Derrida (1930–2004)," *Parallax* 11, no. 1, (2005): 79–87.
18. Derrida, *Gift of Death*, 46.
19. Gary Peters, "The Fear of Fear: The Phenomenology of Death in Heidegger and Levinas," *Contemporary Philosophy* 26, no. 3 (2004): 4.
20. Ibid.
21. S. Lochlann Jain, *Malignant: How Cancer Becomes Us* (Berkeley: University of California Press, 2013), 182.
22. Peters, "Fear of Fear," 4–5. My emphasis.
23. Ibid., 12.
24. Ibid. My emphasis.
25. Ibid., 10.
26. Ibid. Robert Desjarlais, *Subject to Death: Life and Loss in a Buddhist World* (Chicago: University of Chicago Press, 2016).
27. Mikkel, Hastrup, and Sorensen, *Anthropology of Absence*, 5.
28. Marilyn Strathern, *Reproducing the Future: Essays on Anthropology, Kinship and the New Reproductive Technologies* (Manchester: Manchester University Press, 1992), 108.
29. Ibid.
30. Clifford Geertz, *Person, Time, and Conduct in Bali: An Essay in Cultural Analysis* (New Haven, CT: Yale University, 1966), 375.
31. Ibid.
32. Leder, *Absent Body*, 4.

Bibliography

Beck, Ulrich. *Risk Society: Towards a New Modernity*. London: Sage Publications, 1992.
Bille, Mikkel, Frida Hastrup, and Tim Sorensen, eds. *An Anthropology of Absence: Materializations of Transcendence and Loss*. New York: Springer, 2010.
Couch, Fergus, Katherine Nathanson, and Kenneth Offit. "Two Decades after BRCA: Setting Paradigms in Personalized Cancer Care and Prevention." *Science* 28, no. 348 (2014): 1466–70.
Daly, Mary, Robert Pilarski, Michael Berry, Saundra Buys, Susan Friedman, Judy Garber, Mollie Hutton, Noah Kauff, et al. *NCCN Clinical Practice Guidelines in Oncology: Genetic/Familial High-Risk Assessment; Breast and Ovarian*. Fort Washington, PA: National Comprehensive Cancer Network Incorporated, 2016.
Derrida, Jacques. *The Gift of Death*. Chicago: University of Chicago Press, 1995.

Desjarlais, Robert. *Subject to Death: Life and Loss in a Buddhist World*. Chicago: University of Chicago Press, 2016.

Geertz, Clifford. *Person, Time, and Conduct in Bali: An Essay in Cultural Analysis*. New Haven, CT: Yale University, 1966.

Jain, S. Lochlann. *Malignant: How Cancer Becomes Us*. Berkeley: University of California Press, 2013.

Kavanagh, Anne, and Dorothy Broom. "Embodied Risk: My Body, Myself?" *Social Science and Medicine* 46, no. 3 (1998): 437–44.

King, Mary-Claire, Joan Marks, and Jessica Mandell. "Breast and Ovarian Cancer Risks Due to Inherited Mutations in BRCA1 and BRCA2." *Science* 24, no. 302 (2003): 643–46.

Leder, Drew. *The Absent Body*. Chicago: University of Chicago Press, 1990.

Manderson, Lenore. *Surface Tensions: Surgery, Bodily Boundaries, and the Social Self*. Oxon: Routledge, 2011.

McQuillan, Martin. "'Another Death' Jacques Derrida (1930–2004)." *Parallax* 11, no. 1 (2005): 79–87.

Peters, Gary. "The Fear of Fear: The Phenomenology of Death in Heidegger and Levinas." *Contemporary Philosophy* 26, no. 3 (2004): 1–19.

Scheper-Hughes, Nancy. "Dissection: The Body in Tatters; Dismemberment, Dissection, and the Return of the Repressed." In *A Companion to the Anthropology of the Body and Embodiment*, edited by Fran Mascia-Lees, 172–207. West Sussex: Wiley-Blackwell, 2011.

Sharp, Lesley. "Organ Transplantation as a Transformative Experience: Anthropological Insights into the Restructuring of the Self." *Medical Anthropology Quarterly* 9, no. 3 (1995): 357–89.

Strathern, Marilyn. *Reproducing the Future: Essays on Anthropology, Kinship and the New Reproductive Technologies*. Manchester: Manchester University Press, 1992.

CHAPTER 2

Immortality and Existential Terror
Learning the Language of Living Forever

Jeremy Cohen

> Everything that enters into life also begins to die, to go toward its death, and death is at the same time life.
> —Martin Heidegger, *An Introduction to Metaphysics*[1]

I am standing at a small cocktail table in the back of the conference room taking notes. I look over to where John is sitting by himself, and a sense of darkness comes over me. John has bushy white eyebrows, thinning white hair, and a slight hunch. At times it seems that his cane is the only thing keeping him upright. John is quick-witted and in relatively good shape for an octogenarian. He walks two miles a day, and would walk more if he had not broken his hip. When I ask John why he wants to live forever, he tells me that although he sometimes wants to die, the support his military pension provides for his wife motivates him to continue living. As the second day of RAADfest—a yearly conference dedicated to radical longevity and life extension—hits the halfway mark, the attendees are being led in a group stretch. A thousand sets of arms go up, backs are stretched, and bodies loosened. John's cane is leaning against a chair, and he does his best to follow along, arms never able to go too far in any direction, his hunch more prominent now. I write in my field notes that if one person could be given the chance to live forever, it should be John.

As I watch John, I realize that I too am going to die one day, and I am instantly brought back to the hospital room where, a few weeks earlier, my heart was torn with anxiety by the pained expression on my great-uncle's face as I watched him struggle to breathe. Here, at RAADfest, I am witnessing a genuine sense of hope embodied in John that paradoxically reinforces my awareness that my great-uncle's fate will be my own. There is a weight on my shoulders and a sense of morbid dread that follows me until the end of RAADfest. In this chapter I interrogate my experiences with death, along with those of my research community, to complicate the value placed on theoretical frameworks for understanding human motivation in the face of death. Theoretical assumptions, and our own situatedness, paint the varied experiences of death with a broad brush, collapsing the singularity of experience, "the ritual process and the process of mourning."[2] If the study of death in anthropology risks focusing on routine rather than on the singular experience, as Renato Rosaldo has argued,[3] then experiences with death among a group who consider themselves physically immortal reveal the complexity of death for those dying, those who survive the dead, and those who study mortality's epistemic multiplicities.

Anthropology has historically studied death from the idealized position of objective outsider. Understanding death meant exteriorizing the experience through analysis of rituals and symbols and focusing on repetitive recurrences; death mattered only insofar as observable embodied and discursive dispositions allowed.[4] My interactions with my research community, including the panic brought about by fieldwork, have shown me that to study death is not only to include oneself but also to learn how to integrate the variety of experience beyond the self and beyond theory. There is a unique language used within the communities we study, which can act as a shibboleth to demarcate outsiders. I argue that any attempt at learning the language of our communities is a productive step toward empathetic research within the anthropology of death, resulting in steadier moral positioning during fieldwork. At issue is not the search for a correct interpretation of the human response to death but whether theory or personal reflection can always provide an accurate portrait of what it means to die or to lose those closest to us. In trying to learn the language of the communities we study, we risk mistranslating the experience of others, especially when we rely on theory to inform our research. However, even mistranslation is an avenue toward a greater understanding of the singularity of experience. It is in learning the language of the other, and through the development of empathy, that we can begin to gain insight into how individuals and communities experience death, even if we ultimately remain outsiders.

On Being Struck by Lightning

While I believe that we should have open and honest conversations about mortality and confront its inevitability, my feelings about my own death are complicated. I have managed throughout most of my life to place death at a safe distance from my being while immersing myself in its aesthetic allure. The discourse on death that I am familiar with tends to minimize its reality through a lighthearted approach and deliberately morbid aesthetics, such as skull motifs on heavy metal album covers, which it has been argued makes death acceptable.[5] I have not experienced the death of a direct family member or close friend, and the news of the deaths of my paternal grandparents—in both cases relayed to me weeks after their passing—left me with few visible traces of grief. The places where I have met death have been cultural and practical. I have grown up within a music-oriented subculture that venerates morbid imagery and music. My partner works in the funeral profession, and I have accompanied her to numerous industry conferences where I have learned to talk shop with casket retailers and cemetery managers. My wife and I write about death for a popular audience on our website TalkDeath, where we interview funeral directors, green burial advocates, and thanatologists. Our website is positioned within the "death positive" movement, which tends to view attempts at longevity and immortality as byproducts of society's denial of death. I have read Heidegger, Levinas, and Derrida, and I continue to question my parents' judgment in letting me read serial killer nonfiction as a child. As one member of my research community put it, I have "surrounded [myself] with death."

I was also a forestry worker in Northern Canada for almost a decade, where a perilous culture of lack of regard for safety resulted in several close calls with death. The first happened when our driver fell asleep on our way back from a long day of work. I was able to jump over and take control of the wheel quickly enough to avoid having our truck drive over a cliff. Another incident occurred in a remote part of British Columbia where I was planting pine saplings in water-filled trenches with a steel shovel while wearing metal-cleated boots. In the afternoon, a violent storm rolled in. The air was electric, trees were shaking, and within the span of ten minutes, four of us were struck by three different bolts of lightning. A blinding white bolt landed one hundred yards ahead of me, traveled through the ground and up my body, and exited my wrists in two balls of light while knocking me to the ground. We scrambled, drove back to camp, and eventually made the forty-five-minute drive to town to call our families. In the weeks that followed being struck by lightning, I expected an epiphany of the sort supposedly elicited by close calls with death, but none ever came.

It was not until early September 2018 that I experienced my closest encounter with death. Suffering complications brought on by a fall and subsequent pneumonia, my great-uncle was paying his last visit to the hospital. The boisterous, sarcastic, loving gentleman who welcomed us into his home every year for high holidays, and whose pre-dinner ritual involved scotch and baseball, was missing from the husk of a body before me. A pacemaker protruding through his thin white skin, eyes bulging out of his head, he was lucid enough to know that this was not where he belonged. Through his pained and heavy breathing I heard him whisper, "Why am I here ... when can I go home?" My heart sank as I studied the body before me, and suddenly I thought I understood what might motivate an individual to want to live forever. No one deserves the pain that death brings, no matter how great the promise of eternal happiness. While I sensed the distance between my interlocuters and myself collapsing, I would soon learn that the singularity of my experience was not a map through which I could adequately explore the territory of death.

Meeting the Immortalists

RAADfest—organized by the Coalition for Radical Life Extension—is the largest gathering of radical life extensionists, biohackers, and transhumanists in the world. The three-day event attracts around one thousand participants and is attended by some of the most important figures in anti-aging research, transhumanist philosophy, and longevity activism. This quasi-medical conference features full-day speaker sessions, an exposition hall, cocktail dinners, and board meetings for various organizations within the movement, such as the US Transhumanist Party and Humanity+. I spent eight days attending talks and interviewing participants and leaders of various movements, as well as the vendors inside the "Anti-Aging and Age Reversal Exposition Hall." Subsequent to RAADfest, my primary participant observation fieldwork had been with the Arizona-based People Unlimited Inc. (PUI), whose members claim they are physically immortal. I had traveled to Arizona to attend "longevity" events hosted by the community, and I interviewed dozens of individual members while in attendance.

People Unlimited was formed in the 1970s by Bernadeane Brown and Charles Brown, with Jim Strole soon joining and assuming a leadership role. The three founders claimed in interviews and books to have had a "cellular awakening" that led them to become physically immortal. In a 1991 Larry King interview, the founders claimed to have never purchased life insurance; why pay into a system that no one will benefit from? At its height, PUI's three original founders preached their doctrine of immortality to thousands within the United States, Israel, Germany, and the United Kingdom. According to the preface of their 1991 book *Together Forever*, they claimed to know that "there is a biological attraction between [the founders] who will never leave each other by dying—or through any other means."[6] The death of Charles Brown in 2014, and a series of internal crises in the 1990s, have left the group with a diminished but enthusiastic membership. Today, PUI—led by Jim and Bernadeane—are once again building networks beyond their Arizona base. While most of its members do not self-identify as transhumanists, PUI is situating itself within the larger transhumanist movement through outreach and events.[7]

Demographics

I formally interviewed six participants and conducted informal interviews with over a dozen attendees during RAADfest 2018 in San Diego, California, and RAADfest 2019 in Las Vegas, Nevada. I interviewed an equal number of men and women, and participants ranged in age from twenty-seven to eighty-eight. My consultants were Caucasian and American, with the exception of a twenty-eight-year-old African American male and a middle-aged woman from France. I have subsequently made two research trips to Scottsdale, Arizona, to spend time with members of PUI during "Longevity Weekend" and "Longevity Week" events. These events include invited speakers, educational health sessions, and opportunities for "open expressions"—the process of going in front of the group to share one's thoughts and feelings, and, as happened during one of my visits, to air grievances. I have participated in these events through open expressions of my own and by volunteering to help conduct noninvasive medical tests on members. I have formally and informally interviewed dozens of PUI's roughly 160 Arizona-based members. PUI is made up of members as old as one hundred and as young as infants, with most falling between the ages of thirty and sixty-five. There is an equal number of men and women, and the group is made up of various racial and ethnic identities, including Caucasian and Black Americans, Israelis, Venezuelans, Germans, and Australians, among others.

Arizona is a fitting home for this health-oriented community. For instance, my server at the vegan Italian restaurant I attended for lunch one day in Scottsdale is named Kale. As I typed field notes inside a nearby coffee shop, a group of middle-aged women sitting beside me were discussing the benefits of juice cleanses. These health-based lifestyle choices are common and encouraged among People Unlimited, whose members claim to be physically immortal in the present or actively working toward immortality. According to PUI, members' mastery over their bodies at a cellular level represents a new genomic expression that does away with death. This view is shared by many members; however, immortality for most is the outcome of good health, physical activity, and a positive outlook. Members are encouraged to live out immortal futures through everyday actions in the present. In other words, members maintain that they are currently immortal, but at the same time the failure of proper action and thought, and a lack of commitment to antiaging futures, means that they are always susceptible to death. A future-oriented lifestyle, physical connections to like-minded immortalists, and mind/body synthesis are all essential elements in the process of achieving immortality and guarding against death.

Every Death Is a Suicide

For a community that defines itself by its members' inability to die, PUI has had to contend with the death of many of its members. A founder of PUI, Charles Brown, died in 2014 of complications from Parkinson's disease. A member died two weeks before my second fieldwork engagement, another died a few months prior to that, and the oldest living member died in 2019 at 101 years old. Discourses around death for PUI members take on a number of themes. I have heard death described as an enemy, a symptom of our collective negative energy, and a problem in need of a scientific solution. Death is believed by members to be transferred through genetic lines; death is darkness, and death is a tragedy. For some members, because we must be the masters of our own destiny, every death is a suicide. James and Bernadeane told the crowd gathered for a longevity event in Arizona that the largest cult is our society's "cult of death." The three original founders also wrote in *Together Forever* that "death is not natural, even though it has been the norm up until this time. Death has been imposed upon the body. Once this imposition is removed, the body has the ability to function in its true natural state, which is constant rejuvenation."[8] In a certain paradoxical sense, the goal for many immortalists is not to defeat death but to find methods to stay alive. This distinction is important insofar as the latter invokes the feeling of moving forward while the former implies regression.

Saul is a well-dressed and good-looking middle-aged man. A member of PUI for over three decades, he has experienced the changes, deaths, and renewals that all communities inevitably go through. We met for dinner at an upscale farm-to-table restaurant, where we spent several hours talking. I asked Saul about the experience of death for PUI members, and he shared with me that he had been a caregiver for a member of PUI who had died from cancer. Saul was one of the people who drove this member to their doctor appointments, helped them handle their affairs, and sat with them for hours inside the hospital. "Death is a tragedy," Saul told me as he began to tear up. "I just really hate the loss." Saul continued to share reflections with me about his upbringing, early experiences with death, and some of the family dynamics that brought him to PUI. I asked Saul about making sense of the loss given the community's belief in immortality. Saul confided that if there is anxiety around death for members of

PUI, it is not the result of a fear of annihilation but is rather provoked by the possibility that one has not lived a sufficiently immortal lifestyle by eating well, taking the right supplements, being an active immortalist, and always cultivating a positive mindset.

Saul expressed to me a rather pragmatic view of what it means to die and handle death. While he and other community members are actively working toward an anticipated future of physical immortality, death remains an unplanned contingency. Saul looks forward to a time when aging will be reversed through biomedical intervention, but he recognizes that, for now, disease and accidents can still cause unexpected death. As another member told me, "70 percent of deaths are people's own fault [bad habits and giving in to death], 20 percent of people die from things that are out of their control like war and famine, while 5 to 10 percent of people die because shit happens." When I asked PUI member Greg how he makes sense of the death of Charles Brown, or the most recent deaths in the community, Greg told me that "every death is a suicide." Greg went on to explain that someone may claim to be physically immortal but still hide death within themselves in a number of ways. For example, according to Greg, Brown did not take care of himself in his later life. Likewise, Greg told me that a member who died from cancer had issues with greed, while another member who died had hidden many bad habits, so that guilt and stress were the ultimate causes of their cancer.[9] Saul was distressed by such explanations because blaming the sick risks denying them access to the community, a necessary element for achieving immortality. Because of the positive effects of being surrounded by like-minded people, including changes to our genetic makeup and neural activity caused by members' positive energy, PUI members believe that immortality is impossible without an ongoing connection to a community of immortalists. Saul told me that "if we believe that everyone dies, we lose the connection," but that members should also not "lose the connection to the dying." In other words, a community must remain a community, even in death, or risk ostracizing people for a fate they did not choose.

Death Denying or Life Affirming?

In their multitude and variation, members of People Unlimited utilize explanatory models to make sense of death that resemble the explanatory models used in the study of death and dying. For some scholars, "civilization is a structure invented to protect individuals from death."[10] For others, death is not only the "supreme and final crisis of life" but also the source of all religion.[11] The fear of death is portrayed as a "potentially debilitating terror"[12] while paradoxically acting as "the mainspring of human activity" and a primary motivation in human behavior.[13] The awareness of death serves an evolutionary purpose, while expressions of grief are both biological and cultural.[14] According to the philosopher Heidegger, death can be observed but never experienced.[15] For other philosophers, however, death can only ever be experienced by witnessing the annihilation of the other.[16] Interpretations become more complicated when scholars attempt to make sense of immortality. According to some, a future where immortality is possible would inevitably lead to increased fear of death,[17] and people who desire immortality today show "distinct traces of fantasy, cathexis, denial, and over-investment."[18] One theory holds that as organized religion recedes into the background, the need for symbolic immortality increases, suggesting perhaps that transhumanist and immortalist ideologies are part of postmodern strategies for dealing with death anxiety.[19] These theories are often rooted in functionalist accounts that seek to explain individuals' distinct psychological and/or material needs and purposes with reference to bounded moments of observable ritual.

Theory is a necessary element to successful ethnographic engagement; however, the reliance on death denial as a model risks collapsing the singularity of experience. My initial research questions were oriented by my own history within the death positive movement and the belief that death anxiety was an orienting phenomenon for all individuals. My reliance on theoretical models reflected my own inexperience with death and limited my ability to make sense of the intimacy of losing people in our lives. As members of PUI attempt to navigate the less-than-positive intricacies of grief and loss, what, if anything, do these theories—often rooted in psychological models—tell us about the experience of dying, or about the death of the other? What do theories tell us about the pain that comes from missing important people in our lives who have died or the complicated grief or motivation that can come with the guilt of believing death was caused by the deceased's own actions? As C. Jason Throop writes about experiencing the death of others, "Mourning necessarily takes on unique textures and trajectories for each death we live through."[20] Instead of thinking about death and responses to death as an orienting condition only through the lens of theory, perhaps we should ask, as Abou Farman does, "What specific practices does this informatic mode [immortality] generate? What kind of ethics or selves does it develop? What discipline does it demand of its participants?"[21]

For many in my research community, the discipline that immortality demands involves active participation in the community and the performance of immortality through bodily dispositions and discursive formations. Immortality requires an obligation and responsibility to live an ageless life within the norms and mores of the community. If the death of a PUI community member makes someone "hate death" even more, as Saul tells me watching his friend die did for him, we should ask how those feelings are lived out. How do individuals and communities grieve? How does death affect their relationships to each other? While I initially believed that "hating death" would lead to a debilitating anxiety about one's appropriate action in the face of mortality, I came to realize that for many members of PUI, it led to positive possibilities through a future-oriented focus on life and community. Even if theories concerning innate human motivations in the face of death could accurately describe the actions of immortalists, there are unique "informatic modes" that can only be uncovered through direct engagement, which fieldwork can begin to provide. As I came to discover, theory in the study of death is only as useful as empathy and language allow.

"Do Not Go Gentle into That Good Night," or, Death as a Call to Action

I was sitting inside the PUI meeting hall during the community's monthly longevity weekend event. Dozens of chairs were arranged in a semicircle around a wooden stage. There were two tall chairs in the center of the stage; one sat empty, while the other was occupied by a stoic Bernadeane who eyed the crowd and nodded in agreement with Jim Strole's emphatic gestures. Before members could come on stage to "express themselves" or share their emotions with the community, Jim and Bernadeane delivered passionate expressions about immortality, paradigm shifts, and their desire for a strong community. Their speeches and speech-acts set the tone for the performances of members, which often involve passionate displays of tears and movement. Delivered with a force that was not quite yelling but still quite firm, Jim told the crowd, "Don't go gentle into that good night!" At another event, Bernadeane told the crowd, "I am not listening to anyone who says I'm going to die. You can't explain it [immortality]; you have to experience it." During one particularly powerful interview, PUI member Jane asked me if I believed in the possibility of immortality. I shared my reluctance to believe in ideologies of immortality while also expressing my fear of death. Jane told me that it is not death that I am afraid of but the pain that surrounds death. "Death is nothingness," she said, so why fear nothingness? Jane believed that the pain of death, the loss of loved ones, and the pain that dying brings can be averted through a transformation of the self and a focus on the future. If we love life and love ourselves, we can change our genetic makeup and become immortal.

Death for members of my research community is not dealt with in a theoretical fashion. Death is not something to be reflected on in hopes of making it acceptable; death is a call to action. As with the Ilongot whom Rosaldo studied, at stake for PUI members "are practical matters concerning how to live with one's beliefs, rather than logical puzzlement produced by an abstract doctrine."[22] When Jane told me that I should not fear death, she was not arguing for the acceptance of mortality, because to accept mortality as inevitability is to die. Once we remove the power of death over life, our lives become a wellspring of unlimited potential, even if, as the historian John Gray writes, "planning for immortality means spending your life thinking of death."[23] Death is undeniably an orienting problem for immortalists. Yet the more time I have spent with members of PUI, the more death has receded into the background, at least in its explicit manifestations. Instead, individuals at PUI are concerned with larger themes relating to their health, fitness, mental well-being, financial well-being, and community. Death recedes into the background, because to surround yourself with death is dangerous. "Imagine a balloon filled with light. When you focus on death, you are adding drops of darkness into the balloon. Little by little it fills up," Jane told me. Though concerns for health and wellness may nonetheless reflect the human desire to overcome a fear of death,[24] I have come to realize that death denial is a nuanced concept that does not adequately represent how members of PUI create their interior and exterior worlds.

Death and the Other

The audience at RAADfest was constantly reminded that not only is immortality going to be possible within our lifetime—"live long enough to live forever"—but that the community acts as an extended family: "The people beside you in this room, they are your best friends ... your best friend is the person who wants you to live forever." This attitude also helps explain why so many members of PUI—seeking a community that understands them—have moved to Arizona from elsewhere. Members of PUI have friends and relationships outside of the immortalist community; however, most have very strong bonds with each other. They meet twice a week, hold events together, and help each other during difficult moments, and some members even live together. The promise of immortality is thus connected to the relationships formed by members, many of whom have families within the group. The knowledge of death inspires positive action with the goal of maintaining life because a community is nothing without its individual members, and to die is to lose membership to the exclusive club of the living.

Death is fundamentally about our relationships in that it marks an end to the familiar other. One of the reasons why the immortalist relationship to death is complicated is that death is literally the end of relations. Death is painful for many members of the community because many see death as abandonment by their "short-lived" family.[25] Marissa, an older Venezuelan woman, expressed the view that she needs to learn to let go of her sons, because "I am going to lose them, and it's painful." Unlike spiritual ideologies of immortality, there is no reunification for immortalists in a postmortem heavenly realm. With the possibility of reunification removed, when someone dies at PUI—few of whom opt for cryonics—they are *de facto* excluded from a forever-ageless community.[26] By directly confronting the power and potentiality of mortality, the focus on death shifts to a focus on life and the formation of future-oriented ethical, immortal selves, and the promise of the continuation of familiar bonds.

On Learning the Language

A difficult and contentious weeklong event at PUI was coming to a close, and even as an outsider, I had started to think that I was finally learning PUI's intracommunity language. I was able to articulate what members meant when they talked about "leaving the family paradigm," and I began to connect many of the relationships within the group. I had signed up for volunteer opportunities within the community, and I thought that I was beginning to understand how death orients life for many PUI members. However, when Mike took to the stage on the last day, attention turned to me during his open expression against the paradigm of death. "Even if it's a friendly anthropologist who is asking the questions," Mike cautioned in a stern voice, "don't let them put the responsibility of death on you!" Mike was referring to a question I had asked many people at PUI about making sense of the death of fellow members. What I had not realized was that by asking questions about death, I had been asking members to bring up the past, to "bring the names into the room," as Mike put it. During Mike's speech, it dawned on me that this line of questioning might be understood as problematic for a future-oriented community. Because I felt it necessary to have open conversations about death in my personal life, was I assuming PUI members would feel comfortable doing the same? In the moment, I felt the room close around me as I was made aware that as a member of society's "cult of death," and as an anthropologist, I was an outsider. I began to think about how my disposition was coming across to the room: my arms were folded; did that posture make people think I am closed off? If I did not clap, did that generate negative energy? I felt anxious as I thought about the health regimens I *could* be following, and about the fact that my body will one day age and fail me. I thought back to John at RAADfest and realized that the hope that caused me panic was a projection of my own fears around death. I had spent a lifetime thinking about death without being forced to interrogate what death meant for others beyond my own anxieties and aesthetic preferences.

The moments of anxiety that I experienced at RAADfest and during PUI meetings are what Thomas Csordas calls a transmutation of sensibilities, or "when one has an unexpected and striking experience in a modality typical of the setting in which one is working."[27] A transmutation of sensibilities is a moment, positive or negative, when we are pulled out of what may have become routine during our fieldwork. Moments where language failed me, or where experienced-based assumptions were challenged, produced anxiety because they forced me to confront my outsider status and my fear of death. Between the epiphanies that participant observation can bring, "there are moments in the course of ethnographic work that occupy a particular position on the continuum between going native and feeling the absolute stranger."[28] My fieldwork has oscillated between moments of "getting it" and moments of feeling like an absolute outsider when it comes to the study of death, even the moments of "getting it" may rely on assumptions developed from past experiences, which create a false coherence to the narratives we build as scholars.

Freud believed that there existed "different impulses in the mind that the proneness to decay, or precarity, of all that is beautiful and perfect can give rise to."[29] Belief that the fear of death is a "potentially debilitating terror"[30] has made any attempt at circumventing death appear as an unhealthy denial of the inevitable. However, as I discovered, the feelings of anxiety, anger, and rage that death may provoke can in fact be a positive motivator for some individuals. Even if, for some members of People Unlimited, responsibility for death rests on the shoulders of the dying or dead, responsibility for life is a controllable experience for the living. Rather than finding a community whose world is oriented categorically by the denial of death, or by unhealthy motivations due to fear, as so many theories might predict, I found instead that responses to death at PUI reflected the different epistemic values of individuals. Death for many PUI members is foregrounded by human relationships, health regimens, and active movement toward an anticipated immortal future, and it is treated as a motivating condition. This was a counterintuitive position for me, which was only clarified through ethnographic engagements and the questioning of my status within the community. These transmutations of sensibility, especially my own complicated relationship to mortality, forced me to work through my inability to understand the language of death among immortalists. In such moments of mistranslation, I am reminded that I am an outsider not only to a community but also to experiences of death and grief other than my own.

The Role of Empathy

To what degree does empathy allow for meaningful insight into the singular experience of death and mourning? This question remains open. The role of empathy in the study of death is, as Throop highlights, a rather contested space: "Our personal experience of mourning particular others may lead us to overlook the singularities of others' experiences of mourning and the unique circumstances that arise for them in the wake of a loved one's passing."[31] How one develops empathy, and what benefit it may have during ethnographic engagements, has been debated extensively since the reflexive turn in the field. Clifford Geertz believed that empathy was unnecessary to ethnography because to take an emic perspective could leave one "imprisoned within [the subject's] mental horizons."[32] Geertz wondered if anthropological knowledge was *only* ever possible if we had an "experience-near" connection with our interlocutors. Taking the opposite approach, Michael G. Gunzenhauser emphasizes that responsible ethnographic engagement, developed through intersubjective dialogue [language] over a span of time, is primarily empathetic, or what he terms a process of advanced empathy.[33] Unfortunately, "researchers assume they know a research subject through the interview well ahead of any point where it would be reasonable to claim so."[34] Instead, empathy involves an evolving intersubjective process that appears to necessitate shared experience. Empathy opens up modes of enquiry that move beyond static theory, precisely because we can acknowledge the limit of theory within our own lives.

When I entered the field, my questions reflected my own lack of direct engagement with death and my simultaneous assumptions about immortalists' relationship to death. I assumed that death was going to provoke debilitating anxiety for my informants, or that their quest for immortality would stem from a terror that could be articulated. Instead, I was frustrated by their frustration at my obvious and, truthfully, empty questions. My experiences led me to focus my questions on the past. In so doing, I missed what was important to members' own lifeworlds as future-oriented immortalists. Lorraine Code argues that some of the most compelling insights from qualitative research can come when research participants assert themselves as "knowing subjects" against the assumptions of the researcher.[35] Advanced empathy as articulated by Gunzenhauser guards against the impulse to place death-related behavior "at a safe distance from the core of one's own society" or for anthropologists to become a "spectator of, rather than participant in, social reality."[36] Empathy, developed through intersubjective dialogue, is a means of building trust beyond the confines of insider language and a means of overcoming the perils of mistranslation. In moments where language fails us, a framework of intersubjectivity can create a different relationship based on a mutual understanding of each other's differences.

There is more than death that separates me from the community I study. I actively spend time inside cemeteries and participate in death positive events. As PUI members were given the latest information about diet and health during the longevity event, my thoughts strayed to the tantalizing half-eaten slice of cold pizza in the back of my rental car. While the crowd was being told to maintain a positive outlook, I sat and stewed about the person who cut me off in traffic earlier in the day. While I sometimes worry that these differences will cause estrangement from the community, active engagement through mutual dialogue appears to be building an advanced sense of empathy. According to ethnographer Sarah Pink, empathy

> invites us to make correspondences between the experiences of research participants and our own. ... In doing so the technique of drawing from past experiences to understand the principles of what participants are seeking to achieve offers a means of creating bridges between their and the ethnographer's experiences.[37]

Even if members of PUI may not relate to the existential fear of death that was provoked in me at RAADfest, emotional entrance into the community through the fostering of intersubjective dialogue resulted in a kinder and gentler look at the people I study, and it prompted a conscious effort to portray them in a similar fashion. It was by asking the wrong questions that I learned from my initial mistranslations. Death as a mode of enquiry does not disappear but is folded into a number of other concerns. Empathetic ethnography has the potential to break down taxonomies of culture and ritual and religion, revealing actual human beings who are trying to find their place in a world led by the "cult of death."

Conclusion

Debates within the field of anthropology over insider/outsider status have been long running and contentious.[38] As I entered the field, I quickly realized that my outsider status was not ethnic or "cultural" but psychic and discursive. While PUI and the attendees at RAADfest are part of the same Anglo-Western culture I was born into, I have come to realize that there is a language barrier between us. Athena McLean and Annette Leibing note that a byproduct of ethnographic study is that our own shadows inevitably infuse the subjects we study.[39] This is because, as Ellen Badone writes, "to study death as an ethnographer is to come face to face with one's own mortality."[40] We are called to maintain a critical distance from our interlocutors while simultaneously throwing ourselves into their worlds, bringing with us our own cultural baggage. This observation seems especially true in the study of death. Just as ethnographers try to understand "culture" by examining the myriad social, personal, and institutional networks that make up particular systems of knowing,[41] our "very descriptions about the Other are 'haunted' by other voices and visions which lie in our personal histories, often unbeknownst to us."[42] The solution to the problem of experience seems to me to be about language acquisition through intersubjective dialogue and empathy. Our same-culture communities share discursive patterns that are often unfamiliar to us well into our engagements with them. Learning about a community means becoming proficient in their language, speech-acts, and self-understandings and opening ourselves up to an unfolding world, even when we experience failures in understanding.

I began writing this chapter by questioning reflection as a means of understanding the singular experience of death. However, circumstances within my own fieldwork suggested that language and empathy were the problems, and solutions, to our distanced relationship to the death of the Other. Empathy certainly has its limits, and it does not imply total understanding on the part of the researcher, as I have come to learn. In many respects, despite my taste for morbid aesthetics and my own near tragedies, I have remained a spectator of the personal and social realities of death and dying. Even through my participation in the death positive movement, I never had to confront my mortality as I did, surrounded by a group of immortalists and transhumanists. It was through gazing on the face of the other—my great-uncle—and through my relationships with the PUI and RAADfest communities that I began to realize that I will have to face the death of the people I love and the annihilation of my own being. However, reflecting on my own mortality, even with limited direct experience, was about as useful to me as knowing that the fear of death drives human experience. Neither gets to the heart of the singular experience of death, our own or that of others. At issue in this reflection has been the treatment of death as foreign, "out there," and beyond us. We all must cope with the death of others, yet we study dying at some distance from ourselves. Experience was a useful starting point for me that intersubjective dialogue helped elucidate. However, it was not until a channel of empathy was opened up that I could begin, in a limited way, to understand what death was and was not for members of this immortalist community.

The failure of language is instructive and important to ethnographers of death and dying. Realizing that we may not understand our communities "well ahead of any point where it would be reasonable to claim so"[43] can challenge the totalizing nature of theory while developing an eye toward the multitude of human experience. My own questions were initially oriented by theoretical models of death denial, and my questions received frustrated answers because I had not yet learned to speak their language of life. Moments of mistranslation between my research community and myself have been the most instructive parts of fieldwork, as they showed me that responses to death exist outside of bounded, observable moments and forced me to complicate my assumptions. Through the process of language acquisition I realized that the engagement with death among my research community, being different from my own, necessitated a new outlook and new questions. I had come from a death positive mentality that believes that value in life comes from the acceptance of mortality. Learning the language of death among my research community meant that I had to learn the language of life as they understood it. To understand how death is lived out among PUI members and RAADfest attendees, it is necessary to understand how immortal futures are lived in the present. Thus, the anthropology of death, in my experience, has been a process of unlearning the language paradigm I am used to, a paradigm infused with death.

Noting the "staggered existential asymmetry" that makes up life, C. Jason Throop argues that being with others means the possibility that we may outlive them, that they may outlive us, and that in either case the intimate ties that bind people together are always at risk of breaking.[44] To survive the other is "a structuring possibility of every friendship—indeed, of every close relationship. Mourning is thus an anticipatory aspect of intimacy."[45] The extensive literature on modern death denial looks to the systems that made death a problem to be overcome. The belief that one is physically immortal, against all evidence to the contrary, can certainly be understood as a symptom of the modern fear of death. While that may be so, it is also a continuation of a very human impulse. After all, humans have tried living forever, forever. Where once people drank gold in an attempt to stay alive, now many of us exercise, take supplements, and purchase expensive juice cleanses. As Peter Berger argues, "Death presents society with a formidable problem not only because of its obvious threat to the continuity of human relationships, but because it threatens the basic assumptions of order on which society rests."[46] Even if, for some members of People Unlimited, responsibility for death rests on the shoulders of the dying or dead, responsibility for life is a controllable experience for the living. Immortality and the justifications offered for the death of immortalist community members may be ways to make sense of what most of us would deem inescapable. However, what seems to matter the most to my research subjects moves beyond theoretical and experiential assumptions, as the topic of death recedes into the background in favor of a focus on the future.

The job of the anthropologist of death is to learn how to give agency to subjects—to elaborate on the excess of the "singularity of each death"—while capturing what can go unseen by theoretical models that compartmentalize the world.[47] Death by its very nature as an end to experience means that we cannot help but study it at some distance from ourselves, but the anthropology of death can allow for the development of an empathetic outlook that recognizes the varied nature of death and dying. My research has suggested that the avoidance of suffering is a motivating factor for many within the immortalist community, but I was wrong to assume that death would provoke only feelings of anxiety and fear similar to my own. When I watched John stretch at RAADfest, my own terror at the thought of death was projected onto him. Panic at the thought of my own death sits within various epistemic boundaries. These include my historical situatedness, personal beliefs, empathy toward those who hold the desire to live forever, and, paradoxically, death positivity. Where death feels like terror to me, it is a call to action for PUI members.

There exists a multiplicity of identities and responses in the face of death, both for researcher and subject. The singularity of every death can result in a mistranslation of the experience of the other by anthropologists. The desire for immortality may map perfectly onto theories about death denial but tell us nothing about the actual experience of death. I do not know if members of People Unlimited are denying death, but I do know that their living among the cult of death creates active engagements with life. Empathy can become problematic because it may assume a tacit agreement through experience, and it may not account for the complicated relationships we hold toward the goals and beliefs of our research community. Cultivating an empathetic outlook helps us to recognize the varied nature of death and dying, allowing us to think beyond ourselves, while giving us the tools necessary to start to learn the language and, in doing so, to focus on the singularity of experience among individuals rather than treat death as some whole that exists outside of us and them. My own experiences and attempts at translation, limited as they are, cannot provide an authoritative map for the singular experience of death, but I hope I can add topographical elements to make sense of that terrain.

Jeremy Cohen's ethnographic research focuses on communities and new religious movements seeking radical longevity and immortality, as well as the historical and cultural framework of changing North American relationships to technology and death. He is currently ABD in the Department of Religious Studies at McMaster University. He has presented his research at the annual meeting of the American Anthropological Association (AAA), the American Academy of Religion (AAR), and the Society for the Anthropology of Religion (SAR), and has given numerous guest lectures on transhumanism, immortality, conspiracy theories, and the ethics of radical longevity. His research is funded by the Social Sciences and Humanities Research Council of Canada (SSHRC).

Notes

1. Martin Heidegger, *An Introduction to Metaphysics*, trans. Ralph Manheim (New Haven, CT: Yale University Press, 1959), 131.
2. Renato Rosaldo, *The Day of Shelly's Death: The Poetry and Ethnography of Grief* (Durham, NC: Duke University Press, 2014), 128.
3. Ibid., 126.
4. Ibid., 125
5. Christopher H. Partridge, *Mortality and Music: Popular Music and the Awareness of Death* (New York: Bloomsbury Academic, 2015).
6. Charles Brown, Bernadeane Brown, and James Russell Strole, *Together Forever: An Invitation to be Physically Immortal* (Sydney: Pythagorean Press, 1991), 17.
7. Transhumanism is a philosophical and political movement that aims to overcome human mental and physical limitations with the aid of technological and medical advances. Transhumanists look to current and emerging technologies such as cybernetics, nanotechnology, and AI in the hopes of augmenting the human condition, including the eventual defeat of mortality, and the creation of artificial superintelligence (strong AI).
8. Brown, Brown, and Strole, *Together Forever*, 36.
9. In order to protect the identities of individuals, deceased and alive, names and identifying information have been changed.
10. Jerry S. Piven, "Death, Neurosis, and Normalcy: On the Ubiquity of Personal and Social Delusions," *Journal of the American Academy of Religion* 71, no. 1 (2003): 135.
11. Bronislaw Malinowski, *Magic, Science and Religion: And Other Essays* (United Kingdom: Read Books, 1948), 9.
12. Sheldon Solomon, Jeff Greenberg, and Thomas A. Pyszczynski, *The Worm at the Core: On the Role of Death in Life* (London: Penguin, 2015), 1.
13. Ernest Becker, *The Denial of Death* (New York Free Press, 1973), ix.
14. Hannah Waters, "The Evolution of Grief, Both Biological and Cultural, in the 21st Century," *Scientific American Blog Network*, 11 November 2011, https://blogs.scientificamerican.com/culturing-science/the-evolution-of-grief-both-biological-and-cultural-in-the-21st-century/.
15. Martin Heidegger, *Being and Time*, trans. Joan Stambaugh and Dennis J. Schmidt (Albany: State University of New York Press, 2010), xx.
16. Jacques Derrida, *Aporias* (Stanford, CA: Stanford University Press, 1993); Emmanuel Lévinas, *God, Death, and Time* (Stanford, CA: Stanford University Press, 2000).
17. Nicholas Agar, *Humanity's End: Why We Should Reject Radical Enhancement* (Cambridge, MA: MIT Press, 2010).
18. Jerry A. Flieger, "Is There a Doctor in the House? Psychoanalysis and the Discourse of the Posthuman," *Paragraph* 33, no. 3 (2010), 358.
19. Robert J. Lifton and Eric Olson, *Living and Dying* (London: Wildwood, 1974), 12.
20. Devin Flaherty and C. Jason Throop, "Facing Death," in *A Companion to the Anthropology of Death*, ed. Antonius C. G. M. Robben (Hoboken, NJ: John Wiley & Sons Inc., 2019), 166.
21. Abou Farman, *Secular Immortal* (New York: Department of Anthropology, City University of New York, 2012), 38.
22. Rosaldo, *Day of Shelly's Death*, 122.
23. John Gray, *The Immortalization Commission: Science and the Strange Quest to Cheat Death* (London: Allen Lane, 2011, Ebook).
24. Marcel O'Gorman, *Necromedia* (Minneapolis: University of Minnesota Press, 2015). Francoise Dastur, *Death: An Essay on Finitude* (London: The Athlone Press, 2002).

25. "Short-lived" and "deathist" are meant as derogatory terms used by some immortalists to describe outsiders who have accepted death as a natural condition. These terms are also popular among transhumanists.
26. Cryonics is the process of cryogenically freezing the dead (who are referred to by cryonicists as "patients") in the hopes of reviving them when future technology allows. The largest cryonics facility in America, Alcor, is situated in Scottsdale, Arizona, a few miles away from PUI. Many immortalists eschew cryonics because they believe that signing up for the process would mean accepting that physical immortality is not yet possible.
27. Thomas J. Csordas, "Transmutation of Sensibilities: Empathy, Intuition, Revelation," in *The Shadow Side of Fieldwork: Exploring the Blurred Borders between Ethnography and Life*, ed. Athena McLean and Annette Leibing (Malden, MA: Blackwell, 2007), 109.
28. Ibid., 106.
29. Sigmund Freud, "On Transience," in *Freud's Requiem*, ed. Matthew von Unwerth (New York: Riverhead Books, 2005), 217.
30. Solomon, Greenberg, and Pyszczynski, *Worm*, 1.
31. Flaherty and Throop, "Facing Death," 167.
32. Clifford Geertz, "'From the Native's Point of View': On the Nature of Anthropological Understanding," *Bulletin of the American Academy of Arts and Sciences* 28, no. 1 (1974): 29.
33. Michael G. Gunzenhauser, "Chapter Three: From Empathy to Creative Intersubjectivity in Qualitative Research," *Counterpoints* 354 (2013): 61.
34. Ibid., 64.
35. Code quoted in Gunzenhauser, "Chapter Three," 58.
36. Johannes Fabian, "How Others Die—Reflections on the Anthropology of Death," *Social Research* 39, no. 3 (1972): 549.
37. Sarah Pink and Jennie Morgan, "Short-Term Ethnography: Intense Routes to Knowing Short-Term Ethnography," *Symbolic Interaction* 36, no. 3 (2013): 356.
38. Robert A. Innes, "'Wait a Second. Who Are You Anyways?' The Insider/Outsider Debate and American Indian Studies." *American Indian Quarterly* 33, no. 4 (2009); Abdi M. Kusow, "Beyond Indigenous Authenticity: Reflections on the Insider/Outsider Debate in Immigration Research," *Symbolic Interaction* 26, no. 4 (2003).
39. Athena McLean and Annette Leibing, *The Shadow Side of Fieldwork: Exploring the Blurred Borders between Ethnography and Life* (Malden, MA: Blackwell, 2007), 6.
40. Ellen Badone, "Memories of Marie-Thérèse," in *Coping with the Final Tragedy: Cultural Variation in Dying and Grieving*, ed. David. R. Counts and Dorothy A. Counts (Amityville, NY: Baywood Press, 1991), 213.
41. James S. Bielo, *Words upon the Word: An Ethnography of Evangelical Group Bible Study* (New York: New York University Press, 2009), 11.
42. McLean and Leibing, *Shadow Side of Fieldwork*, xv.
43. Gunzenhauser, "Chapter Three," 64.
44. Flaherty and Throop, "Facing Death," 165.
45. Derrida quoted in Flaherty and Throop, "Facing Death," 165.
46. Peter L. Berger, *The Sacred Canopy: Elements of a Sociological Theory of Religion* (New York: Random House, 1990), 23.
47. Flaherty and Throop, "Facing Death," 166.

Bibliography

Agar, Nicholas. *Humanity's End: Why We Should Reject Radical Enhancement*. Cambridge, MA: MIT Press, 2010.

Badone, Ellen. "Memories of Marie-Thérèse." In *Coping with the Final Tragedy: Cultural Variation in Dying and Grieving*, edited by David. R. Counts and Dorothy A. Counts, 213–29. Amityville, NY: Baywood Press, 1991.

Becker, Ernest. *The Denial of Death*. New York: New York Free Press, 1973.
Berger, Peter L. *The Sacred Canopy: Elements of a Sociological Theory of Religion*. New York: Random House, 1990.
Bielo, James S. *Words upon the Word: An Ethnography of Evangelical Group Bible Study*. New York: New York University Press, 2009.
Brown, Charles, Bernadeane Brown, and James Russell Strole. *Together Forever: An Invitation to be Physically Immortal*. Sydney: Pythagorean Press, 1991.
Csordas, Thomas J. "Transmutation of Sensibilities: Empathy, Intuition, Revelation." In *The Shadow Side of Fieldwork*, edited by Athena McLean and Annette Leibing, 106–16. Malden, MA: Blackwell, 2007.
Dastur, Francoise. *Death: An Essay on Finitude*. London: The Athlone Press, 2000.
Derrida, Jacques. *Aporias*. Stanford, CA: Stanford University Press, 1993.
Fabian, Johannes. "How Others Die—Reflections on the Anthropology of Death." *Social Research* 39, no. 3 (1972): 49–61.
Farman, Abou. *Secular Immortal*. New York: Department of Anthropology, City University of New York, 2012.
Flaherty, Devin and C. Jason Throop. "Facing Death." In *A Companion to the Anthropology of Death*, edited by Antonius C. G. M. Robben, 161–74. Hoboken, NJ: John Wiley & Sons, 2019.
Flieger, Jerry A. "Is There a Doctor in the House? Psychoanalysis and the Discourse of the Posthuman." *Paragraph* 33, no. 3 (2010): 354–75.
Foucault, Michel. "Technologies of the Self." In *Technologies of the Self*, 16–49. Amherst, MA: University of Massachusetts Press, 1988.
———. *The History of Sexuality*. Vol. 2: *The Use of Pleasure*. Translated by R. Hurley. London: Penguin Books, 1992.
Freud, Sigmund. "On Transience." In *Freud's Requiem*, edited by Matthew von Unwerth, 215–19. New York: Riverhead Books, 2005.
Geertz, Clifford. "'From the Native's Point of View': On the Nature of Anthropological Understanding." *Bulletin of the American Academy of Arts and Sciences* 28, no. 1 (1974): 26–45.
Gray, John. *The Immortalization Commission: Science and the Strange Quest to Cheat Death*. London: Allen Lane, 2011. Ebook.
Gunzenhauser, Michael G. "Chapter Three: From Empathy to Creative Intersubjectivity in Qualitative Research." *Counterpoints* 354 (2013): 57–74.
Heidegger, Martin. *Being and Time*. Translated by Joan Stambaugh and Dennis J. Schmidt. Albany: State University of New York Press, 2010.
———. *An Introduction to Metaphysics*. Translated by Ralph Manheim. New Haven, CT: Yale University Press, 1959.
Innes, Robert A. "'Wait a Second. Who Are You Anyways?' The Insider/Outsider Debate and American Indian Studies." *American Indian Quarterly* 33, no. 4 (2009): 440–61.
Kusow, Abdi M. "Beyond Indigenous Authenticity: Reflections on the Insider/Outsider Debate in Immigration Research." *Symbolic Interaction* 26, no. 4 (2003): 591–99.
Lévinas, Emmanuel. *God, Death, and Time*. Stanford, CA: Stanford University Press, 2000.
Lifton, Robert Jay, and Eric Olson. *Living and Dying*. London: Wildwood, 1974.
Malinowski, Bronislaw. *Magic, Science and Religion: And Other Essays*. London: Read Books, 1948.

McLean, Athena, and Annette Leibing, eds. *The Shadow Side of Fieldwork: Exploring the Blurred Borders between Ethnography and Life*. Malden, MA: Blackwell, 2007.

O'Gorman, Marcel. *Necromedia*. Minneapolis: University of Minnesota Press, 2015.

Partridge, Christopher H. *Mortality and Music: Popular Music and the Awareness of Death*. New York: Bloomsbury Academic, 2015.

Pink, Sarah, and Jennie Morgan. "Short-Term Ethnography: Intense Routes to Knowing Short-Term Ethnography." *Symbolic Interaction* 36, no. 3 (2013): 351–61.

Piven, Jerry S. "Death, Neurosis, and Normalcy: On the Ubiquity of Personal and Social Delusions." *Journal of the American Academy of Religion* 71, no. 1 (2003): 135–56.

Rosaldo, Renato. *The Day of Shelly's Death: The Poetry and Ethnography of Grief*. Durham, NC: Duke University Press, 2014.

Solomon, Sheldon, Jeff Greenberg, and Thomas A. Pyszczynski. *The Worm at the Core: On the Role of Death in Life*. London: Penguin, 2015.

Sontag, Susan. *Illness as Metaphor*. London: Penguin Books, 2002.

Waters, Hannah. "The Evolution of Grief, Both Biological and Cultural, in the 21st Century." *Scientific American Blog Network*, 11 November 2011. https://blogs.scientificamerican.com/culturing-science/the-evolution-of-grief-both-biological-and-cultural-in-the-21st-century/.

PART II

Caregiving

CHAPTER 3

Living, Caring, and Dying
Music and the House of Endless Losses

Carina Nandlal

Death is a natural part of life. However, living in Australian mainstream society means that dying and death are hidden from view, managed in bureaucratized health institutions and concealed behind the doors of purpose-built aged-care facilities on the urban fringe. The understandable fear of dying becomes magnified by this process of death management. Death becomes something unnatural, and the taboo around death heightens the sense of fear it instills.[1] This fear does not only take hold on the person surrendering to death. Caregiving for a dying loved one is an isolating experience. Fear of death and exhaustion from the rigors of daily caregiving can result in desolation and an almost complete state of emptiness.

My mother has dementia. It is a cruel and unyielding disease that slowly removes physical and cognitive functioning. Every aspect of the person you knew and loved becomes erased. Memory, thinking, and behavior progressively deteriorate. Emotional control and social behavior become so altered that sometimes you do not recognize the person before you as your loved one. Their terrified screams, disinhibited behaviors and powerful aggression constantly accompany the household as an eerie kind of basso continuo. In this chapter I consider my personal responses to caring for my mother during this painful time and discuss how we have created new daily rituals around music to recover meaning at a time of endless losses.

After my mother's diagnosis, my father, sister, and I decided to care for her in our family home. This decision transformed each of us. Many health professionals with the best intentions gently encouraged us to consider placing her in a nursing home. Family and friends warned us to consider our needs and the burden that caregiving creates. But we stubbornly refused to accept the possibility of placing our beloved mother in care. We could not be parted from her while she confronted this most terrifying illness. Instead, we decided to keep her engaged with normal life in our home. We were fortunate to have excellent support from a new government policy to promote care for older people in their own home. Whether intentional or not, the effect of a policy allowing people to age in their own homes brings the specter of death into middle-class suburbia.

My father, sister, and I live in a relentless twenty-four-hour cycle of caring for someone slowly walking toward death. The confrontation with the aging and death of a beloved parent is profound. But it is also coupled with other more mundane perceptions that reveal fundamental conflicts deep inside. Mum's diagnosis of dementia hit our family like a death sentence. We already understood that Mum had an increasing cognitive impairment, coupled with balance problems, frequent falls, and a tremor. Eating became difficult and slowed down. Sometimes I caught her struggling with intense concentration to simply put her right hand on her left. I have seen her frozen on one spot, trying to determine which leg was supposed to move where. She gradually lost her ability to read or walk unaided. As each of these losses occurred, my struggle to cope with them intensified. The weaker she got, the more help she needed, and gradually her needs engulfed our household. As Higgins eloquently describes, dementia "is not confined to those who suffer from it themselves. ... Carers ... are drawn into this engulfing circle of need."[2]

Initially compounding my pain at seeing my mother in almost constant distress was the unacknowledged assumption that my sister and I, rather than our brothers, would devote ourselves to her care. Of course, I recognize that this choice is one that I cannot resile from, whether I fully understood it or not. But informing that choice was the idea that, as daughters, it was our role to be attentive to elderly parents. Grigoryeva argues that "while women provide as much care for their elderly parents as they can manage, men do as little as they can get away with and often leave it to female family members."[3] Having a sister means for men that they are statistically likely to provide less care, yet for women it is the opposite; women with male siblings actually increase the amount of care they provide for their parents to compensate for their brothers' inattention.[4] Grigoryeva states that "sons reduce their relative caregiving efforts when they have a sister, while daughters increase theirs when they have a brother. ... Sons pass on parent care giving responsibilities to their sisters."[5] In my experience, care for an older loved one is a deeply gendered choice whose repercussions ripple out into other facets of our lives.

Caregiving is a "persistently double-edged concept and practice."[6] My brothers' roles in our mother's care always felt to me to be clearly delineated, whereas my caregiving seemed never-ending. I experienced what Code describes as the duality of caregiving; the "warm, feel-good aura" of caregiving and its nurturing modality contrasts starkly with the isolation of its "darker side where women are confined as carers."[7] Others freely acknowledge how difficult the role of caregiver is, but it seems quickly glossed over, as if a deeper acknowledgment of its difficult aspects is taboo. Every progression in my mother's illness correlated to an expansion of my role as caregiver. Maintaining employment while caring provided some relief, structure, and, importantly for me, time away from the house. Yet it came with increased difficulty, as I would transition from my public work-self at the end of the workday into my private carer role. This shift from office to home initially became a site of great emotional upheaval. The tempo of life in each of these contexts is so utterly divergent as to be irreconcilable. Frequently when I moved between these incompatible tempos and their expectations I would be overwhelmed by unending streams of tears. Crying on my commute home from work felt like a ritual cleansing. It happened most especially on Friday evenings, when I feared the terrifying open expanse of time signaled by the weekend. These awful tears were always accompanied by my sense of shame that I could not cope. This was coupled with the bitter recognition that our mother's dying did not affect my brothers in the same way. The brutal waves of my emotions were mine to resolve, and it seemed that no one could share the awfulness of my suffering.

Understanding my emotional responses became significant in learning to cope with my newfound situation. It is a difficult journey from fear of recognition of a problem in a loved one to the despair of a diagnosis of "no hope" that condemned all concerned to a never-ending series of losses and humiliations.[8] As my tears flowed more freely than ever before, I felt despair overtaking me. Becoming entangled in dementia is to bear "witness to the slow dissolution of a loved one."[9] Bearing this witness is painful beyond anything I had experienced. I felt shame when strangers questioned why Mum was distressed, implying that I may be hurting her. Conversely, I felt guilt when someone praised my efforts too much. Underlying all these emotions was despair.

Complicating these emotional entanglements is the context of bureaucratized death management, which encompasses a strange emotional regulation of the dying person and their carers. Once my family decided to care for my mother at home, we had to engage with a bureaucratized health system around death. It felt as though dying had become monetized in a system where care agencies are provided with government subsidies and private money to support people to live in their own homes. Absorbing the responsibilities of full-time at-home care for someone with dementia is challenging, and it is only made more difficult by having to navigate complex administrative processes.[10] Profit, the force that binds "everything within the capitalistic system tightly together ... [means that] what the elderly dementia sufferer gets in the way of care is what the market permits."[11] Care agencies are primarily businesses making deals with authorities to generate profit in exchange for "caring for the elderly."[12] Evans describes this system as one designed for containment and processing of the elderly. Death management structures can be viewed through the mechanisms of power and control fundamental to the prison system.[13] When seen through this lens, regulation and surveillance of the dying patient is paramount.

Time is altered for dementia patients, and the slow pace of living can be at odds with the often "manic pace of staff,"[14] who are overwhelmed daily from dealing with multiple aged patients in a short timeframe. Dementia results in slowness of movement or bradykinesia, rigidity, tremors, and impairment of posture, which progressively slow everyday tasks and fine motor skills, making some movements impossible. Falls are common, and balance is impaired; eating and swallowing become difficult. Meanwhile, searching the sufferer's face for indications of how they are feeling becomes compromised because muscle rigidity can result in a mask-like appearance.[15] Difficulty with communication can lead carers into a "sustained atmosphere of "hysterical merriment." Higgins describes witnessing "jolly carers" who perform a kind of high-intensity automatic happiness with the dying patients to avoid the painful "moments of authentic and healing sadness."[16] Without any slowness or breaks in this frantic tempo, there is no space for genuine connection with the dementia sufferer. This strange emotional context creates psychological tension that does not have an easy mechanism of release. Moreover, flexibility to meet the changing needs of a loved one in the throes of dementia gives way to rigid routines. The inflexible bureaucratic structure that governs death management conflicts with the nature of a person slowly relinquishing life.

Despite these ongoing traumas, there is a soothing and nourishing presence throughout for us—music. Our shared love of music provided us with a tool of communication, an instrument to soothe the savage beast of dementia, and a way to feel whole despite all the losses that dementia brings about. Metcalf and Huntington write that "the issue of death throws into relief the most important cultural values by which people live their lives and evaluate their experiences. Life becomes transparent against the background of death, and fundamental social and cultural issues are revealed."[17] Reflecting on my mother's particular joys in life made us realize how much they were bound to her love of music. It then became clear that music could help and heal us during this time, especially as it has the capacity to provide an emotional outlet and nurture positive feelings.

My mother has loved music since childhood. She was raised in a musical family, and her father had nurtured the dream of his four children playing in a quartet. This ambition was never realized, as by the time my mother had acquired enough skill on the cello to play with the others, they were no longer living under the same roof. However, this did not dampen my mother's enthusiasm for music. Initially she learned the cello in a sidesaddle position, as Mother Teresita, the saintly Loreto nun who taught her, believed it was unladylike for a woman to open her legs to grip the instrument. Once my grandfather discovered this, he promptly moved her lessons to Melbourne with a "proper" teacher, Marianne Maxwell. Eventually she passed the audition to study at the Melbourne Conservatorium studying under the renowned cellist Henri Touzeau, an émigré fleeing war-torn Europe.[18] Mum was part of the Conservatorium orchestra and was a founding member of the Australian Youth Orchestra. She performed under notable conductors including Sir Bernard Heinze, an Australian musical luminary. She went on to teach music at MacRobertson Girls School in Melbourne. Marriage to my father and subsequently moving to Fiji to live near his family also involved carting the precious cello to this inhospitable climate. The cello survived the heat and humidity and remains with us today in our cozy home in Melbourne. My mother was nurtured throughout her life by music, and she nurtured the love of music in her children.

I grew up in a large family, which meant my mother was often busily engaged away from me, managing the chaos of the household. Despite this, my music lessons, recitals, and competitions were all times that we shared together without my siblings. It became special time that I had with her. She patiently drove me to compete in music competitions in various cities and would sometimes sit in the audience and knit, putting down her knitting needles only when my childish footsteps approached the stage. She gently guided my musical progress. No matter how much I stumbled in my performance, she was proud. Mum passed her love for music to me and music provided a special place where I knew I could be with her without other distractions. Music was our shared space. Now, as Mum is slowly dying from dementia, music provides a tranquil space for me to connect with her in the new care rituals of our lives that we have developed.

Being with someone who is dying requires resilience, and music nourishes the resilience of carers for the dying. Its powerful symbolic language allows a sense of self to remain even while thinking skills, cognition, and other functions of the brain are in decline.[19] It seems to me that music can provide a language that helps when words cannot be found. Music can reinforce the sense of self at a time when one's senses, perceptions, and relationships are jumbled, confused, and undifferentiated. The ambiguous nature of music allows it to reach beyond language barriers, and it can provide the emotional vocabulary that is deeply felt and deeply shared. When caring for a dying loved one causes life to seem bereft of meaning and my own identity to dissipate, music can validate my emotions and invite me back to connect with my mother based on our shared experiences. Music has become central to the new rituals of our lives. It calms my mother when she is anxious and gently soothes her before sleep. With the comforting power of music as a presence, I can read my mother's eyes and gentle touch for the things she cannot say. Because of the deep relationship we share, it feels that only I can pick up the tiny flickers of signals Mum is sending. In this silent communication, music can be a profound tool, because music can open the possibility that people with dementia may be able to live a more fulfilling life. Davidson and Krause point out that in Western contexts, we use music to regulate our moods, with different types of music satisfying different needs.[20] As such, music can help to verify and validate a sufferer's emotions and strengthen the bond between Mum and me. It also nourishes and consoles the caregiver at times of acute despair. For our household, it feels as though "we humans are a musical species no less than a linguistic one."[21]

Empathy is essential to being with someone suffering from dementia. Waller highlights that when caring for a loved one with dementia, we must broaden our communication arsenal to emphasize nonverbal signals and utilize empathy to discover the meaning of what the person is trying to communicate. The language of music and its ability to encompass emotions promotes empathy and better communication. Music has a special place to generate, nourish, and nurture empathy. Sufferers of dementia are often not given the dignity of empathy from rigid caregiving institutions. Their state of being is at odds with a time-pressured health bureaucracy, and empathy may be one of the things discarded as the stress of dealing with a person in that condition builds. However, it is essential for carers to nourish empathy. The process of empathizing is one where we retain our distinct consciousness while simultaneously entering imaginatively into the inner state of another to understand how they experience the world. When we return to thinking about ourselves again, we are enriched through this process because we "respect and acknowledge their human dignity and our shared humanity."[22] Empathy means that we understand the human bonds of experience and feelings that we share with others. Music and its role in nurturing empathy with dementia sufferers results in stronger bonds within our family, and our connections become deeper.

Music-related activities may promote empathy, affiliation, and inclusiveness. Involvement with the arts can help make bearable the progression of the illness and can relieve the depression of those with dementia.[23] Listening to music together promotes affiliation between the carer and the sufferer. This connection is crucial to the dignity of the dementia suffer, for, as Tyler states, dementia can be a series of unacknowledged losses.[24] In a culture that dismisses older people, those with dementia are sometimes viewed as "ex-people, empty shells, and bodies from which personhood has been removed."[25] Evans encapsulates the painful reality of dementia and the way it realigns the perception of time as the act of interminable waiting. For dementia suffers, "all rooms are waiting rooms and all time is waiting time ... waiting is a part of their suffering."[26] While waiting in the slowness of this house, it can be painful to get in touch with feelings, but music can bring us into a space of contemplation of our emotional selves. Listening to certain music allows "a cathartic release of psychological tension."[27] Slower-tempo music can make someone feel calmer and more relaxed.[28] In the painful experience of loss and disintegration that accompanies dementia for the sufferer and caregiver, music can create a sense of wholeness. Such musical fulfillment is felt in Fauré's requiem.

Gabriel Fauré (born 12 May 1845, Pamiers, Ariège, France; died 4 November 1924, Paris) was a French composer whose refined and gentle arrangements influenced the course of modern French music. He composed his Requiem in D Minor, op. 48, between 1887 and 1890. The choral-orchestral setting of the shortened Catholic Mass for the Dead in Latin is perhaps his best-known large-scale work. The name "Requiem" derives from the first word of the best known of the introits, or entrance part, of liturgical celebration of Eucharist, which is used on such occasions: *Requiem aeternam dona eis, Domine* (Eternal rest be to us, Lord).

Although some music therapists do not deploy music for bereavement ceremonies such as the requiem in formal music therapy, there are times in caring when we are drawn to the beauty of pieces that encapsulate death.[29] While today this piece and other requiem masses by the canonical composers are most often performed in concert halls, its primary purpose is to accompany the ritual expression of grief and loss. Fauré's Requiem provides a sense of death as eternal rest that consoles the living left behind. Although Nectoux argues that the Requiem was not composed to the memory of a specific person but rather "for the pleasure of it,"[30] it has become a long-held idea that he began this composition as an act of bereavement upon the death of his father.[31] Regardless of this initial inspiration, the work endures as the most famous of Fauré's compositions because of its soulful consolation for those contemplating death.

Music is associated with emotional expression, and in grief it achieves its most searing voice. The "inescapable grief of bereavement and human mortality seems to require musical accompaniment."[32] Listening to a votive mass on behalf of the dead, which is often sung on the day of burial, may seem a strange request from someone who is dying. Yet it is precisely this piece that is frequently requested by my mother. Fauré's Requiem may be a piece written for the act of bereavement; however, its sonorous consolation is a balm to the desolation of caring for a dying loved one. Fauré declared in one interview, "It has been said that my

Requiem does not express the fear of death and someone has called it a lullaby of death. But it is thus that I see death: as a happy deliverance, an aspiration towards happiness above, rather than as a painful experience."[33] The idea of a "lullaby of death" combines an idea of music for soothing children and the music of death.[34] The specific prayerful and contemplative character of these works was achieved through such musical means as slow tempos, the avoidance of strong dissonances and dynamic culminations, the dramatizing of the musical narrative, and the uniformity of energy levels through the repetition of ostinato figures, especially of lullaby motifs, either with a pendular motion to the melody or based on spread chords.[35] The unfolding of a melody through chains of sequences conveys the impression of inevitability as in the long entreaty of the "In Paradisium," which feels like one continuous sentence.[36]

Fauré creates an atmosphere of beautiful peace. The composer said that the work is "dominated from beginning to end by a very human feeling of faith in eternal rest."[37] The peace of the Requiem is a consistent and repetitive rhythmic formula, which once established is maintained for long passages. Rather than monotony, it creates a sense of restful calm. Daring harmonic progressions and sudden modulations seem more surprising because of the static rhythmic flow that induces the sense of calm. Fauré's beautiful piece expresses our humanity. It reveals what is hidden or denied in our humanity and articulates our wish for something better.[38]

Research demonstrates that creative artistic practices and enjoyment of the arts can have a significant role in promoting mental and physical health, as well as general well-being of older people.[39] Meaning, which can be increasingly diminished as patients face death, can be regained through music.[40] Music touches parts of the brain that link what we sense, know, and feel. Being in touch with our feelings is vital for health. Although aspects of self-awareness can disappear in dementia patients, aspects of one's essential character, of personality and selfhood, survive at the same time. So identity is never wholly lost. Oliver Sacks argues that the response to music is particularly preserved.[41] Emotional memory in the brain can be activated by music, and the ability to understand music is not lost in advanced dementia. Smilde argues that music can underpin the creation of new relationships, an increased quality of life, and the self-esteem of people with dementia, and it can also ease depression.[42]

I believe this aspect is vital because dementia sufferers are so easily rendered as less than whole people. "The picture painted of people living with dementia is often one of ultimate suffering, where the person with dementia would lack the capacity for well-being and self-awareness and lose their identity and capacity for learning."[43] Kitwood memorably recounts the popular image of dementia as "the death that leaves the body behind."[44] But even in advanced dementia Sacks argues that there is *always* "a self to be called upon, even if music, and only music, can do the calling."[45] Music can help maintain personhood and dignity while the losses of dementia are increasing. Within the suffering of dementia, music can "create a safe space to explore, enjoy, discover, reminisce, and communicate in new ways." This connection allows sufferers to "[express] their feelings, thoughts, and emotions" while also enabling carers to support the patient by allowing them to make decisions and indicate preferences for the music.[46] In a time in life when almost all decisions seem to be made *for* her, with music my mother can indicate her own choices. My mother demonstrates her preferences by choosing what we listen to. The music she enjoys can calm her anxieties and release tension so that she can rest. Discussing the music that we are listening to together allows me to access something of our shared past. Crucially in my role as a carer, I see that my mother's musical recall can help support the feeling of knowing who she is.[47] We often discuss how to hold a cello's bow or where the hand on the neck might sit when making the notes. Her hands, which are now often paralyzed in rigid positions, can somehow seem freer when she is imitating the sound of her beloved cello. She can beat in time to the music with her foot or nod her head gently with the rhythm. In these small ways, she can access part of her body, memory and emotions that are tied up by the disease of dementia. Music helps us focus on the personhood of the individual with dementia and not on the loss contained within the dementia.

Music also helps with the new tempo of our house. The slowness of life can be difficult yet liberating. The day is carefully calibrated around meals, medications, toileting, and rest. Each step on the progressive journey of Mum's illness requires a gear change as we continue to slow down. However, with music I see that Mum consistently yields instead to the gentle adagio that keeps pace with her internal tempo. This simple understanding is profound. Transitioning the body and mind from the pace of work to the pace of the home requires music and an emotional release. Assisting in the bodily and psychological parts of this process is listening to Bach.

Glenn Gould, the famously idiosyncratic Canadian pianist, made his 1955 debut recording with a spirited rendition of Bach's *Goldberg Variations*, a series of thirty variations on a theme concluding with an aria. In 1955, Gould's performance lasted a spritely thirty-eight minutes. However, the very last recording Gould made was also of the *Goldberg Variations*. In 1981, Gould recorded his final album, and its deliberate fifty-one minutes feel as though each note were played with the intent of a man whose life was ending. Gould died in October 1982, not long after completing this recording. As his extraordinary career was bookended by the *Goldberg Variations*, it is fitting that his second version is somehow a tragic coda attesting to his fascination with the piece.

Aside from other artistic and aesthetic concerns, both recordings are interested in the passing of time. The second recording became a favorite of mine because in its broadness there is a sense of contemplation as Gould looks back upon his life. It encapsulates the transformation of someone at the end of their life. My mother is now in a period of life which is painful for me to fathom, and I cannot speak to her to discover how she really feels. Throughout all of this, my perception of time is radically altered.[48] The pace at which my mother walks is now an almost interminable shuffle. In her shrunken body, with tiny spindles for legs, it takes an age to move a short distance. As she gradually relinquishes walking altogether, there is the matter of hoisting her into her wheelchair and gently guiding her feet, legs, and arms into a position where they will not accidently knock her frail body against the hard edge of a doorframe or wall. This takes time and I have learned to let go of my former impatience and embrace a new sense of time. To care for her means to go at *her* pace. My father, sister, and I have learned to move slowly, deliberately, and with the kind of intent and pace that she displays. Somehow, Gould's second recording of the *Goldberg Variations* helps us negotiate the change in time, pace, and tempo of our lives as caregivers.

In describing Bach's St. Matthew Passion, the "music forms the listener's experience, and in its unique negotiation of the tension between striving and grief, it creates a knowledge of something that has been formerly unknown, something that asks to be integrated in the mind of the hearer."[49] Importantly, Gould also shapes the whole of this complex thirty-two part work into an architectural form that is complete and solid. In so doing, he suggests to us that our lives, with all their disparate and incomplete moments, are somehow capable of being a whole. I find that his recordings suggest a sense of completeness within a quiet momentum that links complex musical ideas. Gould is attentive to the nuances of every note and every moment in the piece. The relationships between these moments are highlighted and stitched together in an intricate mosaic of fugal lines. As Mum's memory fades in the haze of her cognitive dysfunction, I feel that the voice-leading in this work suggests the beauty of a whole life and the completeness of a life. Even if she cannot remember events from her life, this music fills in the gaps with the promise of a completed and coherent life narrative. Our pace of life may be slowed, but Gould's lesson seems to be that at the end of a life, if we are attentive, we can see and hear that the whole of life is somehow unified and complete.

Gould's second, much more spaciously and ominously paced recording of the *Goldberg Variations* is an ode to the slowness of life at the end. Whereas as a young man he lithely dived and wound through the counterpoint of Bach's keyboard piece, his second recording bears the hallmarks of a man coming to the end of his life. Each note sings for its full account, the weight of life existing in every moment. Listening to this recording in a deeper way when caring for my mother is soothing and reminds her of her musical life as a cellist. Moreover, when words fail us, music can say more than is possible between people who love each other and are preparing for the end.

Not everything we listen to is so ominous. A lovely experience for me is discovering a new piece of music with my mother. A long-held favorite composer of mine is Dmitri Shostakovich; however, my mother was unfamiliar with his work and did not play his music. Shostakovich was born in St. Petersburg, Russia, in 1906 and died in Moscow in 1975. A composer who lived in the shadow of Stalinist oppression, he adroitly balanced the insistent requirements of totalitarian political dictatorship over artistic culture with his own irrepressible inspiration for superb creativity to win worldwide acclaim. While many seek hidden messages of resistance against Stalin in his music, what is clear to any listener is how he gently attends to the great human tragedy of even a small, seemingly inconsequential moment. Shostakovich's sorrowful *Prelude* from The Gadfly, op. 97, arranged for two cellos and piano, has now become a favorite of my mother's. The cello voices blend together in a lyrical piece of quiet melancholy. From its opening, the sonorous dual cellos soar in harmony above the intimate piano accompaniment. A short piece of only a few minutes length, Mum especially enjoys the gentle movement of the humble and dignified melody. The cellos gracefully open the piece in a simple note-against-note harmony that mirrors the gentle arc of each other's melancholy. An unassuming rhythm propels the fragile beauty of this melody. As the cellos sweep toward the piece's high point, then surrender the painful moment to a simple resolution, Mum's hand can sometimes flinch as though she were herself playing. She connects bodily to the sound of the cello. The resonance and depth of sound in the cellos playing in simple prosodic harmony in this *Prelude* seem a testament to the richness, grace, and profound strength of my mother herself.

Music connects me to my mother through our shared experience of playing and sharing music together. It allows me to see loss and suffering in new ways. She still expresses her preferences for certain music; she can speak with quietness about why she enjoys something, and her love of the sound of the cello is still obvious in the small movements of her hands that accompany listening to music. At a painful moment in our lives when she is experiencing so many losses, I can connect with her more fully through these physical and emotional reactions. I remember her love of music, and it enriches our existence because of all the losses we have suffered. I cannot have complicated conversations with my mother anymore. She cannot explain to me in depth any aspect of her life or her needs. For many onlookers, she is lost and afraid most of the time. But when we share music in our household, it enriches my understanding of her. Through music we are connected to one another. It fills me with wonder that she was once a cellist, and it connects me to my past where she nurtured my love of music. Listening to music together increases our empathy for others and allows us to access something bigger that enriches our lives. Music allows me to see my mother differently, and it invites me to share in her journey toward death in a rich and complex way. By sharing music with her, I can more deeply grasp her happiness and her pain.

Caring for someone dying is to be transformed. Just as dementia irrevocably alters the mind of the sufferer, being a primary carer for someone afflicted with terminal dementia transforms the mind and heart. To walk toward the dying person rather than shy away from them can be a profound experience that is "mutually gratifying," and one in which the carer can learn not only about the human mind but also about "the unique human aspects of our existence."[50] This experience enriches our existence and can release anxieties about our own mortality. Walking with the dying as a carer, we are nourished and enriched. The caregiving becomes more human as the end of a loved one's life approaches. Death becomes comprehensible, meaning is recoverable and ultimately accepted as a natural part of life.

Carina Nandlal completed her PhD in art history at the University of Melbourne on Pablo Picasso's collaborations with the Ballets Russes between 1916 and 1920. Her published works include papers on Picasso's cover for Stravinsky's work "Ragtime" and the preface for the new edition of Vincent D'Indy's Symphony III, "Short Symphony in a Time of War." Recent academic conference presentations include papers on Picasso and Goncharova's designs for the Ballets Russes, Picasso and Falla's collaboration for the Three-Cornered Hat, and Picasso's guitar constructions. She has been invited to present at the Ian Potter Museum of Art on Marie Laurencin and the Ballets Russes and for the Melbourne Symphony Orchestra's Stravinsky festival.

Notes

1. Therese A. Rando, *Grief, Dying, and Death: Clinical Interventions for Caregivers* (Champaign, IL: Research Press Co., 1984), 7.
2. Robin Higgins, "Foreword," in *Arts Therapies and Progressive Illness: Nameless Dread*, edited by Deborah Waller (East Sussex: Brunner-Routledge, 2002), xiii.
3. Angelina Grigoryeva, "Own Gender, Sibling's Gender, Parent's Gender: The Division of Elderly Parent Care among Adult Children," *American Sociological Review* 82, no. 1 (2017): 116–46.

4. American Sociological Association, "Daughters Provide as Much Elderly Parent Care as They Can, Sons Do as Little as Possible," ScienceDaily, 19 August 2014, retrieved 15 December 2019 from www.sciencedaily.com/releases/2014/08/140819082912.htm.
5. Ibid.
6. Lorraine Code, "Care, Concern, and Advocacy: Is There a Place for Epistemic Responsibility?" *Feminist Philosophy Quarterly* 1, no. 1 (2015): 16.
7. Ibid.
8. Deborah Waller, "Arts Therapies, Progressive Illness, Dementia: The Difficulty of Being," in *Arts Therapies and Progressive Illness: Nameless Dread*, ed. Deborah Waller (East Sussex: Brunner-Routledge, 2002), 1.
9. Higgins, "Foreword," xiii.
10. Ken Evans, "In the Waiting Room of the Grim Reaper," in *Arts Therapies and Progressive Illness: Nameless Dread*, ed. Deborah Waller (East Sussex: Brunner-Routledge, 2002), 15. Ken Evans describes the economic pressures shaping social institutions and the assumption that families are a standardized unit formed by individuals to serve society. In this conception, caring for a dementia sufferer in the home is desirable.
11. Ibid.
12. Ibid., 14.
13. Ibid., 19.
14. Ibid., 22.
15. Jill Bunce, "The Living Death: Dance Movement Therapy with Parkinson's Patients," in *Arts Therapies and Progressive Illness: Nameless Dread*, ed. Deborah Waller (East Sussex: Brunner-Routledge, 2002), 28.
16. Higgins, "Foreword," xiii.
17. Peter Metcalf and Richard Huntington, *Celebrations of Death: The Anthropology of Mortuary Ritual* (Cambridge: Cambridge University Press, 1991), 25.
18. Robin Gray, "Cellist Established Music Camps: Obituary of Henri Edouard Touzeau, Musician," *Australian* 9 (1995): 12.
19. Waller, "Arts Therapies, Progressive Illness, Dementia," 5.
20. Jane W. Davidson and Amanda E. Krause, "Social and Applied Psychological Explorations of Music, Health and Well-Being," in *Music, Health and Wellbeing: Exploring Music for Health Equity and Social Justice*, ed. Naomi Sunderland, Natalie Lewandowski, Dan Bendrups, and Brydie-Leigh Bartleet (London: Palgrave Macmillan, 2018), 33.
21. Oliver Sacks, *Musicophilia: Tales of Music and the Brain* (London: Picador, 2018), xi.
22. Felicity Laurence, "Prologue: Revisiting the Problem of Empathy," in *Music and Empathy*, ed. Elaine King and Caroline Waddington (London: Routledge, 2017), 24.
23. Waller, "Arts Therapies," 11.
24. John Tyler, "Art Therapy with Older Adults Clinically Diagnosed as Having Alzheimer's Disease and Dementia," in *Arts Therapies and Progressive Illness: Nameless Dread*, ed. Deborah Waller (East Sussex: Brunner-Routledge, 2002), 69.
25. Theris A. Touhy, "Dementia, Personhood, and Nursing: Learning from a Nursing Situation," *Nursing Science Quarterly* 17, no. 1 (2004): 44.
26. Evans, "In the Waiting Room," 14.
27. Davidson and Krause, "Social and Applied Psychological Explorations," 38.
28. Ibid., 40.
29. Chava Sekeles, *Music Therapy: Death and Grief* (New Braunfells, TX: Barcelona Publishers, 2007), xii.
30. Jean-Michel Nectoux, "Fauré, Gabriel," *Grove Music Online,* 2001, retrieved 30 October 2019, https://www.oxfordmusiconline.com.ezp.lib.unimelb.edu.au/grovemusic/view/10.1093/gmo/9781561592630.001.0001/omo-9781561592630-e-0000009366.
31. Jakub Kasperski and John Comber, "French Requiems from the Years 1877–1963 as Thanatological Communication," *Interdisciplinary Studies in Musicology* (2008): 144.

32. Helen Hickey and Helen Dell, "Singing Death: Why Music and Grief Go Hand In Hand," *The Conversation*, 24 August 2017, retrieved 18 October 2019, https://theconversation.com/singing-death-why-music-and-grief-go-hand-in-hand-81679.
33. Fauré's original quote appeared in *Paris-Comoedia*, 3–9 March 1954, based on a conversation with Louis Aguettant from 1902, cit. after Jean-Michel Nectoux, *Gabriel Fauré: A Musical Life* (Paris, 1995), 70.
34. Kasperski and Comber, "French Requiems," 147.
35. Ibid., 159.
36. Nectoux, *Gabriel Fauré*.
37. Michael Steinberg, "Gabriel Fauré: Requiem, Op. 48," *Choral Masterworks: A Listener's Guide* (Oxford: Oxford University Press, 2005), 132–33.
38. Richard Wilkinson, "Foreword," in *Music, Health and Wellbeing: Exploring Music for Health Equity and Social Justice*, ed. Naomi Sunderland, Natalie Lewandowski, Dan Bendrups, and Brydie-Leigh Bartleet (London: Palgrave Macmillan, 2018), ix.
39. Rineke Smilde, "Being Here: Equity through Musical Engagement with People with Dementia," in *Music, Health and Wellbeing: Exploring Music for Health Equity and Social Justice*, ed. Naomi Sunderland, Natalie Lewandowski, Dan Bendrups, and Brydie-Leigh Bartleet (London: Palgrave Macmillan, 2018), 142.
40. John Zeisel, *I'm Still Here: A New Philosophy of Alzheimer's Care* (New York: Avery, 2010), 17.
41. Sacks, *Musicophilia*, 372.
42. Smilde, "Being Here," 142.
43. Ibid., 10.
44. Ibid., 141.
45. Sacks, *Musicophilia*, 385.
46. Smilde, "Being Here," 145.
47. Ibid., 143. See also Tom Kitwood, *Dementia Reconsidered: The Person Comes First* (Berkshire: Open University Press, 1997), 82.
48. Rando, *Grief, Dying, and Death*, 8.
49. E. Clarke, T. DeNora, and J. Vuoskoski, "Music, Empathy and Cultural Understanding," *Physics of Life Review* 15 (December 2015): 61–88.
50. Elisabeth Kübler-Ross, *On Death and Dying* (London: The Chaucer Press, 1973), x.

Bibliography

American Sociological Association. "Daughters Provide as Much Elderly Parent Care as They Can, Sons Do as Little as Possible." ScienceDaily, 19 August 2014. Retrieved 15 December 2019 from www.sciencedaily.com/releases/2014/08/140819082912.htm.

Bunce, Jill. "The Living Death: Dance Movement Therapy with Parkinson's Patients." In *Arts Therapies and Progressive Illness: Nameless Dread*, edited by Deborah Waller, 27–46. East Sussex: Brunner-Routledge, 2002.

Barnes, Julian. *The Noise of Time*. London: Vintage, 2017.

Clarke, E., T. DeNora, and J. Vuoskoski. "Music, Empathy and Cultural Understanding." *Physics of Life Review* 15 (December 2015): 61–88.

Code, Lorraine. "Care, Concern, and Advocacy: Is There a Place for Epistemic Responsibility?" *Feminist Philosophy Quarterly* 1, no. 1 (2015): 16–32.

Davidson, Jane W., and Amanda E. Krause. "Social and Applied Psychological Explorations of Music, Health and Well-Being." In *Music, Health and Wellbeing: Exploring Music for Health Equity and Social Justice*, edited by Naomi Sunderland,

Natalie Lewandowski, Dan Bendrups, and Brydie-Leigh Bartleet, 33–64. London: Palgrave Macmillan, 2018.

Evans, Ken. "In the Waiting Room of the Grim Reaper." In *Arts Therapies and Progressive Illness: Nameless Dread*, edited by Deborah Waller, 13–26. East Sussex: Brunner-Routledge, 2002.

Gray, Robin. "Cellist Established Music Camps: Obituary of Henri Edouard Touzeau, Musician." *Australian* 9 (1995): 12.

Grigoryeva, Angelina. "Own Gender, Sibling's Gender, Parent's Gender: The Division of Elderly Parent Care among Adult Children." *American Sociological Review* 82, no. 1 (2017): 116–46.

Hickey, Helen, and Helen Dell. "Singing Death: Why Music and Grief Go Hand In Hand." *The Conversation*, 24 August 2017. Retrieved 18 October 2019 from https://theconversation.com/singing-death-why-music-and-grief-go-hand-in-hand-81679.

Higgins, Robin. "Foreword." In *Arts Therapies and Progressive Illness: Nameless Dread*, edited by Deborah Waller, xiii–xiv. East Sussex: Brunner-Routledge, 2002.

Kasperski, Jakub, and John Comber. "French Requiems from the Years 1877–1963 as Thanatological Communication." *Interdisciplinary Studies in Musicology* (2008): 141–160.

King, Elaine, and Caroline Waddington, eds. *Music and Empathy*. London: Routledge, 2017.

Kitwood, Tom. *Dementia Reconsidered: The Person Comes First*. Berkshire: Open University Press, 1997.

Kübler-Ross, Elizabeth. *On Death and Dying*. London: The Chaucer Press, 1973.

Laurence, Felicity. "Prologue: Revisiting the Problem of Empathy." In *Music and Empathy*, edited by Elaine King and Caroline Waddington, 11–35. London: Routledge, 2017.

Metcalf, Peter, and Richard Huntington. *Celebrations of Death: The Anthropology of Mortuary Ritual*. Cambridge: Cambridge University Press, 1991.

Nectoux, Jean-Michel. *Gabriel Fauré: A Musical Life*. Paris, 1995.

———. "Fauré, Gabriel." *Grove Music Online*, 2001. Retrieved 30 October 2019 from https://www.oxfordmusiconline.com.ezp.lib.unimelb.edu.au/grovemusic/view/10.1093/gmo/9781561592630.001.0001/omo-9781561592630-e-0000009366.

Rando, Therese A. *Grief, Dying, and Death: Clinical Interventions for Caregivers*. Champaign, IL: Research Press Co., 1984.

Robertson, Alec. *Requiem: Music of Mourning and Consolation*. Westport, CT: Greenwood Press Publishers, 1976.

Sacks, Oliver. *Musicophilia: Tales of Music and the Brain*. London: Picador, 2018.

Sekeles, Chava. *Music Therapy: Death and Grief*. New Braunfells, TX: Barcelona Publishers, 2007.

Smilde, Rineke. "Being Here: Equity through Musical Engagement with People with Dementia." In *Music, Health and Wellbeing: Exploring Music for Health Equity and Social Justice*, edited by Naomi Sunderland, Natalie Lewandowski, Dan Bendrups, and Brydie-Leigh Bartleet, 139–154. London: Palgrave Macmillan, 2018.

Steinberg, Michael. "Gabriel Fauré: Requiem, Op. 48." *Choral Masterworks: A Listener's Guide*, 131–37. Oxford: Oxford University Press, 2005.

Touhy, Theris A. "Dementia, Personhood, and Nursing: Learning From a Nursing Situation," *Nursing Science Quarterly* 17, no. 1 (2004): 44–57.

Tyler, John. "Art Therapy with Older Adults Clinically Diagnosed as Having Alzheimer's Disease and Dementia." In *Arts Therapies and Progressive Illness: Nameless Dread*, edited by Deborah Waller, 69–83. East Sussex: Brunner-Routledge, 2002.

Waller, Deborah. "Arts Therapies, Progressive Illness, Dementia: The Difficulty of Being." In *Arts Therapies and Progressive Illness: Nameless Dread*, edited by Deborah Waller, 1–12. East Sussex: Brunner-Routledge, 2002.

Wilkinson, Richard. "Foreword." In *Music, Health and Wellbeing: Exploring Music for Health Equity and Social Justice*, edited by Naomi Sunderland, Natalie Lewandowski, Dan Bendrups, and Brydie-Leigh Bartleet, vii–x. London: Palgrave Macmillan, 2018.

Zeisel, John. *I'm Still Here: A New Philosophy of Alzheimer's Care*. New York: Avery, 2010.

CHAPTER 4

Death and Fulfillment
Mortuary Performance and the Impact on Self

Kalliopi M Christodoulaki

I studied death as a graduate student, or I should say that I tried to study death. I went to a Greek village on the island of Karpathos with the idea that I would learn about their mortuary practices for my master's thesis, but a significant problem arose when no one in the village died. Although it was disappointing, it was during this research that I learned that death could be a social impetus for helping to maintain a sense of community. Several years later, I went back to the same village for a different study, and within a day of my arrival, there was a death—my neighbor, a woman who had happily visited me the night before. Hers was the first of several deaths that year, some of which were very close to me and excruciatingly painful, while others were more distant. I saw how easily I had removed emotion from my previous study of death—no more apparent than in my disappointment in the lack of deaths during my initial field research. While I still understood that funeral services, memorials, and simply speaking about the deceased helped maintain community ties and strengthen familial connections,[1] I also realized how entangled one's identity was with the deceased. This connection between the living and the dead was fostered by those living in the village where I studied. I witnessed delicate performances in which participating individuals tweaked their identity and that of the person who had died. There were also moments when raw emotions made cultural prescriptions and proscriptions of behaviors seem pointless, and other moments when those same traditions gave the griever's emotions a place to shine or hide until the storm had passed. I discovered this all to be true in the most personal of ways.

This chapter focuses on the illness and subsequent death of my beloved grandmother while I was in the field gathering data for my dissertation. While studying questions of identity and social prestige, I was confronted with how the care of my grandmother, both in the final months of her life and in her death, was a series of actions that had shaped my identity and hers. By highlighting our relationship to each other, I added to our social standing in the community where we found ourselves, reinforced the ties that bound us together, and strengthened the love we had for each other. I also shaped my Karpathian identity as I showed that I understood the cultural norms by working to maintain them, thus giving me one answer to the question of "Who am I?" Within this community and for myself, I am the part of my grandmother that lives on. After all, interactions with a person who touched you deeply shape your views of the world and of others, and your interactions with both.

To Give Care

My grandmother was a woman of giving. She tried to help her family in the ways she could: cooking, cleaning, doing laundry, ironing, and raising children. Helping and caring for the household is the traditional role for women in Greece. I had seen my grandmother and my mother follow these roles. Words of love, hugs, and pats on the back were not appropriate measures of care, but cooking, feeding, laundry, caregiving—these were the true markers of love. When my grandmother had her first stroke and lost the use of her right arm, she told me that she was upset because she could no longer help us. She was not consoled when I told her it was our turn to help her. Her worth in her eyes was in giving and her value in doing. By the time I went to Greece for my dissertation fieldwork, my grandmother had had several strokes in New Jersey that left her nonverbal and confined to a wheelchair. The doctors believed the next stroke would kill her, if her heart did not give out first. My mother, the oldest daughter and chief inheritor of my grandmother's landholdings on the island, was, by Karpathian tradition, the one responsible for her care.[2] It was also expected in other parts of Greece that those who receive property should care for those who gave it to them.[3] So when it was decided that my grandmother would spend her final days on the island, we traveled there with her on our little adventure, mother, daughter, granddaughter, and two great-grandsons.

Caring for someone who cannot survive without assistance is an overwhelming task. It consumes you and shrinks your world. The courtyard where my grandmother used to entertain a dozen guests would now be the place she would find only a few of the most dedicated visitors: her sisters, a nephew, a niece, and occasional visitors from the village. We were mostly left alone to administer medicines, feed her, bathe her, and be her companions and consolers. My mother and I performed these duties in part because of the sense of debt we felt toward a woman who had cared for us. Good family members repaid their debts.

My grandmother had done the same for her mother. She was there for her during her last days; bathing her, perfuming her with a special scent from Rhodes, feeding the people who came to visit, and preparing her for burial once the time came. To me, the reciprocity made sense: you bathed me, clothed me, fed me, and cared for me when I needed the help, so I am obligated to do the same. To shirk those responsibilities would make me feel like a bad person. There was also the community that kept close watch. I had heard the villagers speak of others who had not met their obligations to a sick or deceased family member.[4] The critiques were often scathing, and I wanted no part in them.

While I can list the rational reasons for attending to the needs of my grandmother, I also did it out of love. I cared for her, and so began the daily tasks of preparing her clothes, dressing her, feeding her through a feeding tube, combing her hair, and deciphering hand gestures and glances. My mother was her main caregiver, and I assisted when needed. What I remember most vividly is laughing with my grandmother. No longer rushing to do household chores or caring for guests, she had hours to fill. A lot of these were spent in quiet contemplation, but when family came over in the evening to spend time with us or when I had to help her (a woman who hated to be helped), we laughed. My days passed like this for months, caring for a sick woman in her early eighties and playing host to those who would visit her.

My grandmother's impending death watch began on 10 February 2006. I dressed her that morning in a matching nightgown, housecoat, and socks. I said something about the future, but she violently shook her head that that future would not come for her. I left to go to another village for interviews, but by the end of the night she had a devastating stroke that left her in a vegetative state. My interactions with her—the laughter, the smiles, the warmth—were now all gone. There was just a body that did not respond to me or to anyone. I described it in my journal in this way:

> Updates: Warning this is awful!
> Grandmother: pretty much vegetative state [*sic*]. She opens her eyes. She doesn't move at all. If you pick up her arm, it falls limp at her side. The worst thing is wanting someone you love to die, for lots of reasons, but mostly because it is too horrible to see her alive like this. It is playing psychological havoc on my mother and myself.

It must have been after I had written this that my grandmother's good friend came to visit. She told me she was going to share something that would seem a little harsh and unbelievable to me. Her mother had been in a similar state before dying, and she could honestly say now that she wished her mother was still in that state as opposed to being dead. The hard work of caring for someone who was unresponsive, along with the emotional turmoil it caused, seemed worth it to her. She said that I would someday wish this too, being able to know exactly where a loved one was and being able to spend time with her. My grandmother remained like this for a month and a half. What she thought or felt was a mystery. It seemed like she slept a lot, but I assumed this because her eyes were often closed. Later I would feel a sense of guilt for not speaking to her more in spite of her unresponsiveness: an "I love you," an "Everything will be okay," or an "I am here for you," every once in a while, just to encourage her and to let her know I cared. Maybe I had said those things, but I certainly wish I had said them more often.

Just as we had experienced with my grandmother, when a person falls ill enough that death is looming, it is typical for relatives and villagers, especially women, to visit the home and stay at the bedside of the sick individual. Men will also visit, but they usually sit in another room and drink coffee. When asked why the people of the village visit those who are so close to dying, they responded that they felt they should. When asked who would go, they would often answer that it should be the beloved people.[5] In most cases, they said that those who could go, did. At the very least, one person representing a household would try to make a visit. They might do this because of the ties they had to the individual or the family, or to show the community that they had performed their duty. Additionally, such attendance created an obligation for others to visit them when they or their family members were ill.

My grandmother had lived abroad for most of her life, starting at the age of twenty-three. She did maintain a connection to her Greek community, and she visited the island whenever possible, but she was not a full-time resident, which may have caused a decrease in the number of people who felt obliged to visit her during her illness. Another reason for fewer visitors could have also been that the people of the community realized that my mother and I were not accustomed to their traditions and that we might be uncomfortable with their presence in the home. It was understood that Greek-Americans valued their privacy more than those who lived on the island. Regardless of the reason, people who were close to my grandmother commented on the lack of visitors during her final days. In a journal entry I wrote:

> The Blame Game: My mother and grandmother have been in the hospital since Friday, it is now Tuesday, without the typical number of visitors. This absence of visiting relatives was critiqued by the same absent relatives. In other words, one

aunt would criticize the other for not going to the hospital, and during the same conversation explain her own numerous obligations at home as well as ailments.

Waiting for Death

The visitor's presence is important, because, in theory, visitors help the family members of the infirm care for them, but quite often they just sit in the room, talking about everyday village events. These conversations may be of a practical nature, in which they discuss work or family issues. They may also discuss the person who is sick or talk about others in the community. The spouse or the closest relative is not to be left alone with a dying person. Instead the community sets up a buffer, and both women and men try to help the immediate family through their trying time.

As the individual comes closer to passing, a priest is called for so that the dying individual can confess his or her sins, take Holy Communion, and hear prayers that will heal his or her body and purify the soul.[6] Often the family members wait much longer than necessary to contact the priest for fear of upsetting the individual who is on their deathbed. There is also the worry that the mere mention of death will bring it more hastily.

Crying is also avoided during this time, possibly for the same reason, and because it may upset the person who is dying. Margaret Alexiou writes that in ancient Greece, "to weep for someone who was still alive, however great the probability of his death, was a bad omen."[7] This fear continues, and people avoid doing things that might suggest an impending death, but they still make some preparations. For instance, if it is clear that the individual will die, the family and friends remain near. Telephone calls will also be made to alert close relatives to come immediately. Those who are dying should have their closest family around them. It is thought that if someone is missing, the individual will be unable to pass away because he or she will be pining for that family member. It may also be important, because if one cares for a person, he or she should be present when that person dies.

How long it takes for someone to pass away is seen by some as an indicator of what type of life that individual led. A good individual will die relatively quickly and peacefully; a bad person will have a long, painful death. Nadia Seremetakis mentions that a good death among the Mani of mainland Greece is one where there is "an easy separation of the soul from the body."[8] Margaret Alexiou also describes an agonized death as one caused by the unconfessed sins of the dying person or the sins of his or her forebearers.[9]

My field research yielded another reason for prolonging death: several people explained to me, including clergymen, how powerful curses—

either those made by the dying against others or those made against the dying—prevented the soul from leaving the body.[10] A priest recounted to me how he had to be called to pray for the soul of a person who had been in the throes of death for several days because someone had told that person in his youth, "Do not die until a priest reads over you." Once the priest read the blessing, an account he described with great detail and emotion, the individual died.[11]

Another priest suggested that people who expand their property lines onto church property will be found preserved during their exhumation, showing clearly that their soul is restless.[12] They would be punished by God for their transgressions and there would be visible markers of their sin. The reaction among those present ranged from knowing affirmations, to disbelief as one woman said she never believed that people could curse others. The priest assured her that they could. These conversations suggested that one should avoid sinning and the curses of others, while also implying that some information about the moral character of an individual was evident in their manner of death or the state of their corpse. It was seen as important for the dying person to go quickly and peacefully not only for them but also for their family, as a slow death may be taken as evidence that their loved one has sinned.

My mother, being very devout, called the priest to read prayers and give Communion to my grandmother. The only people present were the priest, my grandmother, my mother, my sons, and me. When my grandmother was able to express herself, she showed no indication of being troubled by the presence of the priest. When she was not able to express herself, I believe the benefit of the priest saying a prayer was for the spiritual health of my grandmother and the emotional health of my mother. The latter must have felt less helpless knowing she was providing some assistance to her mother when no biomedical remedy was available to do so.

A few days before my grandmother's death, my mother made the decision to move her to the local first aid center at the suggestion of the doctor. My mother was not sleeping because she was afraid her mother would die. The doctor, fearing for my mother's health, felt that she would find it comforting to have my grandmother hooked up to a heart monitor that would alert us of her condition. On 30 March I received a call to take my children and go quickly to the hospital. We had been there the day before and watched a solar eclipse, faces tilted up, looking through the haze in awe—a moment of respite from the sadness of my grandmother's condition. I rushed there, but with a sense of calm, maybe because the eclipse minimized our miniscule struggles in the vastness of the universe. I saw our family members in the hall of the hospital quietly crying. One told me to hurry into the room. My mother was standing on one side of the bed on which my grandmother lay, and I noticed that the heart monitor had flatlined and was buzzing. I spoke to my grandmother as I rushed in, and there was movement once again on the heart monitor. My mother told me not to talk, to let her pass, but I asked, "Can't I tell her I love her?" My mother relented and nodded, and I said in Greek, "I love you, *yiayia* [grandma]." She left after that moment. The monitor showed a straight line and the buzzer went off after I had said those words to her. I feel that she waited for me, and I love her for it. She let me tell her what she meant to me and gave me the closure I needed in our relationship that I might not have gotten otherwise.

Preparing the Dead

My mom stood rigid, head hanging low with her finger to her lips telling me to not make a sound. We stood there for a few minutes, one on each side of her, and then my mother in a burst of energy said, "Quickly, let's prepare her." We washed her body with soapy water, then wine, and dressed her in an outfit my grandmother had chosen for herself years before. I cannot remember if I cried. I must have—both of us, daughter and granddaughter, quietly crying while preparing the woman we loved to be buried. There was so much to do. Most of it lay squarely on my mother's shoulders. As the primary caregiver, she was at a greater loss. Her entire focus for over a year had been her mother. Now this person, the center of her world, was gone. I found out when writing this chapter that my grandmother's heart had stopped right before I had arrived at the hospital but had started again when my mother pleaded to her, "What am I going to do without you?" My mother felt that, by being emotional, we were making it more difficult for my grandmother to leave us and that she deserved to be at peace when she passed. Neither of us consoled each other at the hospital or in the ensuing days. We each knew the other was suffering and that there was work to be done.

In the past, once an individual had taken their last breath and all those present had had a moment to cry, the room was eventually cleared out. Then two or more women, considered specialists at preparing the body, carried out their tasks. These women were from the village; usually their children were adults and married. They fell into their role of caring for the dead mostly because of their willingness to do so. The woman who did this task in 2002 said she was simply present when a body was being prepared, and she took on the role. When I asked which women do this work, she replied, "Whoever is not afraid." These women are part of the community, and several people I interviewed in 2002 said that they would treat them with more respect because of what they did for the corpse.[13] An elderly man mentioned to me that he refused to hear anything negative about the woman who prepared the bodies of his relatives. Another woman said, "You do not say anything bad [about these women]. They do this for their soul."[14]

Preparing the body helped the soul's journey in the afterlife. Emily Vermeule writes that the ancient Greeks felt Hades would only accept the dead if the body had been prepared.[15] Similarly, the Greek Orthodox parishioners feel that the body must be prepared in order to go before God. The women who did this work were helping the deceased on their journey, and by extension the people who cared for the deceased. Nadia Seremetakis believes this practice "domesticates the corpse" by preventing its pollution from spreading and by keeping the deceased from harming relatives that have not tended to the body properly.[16] She further suggests that "dressing, washing, and laying out the body is also an extension of the kinship ethics of care and tending."[17] To not do so is to neglect one's moral obligation. Moreover, as is common during the care of the infirm, men play a minimal role during these activities. They are never present during the time the body is washed, prepared, and dressed. They may help with the casket and assist in placing the body in it, but before that occurs the body must be stretched out, washed, and dressed by women. My mother and I prepared my grandmother for her funeral. Her niece made some of the funeral arrangements. The men of the family played a rather distant role: moving my grandmother's body to a gurney; driving the pickup truck that transported her to her home; picking up the casket from the manufacturer, placing her in it, and carrying it to the church and cemetery. They did not spend time preparing her.

Once the body is washed, a shroud—a white cloth two to three meters long, divided in two and cut with scissors in the shape of the cross—is pulled over the head of the deceased. After the shroud is placed over the body, it is dressed in clothing. The clothes that the person wears after death and for his or her journey should all be new. Quite often, the deceased has chosen his or her clothing many years before. It is usually bundled up within a large cloth square and placed in a chest or drawer to await the death of the individual. If a widow who has been wearing black dies, she must not be dressed in black. Her mourning period for her deceased husband is now over, and so colors such as navy or gray are more appropriate options.

My grandmother had been a widow for ten years, but we no longer dressed her in black—it felt too foreboding. She had her clothes neatly tied up in a bundle, placed in a drawer in the room where she slept. She had two new turquoise dresses, one with a matching jacket, a full-length slip, other undergarments, and black patent leather shoes. We chose the dress we felt was most appropriate. It was interesting to see her choices in apparel, delicate and feminine, coordinated and respectful, just as she always chose to be. My grandmother also had the sheets ready for her coffin, pretty lace-like fabrics with dainty ribbons along the edges.

I wonder when she had arranged these items in her bundle. It must have been a few decades before her death since the styles were no longer common. I remember people saying that some women would get these items ready soon after their first daughter married. Since birthdays were not celebrated traditionally in Karpathos, it is possible that a daughter's marriage was a time when one's status changed from the woman of the household to that of an elder. Preinheritance in the form of a dowry often meant that a home was given to the eldest daughter. Parents would either stay in rooms attached to the house or build another house for themselves. The daughter along with her husband had the obligation to maintain the home and the property with help from her parents and unmarried siblings. As such, the mother of the married daughter had met her obligation of having a child to inherit the home and other properties. She had raised her. She had found a suitable partner and married her to him. The "hard" work was done; one of her life missions was complete, and now she acknowledged that she would die. She had prepared for it. Each time she would come across her bundle, she would be reminded of the inevitable, and when she told loved ones where to find that bundle, she reminded her relatives of what would happen someday.

After the body is dressed in these clothes, the hands and feet are tied with handkerchiefs or ribbons. The chin is also tied, and the eyes are closed. I was not present when my grandmother was placed in the casket, but my mother tells me of how she used white strips of cloth to tie her wrists and ankles together and that these ties were undone before she was buried. My grandmother did not need to have her eyes closed or her mouth shut, since both were already closed when she died. If they had not been, we would have to do it for her; the living care for the deceased. As Vermeule writes, "The dead are helpless, and need comfort or mothering like infants, from mother or wife, to close the eyes, straighten the limbs, fix the jaw shut."[18] When an individual is not liked by the members of his family or community, it is said that "he will not have someone to close his eyes."[19] Such comments, which refer to the possibility that the deceased will not have someone to care for his body, soul, or gravesite, are common. There is a real concern among members of the community that someone should care for them after death. To refuse such care is to avoid one's responsibility. The importance of the act suggests that to disregard these final obligations is the ultimate form of neglect and represents a stain on one's character. Homer describes this in the *Odyssey* when Agamemnon bitterly recounts from Hades how his wife, Clytemnestra, refused to care for him as he was dying. He describes her leaving his eyes and mouth open as an ultimate betrayal of her duties.

This fear of not having someone to care for their corpse can encourage individuals to avoid certain types of negative behavior, because the improper care of the body is seen as fair payment for past wrongs. It is a final and unforgivable insult made by someone who should have cared for the deceased. In addition, I learned during my fieldwork in 2002 that there is a concern that individuals who die away from the village will not be cared for properly, and lamentations are sung for them. The singer will ask questions such as, "Who closed your eyes in this foreign land?"[20] This may be why there had been a tendency to bring bodies back to the village for burial (when finances would allow) where they were properly cared for.

This knowledge that I gained from my master's research showed me the importance of caring for my grandmother's corpse properly. It helped that my mother showed no fear. She charged ahead, doing what she had done for my grandmother while she was alive. Although my mother was not sure how quickly rigor mortis set in, she had been warned about it, and she rushed to get the body cleaned and dressed before it became an issue. She did so very matter-of-factly, without taking time to think of the loss or question her technique.

Farewells

The practicalities of death certificates and funeral arrangements were seen to by others. It did not take long to arrange things because my grandmother's body was brought up to the village by the afternoon of her death. She was laid out in the main room of the home, a foot or two from where she was most likely born. I looked over her and, before anyone came into the room, quickly took a cream blush I had in my pocket and added the slightest amount to her cheeks. Earlier that day, my grandmother's sister Sophia had called and said with admiration and love of her sister, "Kalliopi had a cheek like a rose petal," referring to my grandmother's flawless complexion often flushed with a hint of pink. My aunt had reminded me of my grandmother when she was alive, when I had only been thinking of her as dead, and I wanted her to be seen in that way by those who would come to pay their last regards. With that silly little addition, I made something that was prescriptive and planned my own.

The people filed in, mostly women. I remained standing near the open coffin, rather angry that the focus was not on my grandmother or on mourning her. When one woman began gossiping, I glared at her even though I knew I was participating in their culture. They were there to support the family but also to be social. This was my first such experience with a corpse in the house. How many of these events had these women attended? How many loved ones had they buried? How used to death were they? So much more than this researcher. The woman made some excuse seeing the expression on my face. I collected my emotions, realizing that I was the intruder here, and left the room. These gatherings were done in a certain way, and I did not know the protocol. My anger was misdirected toward a woman who was doing what she would typically do in this situation. The feelings that I had were directed at death, not at the living.

The attendees knew to come to our home because the quietness of the village was interrupted by the slow tolling of church bells. The community comes to life soon after the bells toll. People go out of their homes and ask others who has died. If no one is around, they will make phone calls to determine the deceased's identity. If possible they will try to visit family members in the afternoon whether or not the deceased is in the village. If the body is not in the house, they will visit for a short time. If the deceased is in the home, they may stay all night to wait with the family as the soul leaves for the afterlife. The community should be present for this journey. Food is provided to all those who stay in the home so no one will get sleepy. Some stay awake and talk quietly or cry, others serve food and drinks, while others prepare for the funeral the next morning. Family members, neighbors, and friends come together to bring comfort to the soul of the deceased, as well as to the family, and show support to the other individuals present. According to custom, the body should stay in the "good" room of the home, on a table with the feet facing east and the head west. Villagers go to see the body and kiss the icon that is laid on the breast of the deceased, something sacred on something that is potentially polluting. This visitation continues until the next day, the day of the funeral and burial.

This is what happened for my grandmother. She lay in the best room in the house overnight, surrounded by family, friends, and neighbors. She would leave her home the next day for her final trip to the church at the center of the village, a trip that she made when alive thousands of times: for Sunday services, for holidays, for her wedding and that of her daughters, for her grandchildren's baptisms, for countless other rites of passage, and for the funeral services of both her parents and other loved ones. One last time, she went through the narrow steps of her community, bidding a final farewell to it.

Mourning and Performance

As her journey on earth ended, my mother and I had a role to play both to care for her and to honor her legacy through a series of rituals and traditions. Wearing black, holding memorial services, keeping lit an eternal flame, incensing her grave, and visiting the gravesite daily were all things that became our new normal. Loring Danforth's work on death rituals in Greece shows how people mediate the differences between life and death, which includes numerous mortuary practices. He concludes that a clear divide exists and that life is in "opposition" to death.[21] While Danforth sees that death rituals enable the relationship between the dead and the living to continue, there seems to be a futility in the relationship, as communication between the living and dead is one way.[22] The Greeks I studied on the island of Karpathos do not necessarily see their relationship as futile or one-sided. The care they give to the deceased long after death suggests otherwise. The great tragedy is not so much that people die—this is understood as a natural event—but that people forget and thus do not honor the dead. During the funeral service, one of the most poignant moments is when the priest and congregation sing about an eternal remembrance of the deceased. Hearing those words, "Eternal be her memory," repeatedly, and chanted by some with determination and by others pleadingly, was emotional for me. Danforth writes, "The dead will never return,"[23] further suggesting a chasm between the living and dead. However, according to the religious beliefs of many Greeks who are Eastern Orthodox Christians, the dead are to return during the Second Coming. In addition, the dead are thought to return in dreams and visions to guide the living. I would suggest that the memorial services that occur on the third, ninth, and fortieth days after death, along with the three-month, six-month, nine-month, and one-year anniversaries of death; the exhumation process and double burial; and the caretaking of the deceased's spirit through a series of obligations would question the clear and permanent divide between life and death. David E. Sutton also found that on the Greek island of Kalymnos "there is no impetus to forget the dead."[24] This is true for family members and for the community as a whole on the island of Karpathos.

Public rituals, including those of mourning, can strengthen social bonds, bringing people together to grieve for the deceased and to console the living, all the while reflecting the social values of the society. Alliances, friendships, expressions of social roles, and the shaping of public perception in the village are created, strengthened, or challenged during these rituals, as attendance and performance are suggestive of family solidarity, status, and community ties. As Fred Gearing proposes, during rituals, a nuclear family performs to an audience.[25] It is here that they show their respective roles in the family as well as their status in it. Looking back on the funeral and the memorial services for my grandmother, I would say there was a performance to show how we were good relatives, good Christians, good villagers. Our performances also displayed the honor that we felt our loved one deserved. For instance, generosity (*philotimo*), a common theme in Greek cultural studies,[26] is a tangible way to express emotions of goodwill. By giving away material goods, one can gain status and create or solidify relationships. After the funeral, one gives food and drink to those who attend. This is done again at the memorial services. How much one gives shows that the person has the ability and the willingness to do so. During mortuary rituals, these displays assure that others will see you, the grieved, as acting appropriately in the role you hold in the community and your family. We gave away things generously after my grandmother's death. It was a way to honor her own generosity, but it was also a way for us to show people how much we loved her. There is also a hope that the deceased feels or senses their treatment, both of the body and soul, along with what relatives do in their name. The soul should be made happy, proud, and comfortable.

The "audience" at rituals also performs for the nuclear family by showing them how they are good neighbors, friends, or relatives. For instance, a relative sent us orange tree leaves from her grove as soon as we returned to the village on the day of my grandmother's death. It was a "gift" to be used in the pillow placed under the head of the deceased. The familial connection was meaningful. It was this niece's last present to her aunt. She was showing her own generosity while also indicating her connection to the deceased. Her gift had both a practical element—to provide cushion in a pillow and a fragrance to help mask odors—and an emotional component as well. The leaves were once alive, now dead, much like the deceased, and the transfer from one person to another was done with sentimentality. Although the mortuary practices deal with the complexities of death, both practical and emotional, they also unite the community through obligations of attendance and participation. It is a way of perpetuating what it means to be a "good" member of the community. It is a time when people perform the obligations to the deceased and his or her family, and also when they display social ties and emotions.

This display is important. I heard several times during my visits to Greece that it is about the image you portray to the outside world. Jill Dubisch proposes that Greek religion also has an interest in the external images, from making the sign of the cross at the appropriate moments to kissing relics or an icon. One must show piety. Greeks feel that the internal state of an individual is inaccessible.[27] Public displays and performances give those present an image of what is considered an appropriate internal state. It is not enough to feel great pain at the loss of a loved one; it should also be expressed. Such an analysis may lead to a better understanding of the behavior seen during rituals, particularly those associated with death, as what one is feeling must be expressed behaviorally in order for the community to appreciate those who are grieving. Some of the displays of grief in Greece, which may include keening, take on an element of caricature to many Westerners who may be used to more subdued forms of expression. When one understands that these behaviors show how one is feeling, or how one ought to be feeling, this display of emotion is appropriate for the situation. In the past, women would take down their hair, loosen their braids, and, while singing lamentations, pull their hair or hit themselves—a violent performance of grief and anger. The women of this village do not currently do this. A woman explained to me, "This is something from before my mother's time. Now they do not even cry properly."[28] Expressing emotion appropriately is expected.

Mourning is a performance showing both grief and respect—respect for the deceased and for the deceased's family. By not mourning properly, one is expressing possible ill will toward the deceased and their family. To do such a thing would encourage animosity and possibly a negative reaction. In some ways, this may be enough of a reason for people to mourn through dress, abstain from activities, or cry at the appropriate rituals. As mentioned in *The Iliad*, after Achilles loses his best friend and comrade, Patroclus, other Greeks mourned the loss for selfish reasons. "Antilochus kneeling near, weeping uncontrollably, clutched Achilles' hands as he wept his proud heart out—for fear he would slash his throat with an iron blade."[29] Thus, weeping may be an emotional release, or it may be a required performance. Many times, I heard women say that they could not go to a festivity because they were embarrassed to do so for fear that the family of the deceased would find out. One woman said that she needed to let forty days pass before she could break her mourning. Another woman responded that she understood but that this year one death followed another, with the village having been in continuous mourning since Easter.[30]

People were also critical of individuals who did not follow what is believed to be the appropriate protocol. On another occasion, a woman named Theano spoke of a family in a neighboring village. She said with disdain that musical instruments were brought to the home of the family in mourning. The women surrounding Theano listened disapprovingly, clicking their tongues and shaking their heads. She went on to say that many people in that village spoke of how inappropriate the behavior was.[31] This family did not mourn their dead properly. If those who inherited were not good mourners of the dead, there would be consequences that involved ostracization, a decline in status, and possibly a decrease in attendance at their own family functions. There may also be spiritual consequences with the neglect of the dead. The deceased could bring bad luck as a form of retaliation or there may be an inability to die peacefully because of neglecting one's obligations to the dead.

This prevailing idea of external images expressing internal states was exemplified for me when I wanted to say some words at a service held in my grandmother's honor to convey how important she was to me and to my family and that she deserved to be honored in such a way. I felt that if I did not do this, her status would be diminished. It is common for people to say or sing a few words at these events as a way of recalling the positive life led by the deceased as well as to express what their loss meant to the speaker and the family. Often the higher the status of the speaker, the better. It is during such public events that the living rework or re-emphasize the deceased's accomplishments in order to maintain, remind others of, or improve his or her status. By extension, my grandmother's status impacts my own status. An honorable forebearer is better than a dishonorable one. I wanted to showcase this with the verses I had written in Greek, and while I felt like crying as I read the words, I did not want to diminish the performance. Each example of her value to me and to my family needed to be spoken out loud, clearly, so that others could understand who she was as a person and what her death meant to those who loved her; to do so I had to balance emotion and performance.

Conclusion

Many of the tasks required to properly care for those who are dying, to prepare the body, and to tend to the soul were done by the women of the family and from the village. The closest relatives of the deceased may be paralyzed with emotion or disbelief at their loss, so others spring into action by remembering, reminding, and orchestrating the various tasks that need to be done. Our extended family helped us perform these many obligations. Without them, we would have been lost. Our family members were also in mourning with us, both visibly and emotionally. Our black uniform became a badge of honor. Our outings became restricted to churches and cemetery visits, which also marked our sadness. In this way, the focus, whether spoken or not, was often on my grandmother. Her presence was in the details.

During this period of caregiving and mourning, with its many rituals and practices, there was an attempt to perform roles that can be seen as fulfilling an obligation and bringing honor to the deceased as well as the living. For instance, I wanted to show that I was a good caretaker, granddaughter, Karpathian, and person. It was a performance, and possible completion, of one's obligations to the people within a family and a community. For this reason, displays of piety, concern, and bereavement send an important message. People are aware that they must act mournful and respectful for others to believe that they feel that way. Fear of the living is understandable, but the dead also need to be placated. The dead are cared for by the living, and if the living fail, the dead respond accordingly. For months after my grandmother's death, we were willingly at her service.

My grandmother did not visit us. We believe we had done well by her. She had done well by us too. More importantly, my grandmother's illness and death taught me a valuable life lesson; the people who are most important in your life are the ones who are present for you when things are difficult. They stop what they are doing and make time for you. They care for you in praxis and not through words alone. If the occasion arises, they may close your eyes and dress you lovingly. They will mourn when you are no longer here and yet celebrate having had the pleasure of knowing you. I learned this only after someone I cared for died. When I studied death, I did so as an observer, distant and unaffected. In my master's thesis, for instance, I used the word "expired" several times. I had completely objectified the dead in a way that I could not do so after my grandmother's passing. Several months after my grandmother's funeral, a young man whom I had gotten to know during my fieldwork committed suicide. He had spoken to me of the truth one cold fall day, insisting that there needed to be more of it in the world. Apparently the world failed him. Several months later, he put several gallons of gasoline in the back of his shiny, black pickup truck and drove it into a ravine. When I went to his funeral, I wept. I cried for him. I cried for my grandmother. I cried for myself. I wept more than was acceptable for someone who was not a relative, and I did not even care that people were watching me curiously. When the young man's aunt hit his coffin, yelling at him and telling him it was wrong to do what he had done, I understood it. I wanted to yell with her. When his parents couldn't raise their heads from grief, weighed down by the loss of someone they loved, I understood their burden, and I felt it. When I realized that I was crying for myself, I understood that death is personal. We calculate the loss to *us*, and we weep because of it. How we understand death and how we deal with it is in large part cultural, but there are visceral emotions that exist, which must be acknowledged. These are often lessons taught by example, as described by Nikos Kazantzakis in his book *Freedom and Death*. A man has died, and his family keeps a deathwatch; among them is a young boy who is aware of his duties to his dead grandfather.

> "Come to bed, my child. It's nearly midnight."
> But Thrasáki refused to obey:
> "I'm watching by granddad," he said. "Father hasn't come. I'm watching in his place."[32]

Kalliopi M Christodoulaki is a cultural anthropologist and independent researcher currently working as a limited term lecturer at Purdue University. She received her doctorate in anthropology from Purdue University in 2010, and her dissertation research focused on gender roles, community identity, and value systems on the island of Karpathos in Greece. Her research interests include religious practices, social identity, and cultural change.

Notes

1. This is the conclusion I derived from my master's thesis data collection and analysis along with the review of work from previous studies and theoretical approaches.
2. On the Greek island of Karpathos, a home and landholdings typically go from mother to the oldest daughter. It is pre-inheritance in the form of dowry and is meant to secure a good husband while preventing the division of property.
3. Loring Danforth, *The Death Ritual of Rural Greece* (Princeton, NJ: Princeton University Press, 1982), 124.
4. Clara M. Christodoulakis, "Ouroboros: The Creation of Community through Death" (master's thesis, Purdue University, 2002).
5. Ibid., 45.
6. Danforth, *Death Ritual*, 38.
7. Margaret Alexiou, *The Ritual Lament in Greek Tradition* (New York: Cambridge University Press, 1974), 4.
8. Nadia Seremetakis *The Last Word: Women, Death, and Divination in Inner Mani* (Chicago: Chicago University Press, 1991), 69.
9. Alexiou, *Ritual Lament*.
10. Christodoulakis, "Ouroboros," 47.
11. Ibid.
12. Once the deceased is buried, they remain so for several years. There is an exhumation of the body that occurs after this time, after which the bones washed and sunned. A priest reads prayers during part of this procedure, and once the bones have been cared for properly they are placed either in a box or a cloth bag to be stored in a special room in the cemetery (if the family has the funds) or thrown in an ossuary pit. This process is thought to be good for the soul. It is also a time when the decomposition is used as a marker of the state of the soul. If only bones remain, the soul is in a good place. If the body has not decomposed, the soul is in a bad place, and family members must do religious rituals along with a priest to help rectify this. The practical benefit of this practice is that it frees up a burial site for the newly deceased.
13. Christodoulakis, "Ouroboros," 92.
14. Ibid., 93.
15. Emily Vermeule, *Aspects of Greek Death in Early Greek Art and Poetry* (Berkeley: University of California Press, 1979), 12.
16. Seremetakis, *Last Word*, 64–65.
17. Ibid., 65.
18. Vermeule, *Aspects of Greek Death*, 14.
19. *Christodoulakis*, "Ouroboros," 50–51.
20. Ibid., 51.
21. Danforth, *Death Ritual*, 32.
22. Ibid., 33.
23. Ibid., 115.
24. David Sutton, *Remembrances of Repasts: An Anthropology of Food and Memory* (New York: Berg, 2001), 38.
25. Fred Gearing, "Preliminary Notes on Ritual in Village Greece," in *Contributions to Mediterranean Sociology*, ed. J. G. Peristiany (Paris: Mouton & Co., 1968), 66–67.
26. See John K. Campbell, *Honor, Family, and Patronage* (New York: Oxford University Press, 1974); Ernestine Friedl, *Vasilika: A Village in Modern Greece* (New York: Holt, Rinehart and

Winston, 1962); Michael Herzfeld, *The Poetics of Manhood: Contest and Identity in a Cretan Mountain Village* (Princeton, NJ: Princeton University Press, 1985).
27. Jill Dubisch, *In a Different Place: Pilgrimage, Gender, and Politics at a Greek Island Shrine* (Princeton, NJ: Princeton University Press, 1995).
28. Christodoulakis, "Ouroboros," 100.
29. Homer, *The Iliad*, trans. Robert Fagles (New York: Penguin Books, 1990), 18.36–38.
30. Christodoulakis, "Ouroboros," 64.
31. Ibid., 65.
32. Nikos Kazantzakis, *Freedom and Death* (London: Faber and Faber, 1956), 436.

Bibliography

Alexiou, Margaret. *The Ritual Lament in Greek Tradition*. New York: Cambridge University Press, 1974.

Campbell, J. K. *Honor, Family, and Patronage*. New York: Oxford University Press, 1974.

Christodoulakis, Clara M. "Ouroboros: The Creation of Community through Death." Master's thesis, Purdue University, 2002.

Danforth, Loring M. *The Death Rituals of Rural Greece*. Princeton, NJ: Princeton University Press, 1982.

Dubisch, Jill. *In a Different Place: Pilgrimage, Gender, and Politics at a Greek Island Shrine*. Princeton: Princeton University Press, 1995

Friedl, Ernestine. *Vasilika: A Village in Modern Greece*. New York: Holt, Rinehart and Winston, 1962.

Gearing, Fred. "Preliminary Notes on Ritual in Village Greece." In *Contributions to Mediterranean Sociology*, edited by J. G. Peristiany, 65–72. Paris: Mouton & Co., 1968.

Herzfeld, Michael. *The Poetics of Manhood: Contest and Identity in a Cretan Mountain Village*. Princeton, NJ: Princeton University Press, 1985.

Homer. *The Iliad*. Translated by Robert Fagles. New York: Penguin Books, 1990.

Kazantzakis, Nikos. *Freedom and Death*. Translated by Jonathan Griffin. London: Faber and Faber, 1956.

Peristiany, J. G. "Honour and Shame in a Cypriot Highland Village." In *Honour and Shame*, edited by J. G. Peristiany, 171–90. London: Weidenfeld and Nicolson, 1965.

Seremetakis, C. Nadia. *The Last Word: Women, Death, and Divination in Inner Mani*. Chicago: University of Chicago Press, 1991.

Sutton, David E. *Remembrance of Repasts: An Anthropology of Food and Memory*. New York: Berg, 2001.

Vermeule, Emily. *Aspects of Death in Early Greek Art and Poetry*. Berkeley: University of California Press, 1979.

PART III

Confronting Death

CHAPTER 5

Crossroads
Life and Death in Indiana

Aubrey Thamann

> Death ... is an event of no mean importance. The nearest relatives and friends are disturbed to the depth of their emotional life. A small community bereft of a member, especially if he be important, is severely mutilated.
>
> —Bronislaw Malinowski, *Magic, Science and Religion*[1]

This chapter is based on my dissertation and doctoral studies fieldwork. Between 2007 and 2009, I conducted fieldwork for an ethnographic study of funeral directors in Indiana. My research took place at several homes throughout the state, where I spent several weeks over the course of those two years. My fieldwork took the form of surveys, interviews, and note taking as I observed funerals, consultations, embalmings, and day-to-day office work. I focused on the importance of the role of the funeral director role in mainstream US culture. In this culture we have compartmentalized death, banishing it to hospitals as we try to stave it off for as long as possible, and we attempt to deny an emotional reaction to the death of a loved one. Malinowski writes, "By setting in motion one part of the deep forces of the instinct of self-preservation, [death] threatens the very cohesion and solidarity of the group, and upon this depends the organization of that society, its tradition, and finally the whole culture."[2] Death threatens our social cohesion, and by trying to deny an emotional reaction to death, we exacerbate that threat. Funeral directors help us to mitigate it.

Inspired largely by Renato Rosaldo's introduction to his book on social analysis,[3] I connected personal experiences with my professional ones in the field while writing my dissertation. What follows is a reflexive discussion, informed by anthropological and thanatological scholarship, of my time in the field.

Becoming Well Acquainted with Death

On 4 August 1969 my paternal grandmother, for whom I was named, died from pancreatic cancer. On 31 December 1987 my paternal grandfather died, and his was the first of many funerals I was to attend throughout my life. On 30 March 2003 my cousin Greg died by suicide. On 1 July 2012 my mentor, friend, and dissertation committee chair O. Michael Watson died from esophageal cancer. These four losses framed and shaped my doctoral studies as well as my relationship with death.

Although the four deaths I just mentioned have had the most profound effects on me, these are not the only losses I have experienced. I attended eleven funerals during the course of my fieldwork—five through my contacts and six personal losses. In the few months that I had to work on revisions to my dissertation, I lost three more relatives. Having death as so constant a companion certainly influenced my research interests, and it was impossible for me not to incorporate those losses into my writing. Like Rosaldo, writing personally about my grief and loss, and at the same time turning my observer's eye on it all, helped me to work through that grief and loss. This became the focal point of my work: funeral directors help us process death because, as a culture that values independence, we have turned away from it. We seem to have lost the ability to find *communitas*. Victor Turner defined *communitas* as an intense, usually spontaneous and unconscious feeling of connection to others, often achieved while enduring a period of liminality. *Communitas* is, as Turner states, "an essential and generic human bond, without which there could be no society."[4] It is that visceral connection we feel with others who are going through a rite of passage with us—and funeral directors help us find it.

I do not think that I had really chosen this project when I started. I cannot even remember how I decided to do this work in the first place, and of course, with a topic like this, everyone's first question is always, "Why funeral directors?" When I started my doctoral studies, I was more interested in examining horror films and folklore. I suppose there is a connection there with death. I wanted to know why people like horror films so much. Why are we obsessed with death yet terrified of it at the same time? Perhaps it came from wondering how others can deal with it day in and day out while I could become such a basket case after two deaths. It might have even come from my long-held fascination with the unique relationship we have with death in mainstream US culture.

Thus, when I first began thinking about what to research for my dissertation, I was primarily focused on how film functions as a vehicle for folklore—specifically how horror films often take motifs from urban legends as their thematic makeup. I began looking at horror films from within the framework of terror management theory (TMT). TMT essentially argues that we are continually struggling between a desire to live a long, valued life and our awareness of our own mortality. In an effort to mitigate this struggle, we have developed culturally based worldviews that give our lives meaning.[5] Horror films resonate for us, then, because we are able to face our own mortality and defend our value vicariously. We do not have to continually validate our existence personally or physically. When the monster (representing death) ultimately loses in the end (whether by dying or merely failing to kill the protagonist), then our confidence in our worldview that our lives are meaningful is reinforced.[6]

It was difficult at that time, though, to pin down a specific group of people or culture about whom to conduct an ethnographic study. So I asked myself about the root of my interest in this particular topic. Primarily, I was interested in what I saw as America's death phobia. My next question was, who deals with death on a regular basis? The first answer that came to me was funeral directors. I then set out to discover how funeral directors, as a group, handle working with death for a living, as members of a death-phobic society. I had some selfish motives as well—keep in mind the high number of deaths in my life that I mentioned. I think I was looking for some cathartic experience that would help me to better process loss.

Initially, I still wanted to focus on horror films, but at this point it was more about images of funeral directors in our popular culture. I wanted to know what they thought about those images, how they worked to combat them (if they did), and what their own sense was of who they were. Although the answer to this last question became a central theme to what I was uncovering through my fieldwork, what I was observing throughout my time in the field led me to much deeper meanings behind the role that funeral directors play in our society.

Fearing Death

When I began my research, I had already developed some obsessive-compulsive behavior about death that continued for several years, which only began to fade as I was processing everything I had learned throughout my research. I had terrible anxiety about death. Not my own, but that of my family and friends. And I had my rituals. I could not leave the house in the morning, for example, without saying "Good-bye, drive safe, have a good day, I love you" to my husband. If I did this, then got caught up in doing something else before I left the house, I had to go back and do it all over again. I was afraid that if I did not, and something happened to him, I would not have said good-bye. Even though, of course, I did—fifteen times. I had never had so much to lose—I grew increasingly afraid of what might happen to him, and the need to say good-bye to him properly became an obsessive compulsion.

I think my anxiety began when I came home from a wedding in St. Louis to the news that my cousin had shot himself. I had just spent my first weekend away with my husband—although we were just dating at the time—at his cousin's wedding. When I got home, my mother was the only one there. She asked me rather quietly if I had had a good time and how the wedding was. She then told me that my cousin Greg had shot himself. I remember asking if he was dead and my mother responding, "Well, yeah, he committed suicide." I sat down on the couch, in shock. My first thought was that my cousin's mother was next, still grieving from the loss of her husband only two years before. I remembered how Greg had repeatedly invited me over for dinner with him and his family. I never went—was this partially my fault? When he stopped by my apartment to bring me my mail as part of his carrier route, why had I never noticed that he was depressed, or that he had lost too much weight? Why the hell had no one else noticed the signs we all learn about in eighth grade health class? I remembered the first and only time I had ever been on a motor-cycle—I was eight, and Greg took my sister and me around his neighborhood. I remember wondering how on earth they were possibly going to do an open casket, since he had shot himself in the head. At the funeral itself, I remember his wife running around, slightly hysterical, showing other mourners those photographs clutched in her hands, photos of happier times, bowling, drinking, Greg's earlier days with his rock n' roll long hair. I remember kneeling in front of Greg's casket, asking him why, asking him if he realized what he had done, how he could so completely destroy so much for so many people. My Euro-American sense of distaste for the dead keeping me from kissing him on the cheek, remembering my father kissing his father on the cheek at his funeral, wanting to do it, unable to, settling for a hand on the chest. Saying good-bye. My mother asking me at the funeral, as I am sobbing, if I am alright. How could she ask me that? Did she not realize where we were? Or why? Me singing "Amazing Grace," a song I have come to despise with all it represents. Breaking down once I returned to my pew.

Greg's was the last death in a long series that year—a great-uncle, a friend at work, the family dog, and then my cousin. I remember my father's toast at Christmas after all of this had happened: "Well, it hasn't been a good year. Let's hope the next one is better. To Dickens." That was our family dog. Though he did not mention his godson, my cousin, I know we were all thinking of him at that moment. I think it was just easier for him to mention the family dog. None of us had known that Greg was depressed, except his wife, who had not told anyone. I think it is pretty easy to be in denial about the real depression of someone you love, particularly if it is someone like Greg, who was always a lot of fun to be around. Before Greg died, I had been pretty okay with the idea of death. I had lost two grandfathers, a few great-aunts, an uncle. I thought I had come to terms with death—everyone I knew who had died up to that point had been sick or old, with the exception of my coworker. I knew at least they were not suffering anymore, so, to me, death was not a bad thing. I knew it could be hard on the people left behind. I had to sing at one grandfather's funeral as well as my uncle's, and that was really rough. But I was not afraid of death. I was not afraid that my husband or friends might die soon, or my sister, or even my parents. And then my mother: "How was your trip? I need to talk to you about something."

I am extremely uncomfortable even now, years later, talking about his death objectively. In my family we talk about "when Greg died" or "when Greg did what he did." In death positivity circles, they have pushed the phrase "died by suicide" instead of using the term "committed," because "committed" evokes crime or sin; it is a term that blames. For the longest time I willfully chose "committed" because my grief over his death vacillated between guilt and anger. I still feel the guilt that I think all suicide survivors must feel—if only I had hung out with him when I was living in Cincinnati. If only I had tried to spend more time with him. If only I had recognized his depression the few times I saw him that year. It might be that the guilt that I have since carried created my obsessive-compulsive habits when it came to saying goodbye to family and friends. I think I was stuck in phase three of grief, bargaining: hey, universe, if I make sure to follow the right rituals, no more deaths, okay? The last time I saw Greg, he was delivering my mail, and we just stood in my doorway, chatting. I am sure I invited him in and he refused because he was on a schedule, but that image is something I keep going back to whenever I think of him. With his death, my debilitating fear of death and loss had begun.

Denying Death

> Men do not weep for the dead because they fear them; they fear them because they weep for them.
>
> —Émile Durkheim[7]

Most cultures fear death; indeed, terror management theory would argue that the very reason humans universally believe in some form of afterlife is to offset our fear of just ending. However, it was in the West, specifically in the United States, that we began to work to stave off death indefinitely. Medical and technological advancements prolong the life of our physical bodies, even well after our minds are gone. Jack B. Kamerman argues that "American culture defines death as the failure and life as the goal, and when life is so valuable, death becomes unthinkable."[8] Geoffrey Gorer talks about death as the new taboo, akin to pornography.[9] We do not want to talk about it, because to talk about it makes it real. Death as a natural process has become disgusting to us, as well as a seeming failure of will, because it is less common at younger stages of life.

Beginning in the 1930s, we moved death from the family home to the hospital or nursing home, so the responsibility to care for the dying is now in the hands of doctors and nurses. Because we have lost touch with death as an everyday occurrence, we have begun to deny its existence. In their history of funeral practices in the United States, Habenstein and Lamers write, "The modifications and developments in the organization of American funeral practices has led to a vastly different response to the problems of death and the disposal of the dead."[10] Caring for the dying and disposal of the dead is no longer in the hands of the families of the deceased.

Philippe Ariès argues that in the non-US West, death is completely denied—there is no viewing of the body, and wakes are on the decline.[11] But in the United States we insist on viewings, and thus embalmings are part of the process. Why? According to Ariès, this is what makes our relationship to death unique. We acknowledge death, but we insist on transforming it rather than trying to make it disappear altogether. In my experiences, both personally and professionally, the funeral director is able to stage a life-focused scene through the process of embalming. Increasingly, this living tableau is meant to represent the individual personality of the deceased. People are buried in their favorite team sweatshirt; coffins can be individualized to represent hobbies of the deceased; props are sometimes brought in. In some funeral homes, the living tableau is taken one step further to make it seem as though the deceased is attending his or her own funeral.[12] Again, why? Why do we go to all this trouble to create these types of scenes? Ariès argues that it is emotion we are afraid of rather than death per se. He writes of the "interdiction of death in order to preserve happiness"[13] and how this ultimate denial changes our relationship to death: "The definitive nature of the rupture has been blurred. Sadness and mourning have been banished from this calming reunion."[14] In other words, death is sad, and emotion must be avoided at all costs, so death is transformed to resemble life more closely. This practice makes it easier to maintain composure at a funeral.

Yet, this only pushes the question further—if we accept Ariès's argument that it is really emotion we are afraid of rather than death, then why are we so afraid of emotion? I believe it is due to the focus on the individual in our society. Individualism and self-reliance are core values in mainstream American culture. As Emerson wrote, "It is only as a man puts off from himself all external support, and stands alone, that I see him to be strong and to prevail."[15] Connecting Emerson's self-reliant individual to Ariès's assertion about death, if we are overly emotional at a person's death, then that demonstrates we were at the very least emotionally connected to that person. Depending on our relationships to others is in opposition to the traditional American concept of the individual. As discussed above, individualism is so important to us that our funerary ritual, in place for the living, has become a showcase of the deceased's personality rather than an event centering on the needs of the bereaved. An effect of this is that we then struggle to achieve a much-needed, visceral connection with our fellow mourners. Roy and Jane Nichols, funeral directors who wrote an essay for Elisabeth Kübler-Ross's book *Death: The Final Stage of Growth*, argue that "people need to come to grips with the reality of death. This acceptance must not only be intellectual, it must also be emotional. What appears to be acceptance can be deceptive and can be very, very destructive when the acceptance is only intellectual."[16] Acceptance of death must include an emotional reaction to the death, so if we attempt to banish emotion from the process, then the death is not real. If we do not process the death as real, then we run the risk of an uncompleted social drama (which is any social process that generates a social conflict), which in turn severely hinders our ability to heal, maintain, or forge deep connections with others experiencing the same loss. If we are unable to make those connections, also known as *communitas*, then we run the risk of losing social cohesion altogether. It is my argument, then, that funeral directors, by performing certain roles from within their liminal status, help us to achieve *communitas* following a death.

One death for which I did not get to experience *communitas* is that of my paternal grandmother. I was jealous of other kids who had all four of their grandparents. I never knew her; she died before I was born. My father and aunt talk about how amazing she was, how kind and generous. My sister reminds us every Christmas how they had sloppy joes for Christmas dinner. My aunt used to share a joke that my grandmother would make, about being named Mary Magdalene, about being the "Great Sinner." I was named after her. The way my dad tells it, Aubrey Mary did not flow right, so they changed it to Aubrey Marie. I wonder if she related to the first Mary Magdalene or if she felt a connection to her. I wonder what motivated her to make that joke. I have a photograph of my dad's family when they were kids. My uncle, who also died before I was born, looked so much like his mother. He was the only one; I wonder if this bonded them. I have another photo of my grandmother, on her wedding day. At my wedding, I borrowed from my sister a cameo ring that had belonged to her. This is what I have of her—snippets of stories, photographs, personal artifacts. I cannot make her real, no matter what I do. I cannot make my grandmother, lost to cancer far too young, real, yet her death affects me profoundly. I mourn for never having had the opportunity to mourn for her. I did not get to experience her funeral, so I did not go through the rituals of letting go, of saying goodbye—for me there was no opportunity for *communitas*.

Although *communitas* is the intended result of funeral ritual, a death can create rifts between survivors, particularly if they disagree on how to give a funeral or how to mourn properly. As I was finishing some revisions on my dissertation, my maternal grandmother was in Florida with my uncle, and she was dying. She had been suffering dementia for several years. I am not sure if my mother's relationship with her brother will survive their mother's death. They fought over where my grandmother should live once she began showing signs of dementia. They fought over her care while she was living at my uncle's house. And then they fought because they could not agree on how they should be grieving. My uncle wanted my mother to be more upset. He would call her up, crying. He kept taking photos of this shell that used to be my grandmother and sending them to my mother. She did not want them. She would say she lost her mother years ago. She wanted it all to be over. Neither she nor my uncle could comprehend how the other was grieving.

Like my mother and her brother, we all grieve in different ways, for different losses. This is one of the ways in which a death can cause breaks in family ties, and funeral directors do what they can to lead mourners through these differences. Throughout the course of my fieldwork, I noticed that the funeral directors would adapt their behavior to fit however the families they were working with might be grieving. If the family needed levity, the funeral directors would be more jovial, make some jokes, talk about sports, pat people on the back as if they were old friends. And if the family needed to cry out and fall to their knees, the funeral directors would be there to pick them up when it was time.

This seemingly innate knowledge of what the families might need permeated every aspect of the funeral process. Although I was usually allowed to sit in on consultations to observe, there was one instance where I was asked to sit in a back room where I might listen in, but the family would not be able to see me. The funeral director I was working with told me that he thought it was going to be emotional and might be awkward for the family if I were there. This was a small town, and they knew the funeral director but did not know me at all. Afterward he told me about this family. The man who had died had hanged himself while his wife was camping with her boyfriend. Their daughter found him. The director wondered aloud how the mother could tell her daughter where she was while her father died, and I could see why he would not want me sitting in the meeting with the family, someone who was, unlike himself, a total stranger.

The most memorable of all the consultations at which I was present was one following the death of a newborn, and it was this meeting that demonstrated most clearly to me that funeral directors provide such an important service to us. The parents were a very young couple, maybe eighteen or nineteen years old. Apparently the baby had died within seven hours of being born. I observed Donald,[17] the funeral director, working with this particular family, noting how he spoke, how he utilized body language, and what words or phrases he chose to use. He spoke softly the entire time, which was very different from his usual gregarious nature while in the office. He made sure to look each of them in the eye, even though I could tell that was difficult for the parents. The teenage girl's mother was there as well, and Donald included her in the conversation by making sure to look into her eyes as well when he was speaking with her. He also consistently reminded them that everything was their choice, making sure to give them what they really wanted. They seemed so lost, so he did offer suggestions, but anytime he did that, he reiterated that the choice was theirs to make. While telling them about how the ceremony would go, Donald mentioned to them that the officiant had been through quite a lot herself, and that she would do an excellent job for them because of her own experiences. At one point they were discussing whether or not to have an open casket. Donald needed to check on the condition of the body to proceed on that particular conversation, so he brought me down to the embalming room with him. This was a particularly difficult moment for me, but Donald continued to maintain the manner in which he was presenting himself to the family. I had to look away the whole time. It took everything I had to keep from crying. As gentle as he was with the couple, he was even gentler with the baby, as though he were handling a living infant. He carefully put moisturizing lotion on the baby's face, but in the end assessed that an open casket would not be an option, as the baby had not been embalmed. Later someone told me that everyone in the building cried as they watched Donald, who is a large man, bring this tiny baby down to the embalming room, cradling him so gently in his arms.

Later I asked Donald how the baby died. He gave me a funny look and said something like, "Don't you know? God took that baby up to heaven." I realized as soon as he said this I should not have asked. It was tacky of me. He never brought up how the baby died, out of respect for the family. This memory is difficult for me to write about, because it must have been such a heartbreaking loss for those young parents. I once confided in my committee chair that I was afraid of crying in front of my consultants because I was worried it would seem unprofessional. He told me that if I needed to cry, I should go ahead and do it—all it would do is show that I am human. But it is hard for me to be that nakedly human in front of others, and I think that is what funeral directors are trying to mitigate—it is difficult for all of us to be so human and vulnerable, to admit that we *needed* that person who died. Every single funeral director I worked with told me that they work with the living, not the dead. In constructing the role of the funeral director, we seem to have created a failsafe for making sure we still properly process death, even while we deny its reality. We developed into a culture in which we struggle to achieve that connection, that *communitas*, but we then created a figure who would help us do so. In addition, funeral directors are necessarily liminal—they have to work in that space that we do not want to enter, whether because death is ultimately profane or because it brings out emotions we do not want to feel. The funeral director enters that liminal space for us and brings us out on the other side.

Performances of Mourning

Throughout my dissertation, I focused on the performative aspects of the funeral—how the funeral director, those in mourning, and even the deceased play certain roles as we perform our various funerary rituals during this final rite of passage.

In doing my background reading for this ethnographic project, I came across a lot of references to performance theory, which uses language centered on ideas of performance to discuss ritual and social drama. Mortuary ritual, then, is broken down as a social drama, which Victor Turner defines as "units of aharmonic or disharmonic process, arising in conflict situations."[18] As social drama, the event of a death, as well as the performances of mourning and funerary ritual, can be critiqued in terms of the performed actions associated with them. Turner writes, "I like to think of ritual essentially as performance, as enactment, and not primarily as rules or rubrics. The rules frame the ritual process, and the ritual process transcends its frame."[19] Turner is arguing that ritual is essentially performance because it is never fully circumscribed by its rules. People follow the idea but always make the ritual their own through their performance of it. It is this assertion that informs my own analysis of the ritual data that I collected—data that I analyze through its performances.

Turner addresses the four main phases of a social drama: breach, crisis, redressive action, and reintegration. In these terms, the death is the breach of social relations. The crisis, which can be different for each person affected, involves the time between learning of the death and the performance of the funeral ritual. Is the person next of kin? Will that person be planning the funeral or be merely expected to attend? The crisis can be even deeper—if there is bad blood between the deceased and someone who survives them, in what capacity does that person show up, if at all? The redressive action would be the funeral itself, held for a symbolic act of processing the loss. Reintegration can also be complex—Turner discusses it in terms of whether or not the offending party (the deceased) would be reintegrated back into the community or if a small group would secede from the primary one.[20] In dying, the offending party can never be reintegrated back, but the funeral can offer a chance to formally accept the death as a permanent loss.

The mourners themselves also perpetuate a breach of social contract— we are touched by the death of our loved ones, and in our culture that touch is feared to be contagious. We do not know how to act around those in mourning, what to say, how to help, or if we even should help. The funeral functions for those outside the affected ring as a redressive action that allows those in mourning to return to regular society. We are compartmentalizing our grief within the confines of the funeral process, and once it is over, we are expected to reintegrate back into our daily lives, having moved on from our loss.

Initially, I was skeptical about applying performance theory to funerary ritual, seeing it as something that likely did not apply to funerals and those in the funeral industry. My opinion changed on my first day of fieldwork, during which I was able to witness a funeral. Everything was already set up when I got there; typically, at this particular funeral home, this work is done the night before. When the funeral was over, I was asked to stay behind, as it was not clear if the family would be comfortable with me attending. The following passage is from my notes that day:

> Afterwards, Susan just cleaned up. I asked if I could help. I didn't do much. I get the sense she always stays here for this part, to clean up. I never liked the performance theory thing, but I should look into that. She was breaking down a set. She was folding up the chairs, putting the CDs away, organizing items left behind by the family for when they return. It reminded me of watching my theater crew friends after a play they worked.[21]

From that point on, I saw the performance in every aspect of the funerary ritual, exemplified by both mourners and funeral directors alike.

I have performed several roles at quite a few funerals in my own life and witnessed others' performances. Following a funeral I attended through Jefferson and Richardson Funeral Home,[22] I sat in my car and made the following notes: "Well, I made it to my car before I cried. I keep thinking about Greg's funeral. Sandy with those photos, me singing 'Amazing Grace,' the flag ceremony. It's amazing to me that 6 years later I still cry."[23] Most funerals remind me of Greg's, even though I had been to quite a few before his. I included this excerpt because it is the performances I remember the most. The performance of my cousin-in-law as the grieving widow, sharing photos of Greg in happier times, trying to get everyone to look at them and remember him as he was. My own performance as role of grieving cousin, and having to set that role aside in order to sing "Amazing Grace" at my aunt's request. And the most powerful part (for me) of the entire ceremony—the flag folding the military does at funerals. I remember that soldier getting down on one knee and asking Greg's oldest son to take the flag in honor of his father's service. Sixteen years later and that is still difficult to write about.

My first funeral, that of my paternal grandfather, included a sort of "changing of the guard" from his Knights of Columbus pals.[24] Two at a time stood flanking his casket, each with a Knights of Columbus sword, although I cannot remember if they were in hand or in a scabbard hanging from their belts. I remember thinking my Grandpa must have been an important man to warrant such protection. As I got older and family members realized I could sing, I began my own performances, beginning with my Uncle Tom's funeral and including four more: those of my maternal grandfather, two cousins, and my husband's maternal grandmother, at whose service I sang the entire Mass.

But there were other aspects to these performances, often done unconsciously, things we all do in preparation for and during funerals without thinking too deeply about them—Goffman's "personal front" aspect of our daily performances as social creatures.[25] The American funeral is a staged reality—it involves embalming and putting makeup on the deceased to create a living tableau, as well as costuming the deceased, the mourners, and the funeral directors; even mourning itself and the roles we are cast in when someone we know dies are all aspects of this performance. The makeup on my cousin's face and head to hide the bullet wound of a self-inflicted gunshot. My uncle and later my cousin each in their favorite sports team's sweatshirt, so we could remember them as they really were. Wearing black, and listening to people commenting on the occasional jeans and cowboy boots that crop up at my working-class family's funerals. My cousins walking my aunt around at her husband's funeral, flanking her like the Knights of Columbus did the casket at her father's, holding her up, protecting her from that death the only way they could. And later, at one of those cousin's (Greg) own funerals, I remember weeping, wracked with guilt, sorrow, and anger at his suicide, and my mother asking me if I was okay, in hindsight presumably because I was transgressing my expected performance of quiet crying, which is what transpires at most Caucasian Christian American funerals. I can recall good homilies and eulogies, and bad ones. In my fieldwork, I was able to witness not only performances like these but also those of funeral industry workers, both behind the scenes and up front during funerals themselves.

Transforming after Death

> Undoing, dissolution, decomposition are accompanied by processes of growth, transformation, and the reformulation of old elements in new patterns.
>
> —Victor Turner[26]

Transformative moments happened often during the course of my fieldwork, as well. The first embalming and body preparation I witnessed was particularly meaningful, and I dictated the following notes as I was driving home that afternoon:

> Okay, this is, I'm just going to dictate some field notes as I drive home. So I actually got to see an embalming. ... So he put him on the table, and he lifted him from the hospital gurney. He lifted him onto the embalming table, and made a comment about how he was sorry the table wasn't as clean as it should be—apparently the last body wasn't as cleaned as he would have liked her to be. So that was interesting, and then he undressed the man and cleaned him off as he went. I guess I kind of expected it to go from body odor smells to chemical smells, and while he was *using* the chemicals they smelled, but the embalming liquid didn't smell at all that I noticed. The only one I could smell was one particular cleaning agent that looked like Windex that was particularly, you know, you could smell that but maybe I was just in a specific spot in the room that I didn't smell it as badly because at one point, Bob came in and we were chatting and he had to open up the vent because he said it was burning his eyes, so but anyway. Paul kept saying why don't you come over here and look at this, see what I'm going to do, it was really interesting, it was like I was an intern, and he was teaching me like, this is what we do, why we do it. Talking about pulling out the artery and the carotid and the big vein is in your neck, and pulling them out, and draining the blood out of one, and pumping the embalming fluid into the other. He was a very good instructor. For example he was talking about, sometimes their eyes pop open so we put this sticky stuff on the caps and stick them under the eyelids and it keeps the eyes shut. He showed these tricks they have, shoving cotton in the mouth, for example, so it's puffed up. The guy didn't have any teeth, so they put cotton in the mouth to make it not so sunken in. He kept calling him by name. He kept saying, so Mr. So and So, we're going to do this now, and we're going to do this to you, and stuff like that. I think that's interesting because when I interviewed Paul, he was talking about how one of the ways to distance yourself from that process is if you're not religious the body's just a shell. It's just a thing and it doesn't matter anymore. If you are religious, the person's not there anymore anyway, their soul's moved on, so again it's just a shell. It's interesting to me that he would say that, and I did notice that he would deal with, he sort of compartmentalized the body in a way. He cleaned the head, did the lips, the eyes, the cheeks (set them), then moved on to the hands and arms. It might be a case of where he's doing things the most efficient way, but it seemed, especially when he was dealing with the head, it seemed particularly compartmentalized, which would support the shell idea. But on the other hand, to keep referring to the man by name and keeping him in the process, it was kind of interesting—telling him what he was going to do to him and stuff like that. ... So, he kind of mixed in

the embalming chemicals and let them sit for a while, and started draining out the blood, and then started putting in the embalming fluid, and then the last thing that he did, as I said he kept washing and cleaning the body throughout the process, and then the last thing he did, oh and something else he did which isn't a personal touch of his, per se, but something that he personally insists on is sticking cotton behind the ears so as the embalming fluid's going in, sort of making the body kind of stiff and stuff, it keeps the ears out, rather than back, so that they look more normal, like they would be if they were standing up. So that was interesting. And then he really ... I don't know if I'm projecting which is entirely possible, but he seemed to be simultaneously treating this man both as a body and as a person. Like where he needed to treat him like a person he was treating him like a person, and where he needed to treat him like a thing he was treating him like a thing. ... He then dried him off, cleaned off the table, cleaned up after himself, cleaned up all the equipment and all that stuff. Again, not nearly as gross as I thought it was going to be. ... Then he put the sheet over him up to his neck and that was it. It took about an hour and a half I think, and he was telling me what he was doing step by step, and it was good.[27]

I included this long stretch of my field notes because this was my reaction as audience to Paul's ritualized performance of embalming a body for display during a funeral. There were two layers of performance going on here—Paul's usual ritualistic work of embalming, and his inclusion of me in the process, explaining to me step by step what he was doing. He moved back and forth between these two layers. I entered into the embalming room having no idea how central that process is to the work that funeral directors do. I assumed that it was for sanitation first and foremost, performed essentially to allow for an open casket. I was a naïve outsider, and then I was, albeit merely symbolically, initiated into those who know. Following Richard Schechner, the embalming had elements of both social and aesthetic drama, because it felt like a rite of passage to me, and I did witness an extreme event and reflect on it. In both ways, my consciousness was transformed.

In his text *Performance Theory*, Schechner discusses the transformative power of performance, and how any performance, whether it is social or aesthetic drama, enacts a change on its audience. Whether or not that change is permanent or temporary depends on the performance. He argues that the function of performance is to provide "a place for, and a means of, transformation."[28] In comparing the two, he writes:

> Rituals carry participants across limens, transforming them into different persons. ... Aesthetic drama compels a transformation of the spectators' view of the world by rubbing their senses against enactments of extreme events, much more extreme than they would usually witness. The nesting pattern makes it possible for the spectator to reflect on these events rather than flee from them or intervene in them. That reflection is the liminal time during which the transformation of consciousness takes place.[29]

For Schechner, transformation is the entire point of any performance, whether it changes our social status, our way of thinking, or even ourselves in general, just being different because of having witnessed the performance.

Although I tend to agree more with Goffman's idea that any influence on the observer/audience is intentional, rather than specifically transformative, what I like about Schechner's argument here is the idea that liminality can be extended to the audience of an aesthetic drama, so transformation, while maybe not the intention of the performance, will occur regardless. Moreover, even though the intent of a rite of passage is a change in status, the participants in these rites undergo a transformation of consciousness much like the audience of an aesthetic drama. They emerge knowing what they did not know before; they reflect on what the rite meant and how they are now different.

Much like Schechner's aesthetic drama audience, I was shown an extreme event and was able to reflect on it. I use the word "extreme" here because it was a close-up view of what the embalming process actually is. More accurately, it was extreme because although the practice of embalming is one of the ways in which we deny death, to do an embalming or any death work is to squarely face it. By observing the embalming, I faced death. I then thought about the experience and tried to make sense of it, and I am considering it more deeply now. For example, at the time I was narrating my thoughts, I felt that Paul might be in some sense code-switching—treating the deceased alternately as a person or a shell, as various steps warranted. He often addressed the man by his name and included him in my instruction. He was telling us both what he was doing. On the other hand, as he cleaned the body from head to toe, it seemed very compartmentalized to me. For example, calling the man by his name seemed to be common practice for Paul in his work. He may not say those things aloud when he is alone in the embalming room, but I would venture to say that he thinks them in his head. In the funerals I have observed since, I have noticed that the funeral directors always address the deceased by name. It is important for the mourners to think about the person rather than the shell, so it is important for the funeral directors, who always insist they work with the living, to do this.

On the other hand, witnessing the embalming was like a rite of passage—I felt as if it made me a real anthropologist. I entered the room as a student and left feeling as if I was doing real work. It was particularly significant because I was initially afraid I would not get much access to the behind-the-scenes work. Being able to witness the embalming made my fieldwork real to me in a way it had not been through initial interviews. Though certainly not as stressful or dangerous as many initiation rites, it was definitely a challenging experience. As a member of our death-phobic culture, I am just as uncomfortable around it as anyone else. For example, at the beginning of my notes, I mention that if I was able to see the man's face, I would be ok, because I could see he was a person and not just a dead body. A dead body equals death, and death is scary and unclean. Not having trained the way morticians do—and honestly never even having taken an anatomy class or dissected an animal in biology—I had not had any experience that might have lessened my discomfort in watching the embalming. So when Paul cut into the man's neck to pull out the artery and vein, I struggled to maintain my composure. Most cultures outside of the West take care of their own dead and do not embalm. Some within the West have not adopted the practice of outsourcing death work either. Each of these smaller, uncomfortable moments within the larger experience lent to it the feeling of passing some sort of test, not only as an anthropologist but also as a human, experiencing something that not a lot of people in our culture get to experience.

Conclusion

> *Communitas* ... is almost everywhere held to be sacred or "holy," possibly because it transgresses or dissolves the norms that govern structured and institutionalized relationships and is accompanied by experiences of unprecedented potency.
>
> —Victor Turner[30]

During the writing phase of my dissertation, my mentor and committee co-chair, O. M. Watson, died not long after being diagnosed with esophageal cancer. I was able to get one chapter to him after he asked me to send him whatever I had written. I do not know if he ever had a chance to read it as he died shortly after I sent the email. A small part of me still feels like I failed him. He had no funeral, per his request—his daughters threw a party so we could celebrate the life of the man we all loved and admired. In her book *The American Way of Death*, Jessica Mitford argues that the funeral is a scam perpetrated by greedy businessmen who take advantage of people in their time of grief.[31] In all twenty-five of those deaths I mentioned, the only one for whom a funeral did not seem appropriate was O. M. He was not a formal person, and he would not have been comfortable knowing we were all silently weeping or even somberly reflecting on our time with him. He asked for us to have a party, so we did—we drank, we laughed, and we remembered. We all need a chance to say good-bye in whatever way works for us. And since most of us try as hard as we can to never think about death, we do not always know what the best way might be. In my time in the field, and in my personal experience with death and grief, I have seen that Mitford was wrong. Funeral directors, who do indeed work for the living, can help us find the best way to say good-bye to our dead and connect us with others who are left.

In the time it took me to revise my dissertation, three more people in my life died. In February 2016 my aunt lost her life to cancer. In March another aunt suffered a stroke, then died after a week of hospice care. In May, while driving home from a weekend spent in Cincinnati with family, I received a phone call that my grandmother, who had also been recently placed under hospice care after her condition rapidly deteriorated following years of suffering from dementia, had finally succumbed. All three of these deaths brought about relief in their own ways. Untreatable cancer, the deepest, darkest depression I have ever witnessed, and the complete loss of faculties were not, in my opinion, truly livable situations.

Still, I loved all three of these women, and I was saddened by each loss. The first aunt donated her body to science, and my uncle chose not to have a funeral for my grandmother. He drove her cremated remains and those of my grandfather from Florida to Cincinnati, where we had a memorial service followed by the interment of both grandparents' ashes. However, we had a full funeral for my other aunt. After working on this project for so many years, it was difficult to shut off the part of my brain that insisted on observing the different actions the funeral directors took to care for my family. Once again, I watched two men, the current generation of funeral directors from a funeral home my family has turned to many times, shift fluidly from directing us all to move to certain rooms, recite certain prayers, and note the guest book and prayer cards to fading into the background as we said our goodbyes, comforted each other, and laughed while sharing memories.

My aunt had left the Catholic Church decades ago upon being "excommunicated" by her local priest when she remarried following a divorce. After her youngest shot himself, she began reconnecting to the faith of her childhood, so there were certain requirements she insisted on for her funeral—some of those earlier patterns that traditional Catholic funerary ritual adhered to, and they were there: the kneeler in front of her coffin, the rosary wrapped in her folded hands. But she also wore her Poopsie sweatshirt ("Poopsie" was what she called my uncle), and photos of her family rested underneath her hands. The funeral directors had given her both a traditional and an individualized funeral. They had also given us a chance to reconnect—my cousin-in-law, estranged from my aunt (and thus my immediate family, as my aunt was always with us for family get-togethers) following the suicide of my cousin, was there, mourning along with the rest of us. Family I had not seen in years gathered together for my aunt's final send-off. We each took our turn saying our good-byes, but because my aunt had been so well taken care of by the funeral home, we were able to focus on each other rather than a bad embalming or a mishandled eulogy. My cousin died by suicide the year I began my doctoral studies, and it created a social breach that we had not been able to resolve for thirteen years. His mother died the year that I finished my studies, and the unresolved social breach created by my cousin was finally mended with the help of these two funeral directors. They joked with us, prayed with us, expressed sympathy for us; they took charge when we needed them to, and they disappeared into the background when we needed to focus on each other. Their work with my aunt and with us helped us connect in that deep, visceral, meaningful way that is *communitas*.

Aubrey Thamann is an American studies scholar and anthropologist. She received her doctorate from Purdue University in 2016. Her dissertation was an ethnographic study of funeral directors in Indiana, focusing on the social role they play in offering us the much-needed shared experience of collective grief in the funeral. An interdisciplinary scholar at heart, Thamann has begun research into the fields of fat studies and food studies, specifically exploring where these fields intersect.

Notes

1. Bronislaw Malinowski, *Magic, Science and Religion: And Other Essays*, with an introduction by Robert Redfield, 2nd ed. (Prospect Heights, IL: Waveland Press, 1992), 52.
2. Ibid., 53.
3. Renato Rosaldo, *Culture and Truth: The Remaking of Social Analysis* (Boston: Beacon Press, 1989).
4. Victor Turner, *The Ritual Process: Structure and Anti-structure* (Chicago: Aldine Publishing Company, 1969), 97.
5. Jamie Arndt, Jeff Greenberg, and Alison Cook, "Mortality Salience and the Spreading Activation of Worldview-Relevant Constructs: Exploring the Cognitive Architecture of Terror Management," *Journal of Experimental Psychology* 131, no. 3 (2002): 307–24.
6. Daniel Sullivan, Jeff Greenberg, and Mark J. Landau, "Toward a New Understanding of Two Films from the Dark Side: Utilizing Terror Management Theory to Analyze *Rosemary's Baby* and *Straw Dogs*," *Journal of Popular Film and Television* 37, no. 4 (Winter 2009): 189–98.
7. Émile Durkheim, *The Elementary Forms of Religious Life*, trans. Karen E. Fields (New York: The Free Press, 2001), 401.
8. Jack B. Kamerman, *Death in the Midst of Life: Social and Cultural Influences on Death, Grief, and Mourning* (Englewood Cliffs, NJ: Prentice Hall, 1988), 30.
9. Geoffrey Gorer, "The Pornography of Death," *Encounter* 5, no. 4 (Oct., 1955), 49–52.
10. Robert W. Habenstein and William M. Lamers, *The History of American Funeral Directing* (Milwaukee: Bulfin Printers, 1955), 196.
11. Philippe Ariès, *Western Attitudes toward Death: From the Middle Ages to the Present*, trans. Patricia M. Ranum (Baltimore: Johns Hopkins University Press, 1974).
12. "Dead People Get Life-Like Poses at Their Funerals," ABC News, retrieved 23 March 2016 from http://abcnews.go.com/US/dead-people-life-poses- funerals/story?id=23456853.
13. Ariès, *Western Attitudes toward Death*, 94.
14. Ibid., 102.

15. Ralph Waldo Emerson, "Self-Reliance," in *Essays* (Boston: James Munroe and Company, 1841), 72–73.
16. Roy Nichols and Jane Nichols, "Funerals: A Time for Grief and Growth," in *Death: The Final Stage of Growth*, by Elisabeth Kübler-Ross (New York: Simon & Schuster, Inc., 1975), 91.
17. A pseudonym.
18. Victor Turner, *Dramas, Fields, and Metaphors: Symbolic Action in Human Society* (Ithaca, NY: Cornell University Press, 1974), 37.
19. Victor Turner, "Social Dramas and Stories about Them," in *On Narrative*, edited by W. J. T. Mitchell (Chicago: University of Chicago Press, 1981), 155–56.
20. Turner, *Dramas, Fields, and Metaphors*, 37.
21. Field notes, Colley, Frank, and Froebisch Funeral Home, 4 March 2009, pseudonyms used.
22. A pseudonym.
23. Field notes, Jefferson & Richardson Funeral Home, 10 March 2009.
24. The Knights of Columbus are a Catholic fraternal organization.
25. Erving Goffman, *The Presentation of Self in Everyday Life* (Garden City, NY: Doubleday Anchor Books, 1959), 24.
26. Victor Turner, *The Forest of Symbols: Aspects of Ndembu Ritual* (Ithaca, NY: Cornell University Press, 1967), 99.
27. Field notes, Colley, Frank, and Froebisch, 9 March 2009, pseudonyms used.
28. Richard Schechner, *Performance Theory* (London: Routledge, 1988), 193.
29. Ibid.
30. Turner, *Ritual Process*, 128.
31. Jessica Mitford, *The American Way of Death* (New York: Simon and Schuster, 1963).

Bibliography

Ariès, Philippe. *Western Attitudes toward Death: From the Middle Ages to the Present*. Translated by Patricia M. Ranum. Baltimore: Johns Hopkins University Press, 1974.

Arndt, Jamie, Jeff Greenberg, and Alison Cook. "Mortality Salience and the Spreading Activation of Worldview-Relevant Constructs: Exploring the Cognitive Architecture of Terror Management." *Journal of Experimental Psychology* 131, no. 3 (2002): 307–24.

Durkheim, Émile. *The Elementary Forms of Religious Life*. Translated by Karen E. Fields. New York: The Free Press, 2001.

Emerson, Ralph Waldo. "Self-Reliance." In *Essays*, 37–73. Boston: James Munroe and Company, 1841.

Goffman, Erving. *The Presentation of Self in Everyday Life*. Garden City, NY: Doubleday Anchor Books, 1959.

Gorer, Geoffrey. "The Pornography of Death." *Encounter* 5, no. 4 (October 1955): 49–52.

Habenstein, Robert W., and William M. Lamers. *The History of American Funeral Directing*. Milwaukee: Bulfin Printers, 1955.

Kamerman, Jack B. *Death in the Midst of Life: Social and Cultural Influences on Death, Grief, and Mourning*. Englewood Cliffs, NJ: Prentice Hall, 1988.

Kübler-Ross, Elisabeth. *Death: The Final Stage of Growth*. New York: Simon & Schuster, 1975.

Malinowski, Bronislaw. *Magic, Science and Religion: And Other Essays*. With an introduction by Robert Redfield. 2nd ed. Prospect Heights, IL: Waveland Press, 1992.

Mitford, Jessica. *The American Way of Death*. New York: Simon and Schuster, 1963.

Nichols, Roy, and Jane Nichols. "Funerals: A Time for Grief and Growth." In *Death: The Final Stage of Growth*, edited by Elisabeth Kübler-Ross, 87–96. New York: Simon & Schuster, Inc., 1975.

Rosaldo, Renato. *Culture and Truth: The Remaking of Social Analysis*. Boston: Beacon Press, 1989.

Schechner, Richard. *Performance Theory*. London: Routledge, 1988.

Sullivan, Daniel, Jeff Greenberg, and Mark J. Landau. "Toward a New Understanding of Two Films from the Dark Side: Utilizing Terror Management Theory to Analyze *Rosemary's Baby* and *Straw Dogs*." *Journal of Popular Film and Television* 37, no. 4 (Winter 2009): 189–98.

Turner, Victor. *The Forest of Symbols: Aspects of Ndembu Ritual*. Ithaca, NY: Cornell University Press, 1967.

———. *The Ritual Process: Structure and Anti-structure*. Chicago: Aldine Publishing Company, 1969.

———. *Dramas, Fields, and Metaphors: Symbolic Action in Human Society*. Ithaca, NY: Cornell University Press, 1974.

———. "Social Dramas and Stories about Them." In *On Narrative*, edited by W. J. T. Mitchell, 137–164. Chicago: University of Chicago Press, 1981.

CHAPTER 6

"What Has the Field Done to You?"

Researching Death, Dying, and Bereavement between Closeness and Distance

Ekkehard Coenen

Exploring phenomena in the context of dying, death, and bereavement does something to humans. After all, every death researcher in the field is confronted with events that are often marginalized and considered taboo in society.[1] Also, these experiences are connected to existence itself. In the end, every researcher will die once, every researcher will experience the death of people he or she knows, and every researcher will once mourn.[2] Accordingly, death research gnaws at the subjectivity. At the beginning of the research process, each scientist has a plethora of known and unknown presuppositions, stereotypes, moral values, and motivations, among others.[3] These influence, on the one hand, research activities and, on the other hand, one's attitude to the actions that one can observe in the field.

In what follows, based on some of the experiences I have had in my ethnographic observations in the funeral system, I would like to show that research in the field of death, dying, and bereavement is always a risky endeavor between closeness and distance, between emotional incorporation and unsympathetic rationality. The closeness or the distance of the death researcher to his or her field has a great influence on the language with which he or she describes the object of investigation and—literally—*comprehends* it. If the field researcher is still unfamiliar with the field, he or she only has a vocabulary available that may not have any connection to the observed death phenomena. The field observations and the field report can be correspondingly undifferentiated. From this perspective, dying, death, and bereavement can be described as highly emotional and tabooed areas of society. Unfortunately, they also can persist in this semantic. On the other hand, if the researcher approaches the field, participates in the everyday interactions and problems, and shares the worries, fears, and challenges of the field participants, he or she may be able to adjust to the people of the field of investigation.[4] Dying, death, and bereavement are then observed from the point of view of the field actors and described with the corresponding terms. However, there is a danger that the descriptions and observations may follow the logic of the field too greatly and thus be incomprehensible or disturbing to external parties.

In the following pages I will describe how my perception of this tightrope walk was shaped during my funeral ethnography. For this, I refer to autoethnographic data that I collected during a six-month internship at a funeral home in Germany. I will show that the initial phase of my research in the field of death, dying, and bereavement was enormously influenced by emotional stress. I was highly touched by the interactions with the bereaved and my work with the dead.[5] Thus, I could not completely understand the behavior of funeral directors. I noticed that I was too distanced from the field and its inner logic. In consequence, I decided to go deeper. I immersed myself in the field, became a funeral director myself, and found a way to understand the statements and actions of my colleagues. Then I left the field and tried to find an adequate language for my new insights. In doing so, my experiences and a new relationship to the dead influenced my writings. As I was now situated within the field, I found that some of my formulations and opinions shocked other researchers who were unfamiliar with death studies. I had to learn to distance myself from the field again—while simultaneously preserving my experiences—to be sensitive to the emotions of external actors and to find a language that links my changed relationship to the dead and the (non)understanding of people unfamiliar with the funeral system.

Part One

In 2014, I was looking for a suitable topic for my master's thesis. At that time I was very interested in how people can create something vague and barely tangible, like an atmosphere[6]—and indeed, a specific atmosphere. I wanted to know what techniques and actions generated and maintained certain feelings and sensations in a situation.[7] But what could be a suitable subject for my investigation? Different situations flashed into my head: concerts, fairs, demonstrations, boxing matches, church services, and many more. In a conversation, my partner and I finally talked about funeral services. As individuals who had little experience with burial and death, the emotions that prevailed at funerals seemed obvious to us. But how exactly they were produced was beyond me. It was not long before I decided to enter the research field of death, dying, and bereavement—I was excited to find out how and why something like a mourning "atmosphere" was made. After all, I had no idea how difficult it would be to appropriately understand the field actors and adequately reconstruct the meaning of their actions.

Before entering the field, I had many presuppositions and, admittedly, prejudices about the processes that occurred on the backstage of funerals. For me, the ideal type of funeral director was objectively distanced, calm, purposeful, and always serious. How should I know it differently? I had not had any contact with any funeral directors. I knew only of caricatures from nightly thrillers who stand wordlessly—and thus also characterlessly—at the edge of a murder scene until called for to remove the body. Until then I was unfamiliar with the TV series *Six Feet Under*, which exceptionally attributes a personality to funeral directors. The funeral director was for me a strange being that I had to get to know during my field stay.

The same was true of the funeral services. I had an approximate knowledge of what was considered "proper" protocol at a funeral service—at least I thought I did: wearing black clothes, exhibiting immense restraint, speaking in a low voice, expressing words of condolence, and giving flowers as a sign of compassion. By contrast, I had no idea what it looked like behind the scenes of the funeral system. What actions were necessary in order to realize a memorial service, to establish a certain emotionality in the situation, and, despite all the work involved, to adhere to the required piety? In short, I hardly knew anything about the processes involved.

To collect data for my master's thesis, I decided to conduct problem-centered interviews[8] with funeral directors, cemetery and crematorium staff, pastors, and funeral orators in Thuringia, Germany. I hoped to gain insights into the working methods of the professional actors. How did they create an atmosphere during their funerals? What did they pay attention to when planning and holding a memorial service? What were dos and don'ts within the funeral system? How did they deal with the mourners in these situations? I cannot say that my interview partners made it difficult for me. They were all diligent speakers, and I think they did their best to bring me closer to their work processes. However, after my interviews, I still could not understand how exactly "sad," "dignified," or "comforting" atmospheres, as they are mentioned in the numerous advertisements of funeral companies, are formed. I found it difficult to gain an impression of the concrete funeral processes simply through expert interviews. They helped me to reconstruct how the professional actors saw their work, but I did not have the concrete experience of these situations. Just because I talked about the ambience of burials, I did not know how the atmosphere felt. The mere talk about the mourning atmosphere was far too distant from the actual happenings in the field.

Regarding this problem, and on the advice of a funeral director, I covertly took part in mourning ceremonies in order to gain an impression of the concrete processes. She told me it would not be noticeable if I joined the funeral community. During the first funeral, in which I participated as an onlooker, I felt very anxious. It made me uncomfortable that I, as an unaffected stranger, was participating in the suffering of others.[9] While all those around me were crying, embracing, gloomily hanging their heads, and looking so deeply sad, I could only begin to understand their actions. This does not mean that I did not sympathize. Quite the contrary: I felt the oppressive atmosphere and was immersed in the emotionality of the situation, but it only made me feel sad—sadness, but no grief. I had experienced no loss, and therefore I could not feel like the bereaved did. We were anchored in different lifeworlds. While my lifeworld seemed intact and gave me no reason to mourn, their lifeworlds were deeply broken. The acts of mourning I witnessed were no different from those I knew from various films, TV formats, newspaper articles, and novels. They were, for me, an expression of a specific role action,[10] but I lacked access to the subjective knowledge that underlay this action. It seemed too easy for me to simplify the bereaved as grief-stricken to explain the way they behaved. What does it mean to feel grief? What did the funeral directors feel in this situation? During the funeral, they stood without showing any emotion in the mourning hall. At the grave, their faces were also like stone. While I did not grieve, I still felt sad. The funeral directors seemed completely detached. Why did they seemingly act so callously? Did they not feel anything in this situation?

Irritated by this observation but also fascinated, I expanded my presence in the field. Not only did I attend funeral services but I also began to observe the backstage of the funeral service in consultation with cemetery staff, funeral directors, funeral speakers, and clergy. As an outsider, however, I received only brief insights into the work processes immediately before and after the funeral services. In these situations, the professional actors were far too busy, stressed and in a hurry, and they could give me very little information. After all, they were only given fifteen minutes at the local cemetery to prepare the funeral ceremony. They were simply not in the state of mind to talk to me. Instead, they quickly built the decorations for the memorial service, positioned the casket or urn in the mourning hall, arranged the flowers of the arriving mourners, and discussed the final details of the process. Gradually, I realized that the funeral directors were not completely detached and emotionless when doing their job—they just had other problems. Instead of dealing with a bereavement, they had to ensure within a very short time that their clientele could carry out a successful funeral ritual.[11] They were in great deal of stress—not only because of the shortage of time available to them in the cemetery but also because they were careful not to let anything go wrong.[12] But despite this insight, it was difficult for me to understand how the professional actors could dissociate themselves so much from the bereavement. After all, the focus of all this activity was a dead human. The survivors were in a state of emergency. They were completely distraught, disoriented, and needed help. It was not possible for me to keep my distance. Therefore, at each memorial service I attended, I also felt the tense atmosphere and became sad.

In order to gain more impressions about the field of death, I enrolled in a seminar on the cultural history of the funerals organized by the Department of Cultural Anthropology and Cultural History at the Friedrich Schiller University of Jena. Together with my fellow students, I got to know the origins of our current burial culture and read studies like Ariès's *Western Attitudes toward Death*.[13] We visited museums where we dealt with the different historical death images and analyzed the various burial artifacts. We also toured a local cemetery. There we were shown how a cemetery is built, what the historical development behind it is, and what problems cemetery workers face today. At the end of the cemetery tour, a caretaker asked us if we would like to go to the crematorium to see how the stoves work. None of my fellow students wanted to take up the offer because they all had to go to subsequent courses and had no time left. Thus, my partner, who had accompanied me, and I went with the employee to the back rooms of the crematorium.

The crematorium was an old brick building with soot-black walls. It was not well maintained and looked like an old factory building. As the cemetery employee explained the construction of the crematory ovens, a cremation process was just ending. Another employee pushed a coffin into the room where we were standing. He flipped open the lid of the coffin, giving me a quick glimpse of the corpse inside. I saw a gray-haired woman with folded hands wearing a shimmering white corpse shirt. At that moment I was very shocked. So far I have seen only a few "real" dead—not including the staged corpses of TV programs and movies. The sight of the woman haunted me in the coming days; I regularly thought about the scene and felt traumatized. Once again I wondered how professional funeral workers were able to handle the deaths so distantly.

To better understand the funeral directors and cemetery workers, I decided to attend a course at a funeral home training center. For the most part, the course group consisted of sixteen- to twenty-year-old trainees who had worked for a funeral home for a year. As I sat between the young people, I marveled at the anecdotes they reported from their workday. Although they were all about ten years younger than me, their dealings with death seemed to me to be highly reflective. I realized that they are by no means emotionally distant but are often confronted in everyday life with events that strongly affect them. On the other hand, a distanced tone always arose in the discussions, making me question: How can these young people speak so objectively of their work with the dead?

Despite this strange experience, I succeeded in generating a theory for atmospheric production in the context of funerals based on my fieldwork. I wrote my master's thesis and successfully defended it.[14] Nevertheless, many questions remained. The professional handling of the deceased, the emotions involved in it, and the objective-rational distancing of the funeral directors was a mystery for me, which I wanted to explore further.

Part Two

After completing my master's degree, I decided to allow the questions that arose from my observations in the field of death guide me. Looking back on my previous research process, I noticed that, to that point, I had been restricted by an epistemological limit. The behavior of the funeral directors seemed strange to me, but I had no direct access to their environment. All the experiences I gathered in funeral services resulted from a detached role. I was always the uninvolved visitor. I had no existential interest in truly participating in the rituals and work processes. Instead, I watched like a fly on the wall, quietly and secretly, making my field notes and sketches. On closer inspection, I realized that the data I collected could not explain to me in depth why the funeral directors behaved in a certain way. Through my observations, I had no access to their subjective stock of knowledge, and in the interviews I conducted with the field actors only simple descriptions emerged, essentially serving to explain to a layman like myself the everyday practice of burial. However, these were descriptions of funeral behavior in a scientifically framed situation where experts are questioned by a layman, not descriptions that came directly from practice, thereby becoming detached from the situation and the context. The same was true of my visits to funerary culture museums and participation in the guided tours of each cemetery. Even in these situations I could only imagine what it is really like to organize the disposal of a corpse and the bereavement work.

Consequently, I dove deeper into the field in order to witness the funeral processes and to perceive the associated interactions. For this purpose, I wanted to involve myself as much as possible in many aspects of the funeral system. To accomplish this, I decided to play a role that enabled me to do what is "common" in funeral services—those activities performed by professional actors—and to observe myself doing so. I decided to work for a funeral home and to become a professional death worker myself.

With this idea in mind, I called one of the funeral directors, Thomas Schmidt,[15] whom I had already interviewed as part of my master's thesis, and asked him if I could work for free and collect data for scientific purposes. After a short hesitation, he invited me to a conversation in which I could explain my reasons in more detail, and we clarified the formalities of my work in his company. After I had explained to him my proposed study and the background of my methodical approach, he showed great interest and allowed me to work for him as an "intern" of the funeral home. This finally gave me the chance for an existential inside view of the funeral system.

Thomas allowed me to get used to the tasks in his company. On the first day, I just "stayed" in a funeral conversation and observed the talk between Thomas and the bereaved. My new boss and I were sitting in his office, and I looked out the window and saw two black-clad women approach the funeral home. "Ah, clientele!" Thomas said in a more or less pleased tone. I was irritated by his tone but said nothing, and I asked him how he knew that the women wanted to go to his office and not to the cemetery, which was right next to the funeral home. "Black-clad women with an envelope. This indicates clientele," Thomas replied. "Over time, you just develop a sense of how customers and cemetery visitors look." Indeed, the two women turned toward the funeral home entrance, and I opened the door for them. Thomas and I greeted them, and they told Thomas that their father had died. He asked them to sit down, handed each of them a coffee, and discussed the way forward with them.

Already this first funeral conversation, which I was able to witness, challenged me emotionally. I had to watch my new boss talk to two completely distraught women who had not yet processed their father's death. Tears flowed, handkerchiefs were drawn, glances were lowered, voices trembled, and the conversation often had to be interrupted because one of the two women could no longer concentrate and gave in to her grief. This scene took its toll on me that day. When I wrote my field diary in the evening, my notes mostly revolved around this conversation. I tried to describe the course of the conversation as neutrally as possible, but, nevertheless, my notes were highly permeated with my subjective sensitivities. The description of the interaction, the choice of the urn and the flower bouquet, the selection of the funeral orator, and the discussion of the other formalities were underscored with a tone of sadness. My field report had the bitter connotation of mourning in the terms and descriptions I chose. However, I only became aware of this some months later when I returned to my notes for data analysis. The following passage clearly illustrates an example; in it I am sitting on a bench at a cemetery in front of the mourning hall:

> A graveyard visitor came up to me with heavy footsteps. He indicated that he was looking for something and spoke to me. But he was too quiet, and his voice was so sad that I could not understand him. After a short moment, he told me that he was

at the cemetery to talk to a funeral orator I know. He had forgotten to pick up the bill from him. Actually, this man just wanted to see if flowers were placed on the grave of his wife, whom he had buried the day before with the mentioned funeral orator. Dolefully, he said to me, "It is not easy to bury the woman." As he uttered those words, I could see tears in his eyes. His voice faltered. I realized how I had to fight back tears. I had to stop for a moment and avert my eyes from him. When I had myself under control again, I pointed in the direction in which I had just seen the aforementioned funeral orator. The man left, and I sat on the bench in front of the mourning hall for a while. Suddenly, I felt very depressed. I never thought that during my observations I would sympathize so much with the others.

This situation overwhelmed me. For a long time, I did not know how to handle these types of intense emotions in the field. Often it was hard for me to talk to the mourners and keep my composure. I registered these intense experiences in my diary entries. As I read through them again, I came across a variety of similar descriptions that not only showed that the field actors were suffering but that I, too, was sympathizing with them. I was often on the verge of crying.

On my second day, Thomas wanted to pick up the abovementioned deceased father from the local hospital. He asked me if I would like to "tackle" this task. Would I go by myself? Was I prepared to touch a corpse—the dead body of a person I did not know and from which I could only gather some data from the insurance card and the death certificate? I did not believe that I was. When I hesitated, Thomas said he could pick up the corpse with a colleague from the cemetery while I just accompanied and watched them. This option seemed much more pleasant to me. I agreed.

So it happened that the following day I drove with Thomas from the cemetery office, where we were joined by a cemetery employee, to the hospital. As we parked in front of the back door of the pathology lab and took the empty casket out of the trunk, I realized how I was getting more and more queasy. I knew that the deceased had died of heart failure, but all sorts of pictures were playing in my head.[16] This "death cinema" was likely instigated by the countless crime and horror films, computer games, and novels in which I had encountered bodies in the past. The further we entered the premises of the pathology, the more oppressive the whole situation seemed to me. When we finally met a pathologist, who opened the door to the cold rooms, I felt an impulse to escape. I did not want to see the dead body. I was terrified. Nevertheless, I had enough self-discipline to force myself to stay. But I was conspicuous in the corners of the room where the cold stores were. And so, standing as far away as possible from the cold stores and the corpses inside, I watched the action.

Again and again I heard from the death worker, "One does not forget his first corpse." When I think back to my stay in the field of death, dying, and bereavement, I must agree with that sentiment. I admit that only a few situations have been written into my memory in such detail. I remember well—or at least I think I do—the smell in the pathology lab, the grayish-white taps on the wall, and the sterile light that shone from the ceiling and completely illuminated the room. I can still see in my mind's eye how the pathologist, quite serenely, drew a document from a pile of files on a table, handed it to Thomas, and then left the room. Thomas opened the cold room on which was written the name of the deceased we were picking up. A steel table emerged, which he pushed out and lifted onto a cart. I just stared at the soft shroud lying on the table, showing reddish-brown and yellowish-green discolorations in some places. The colleague whom we had picked up from the cemetery took the sheet aside. It was then that I first caught a glimpse of the yellowed, lifeless feet. Gradually, I saw the rest of the body: the knees, thighs, hips, the bloated tummy, the hematoma-ridden chest, and finally the pale face, with its open mouth and closed eyes. My eyes alternately focused on the face, which had patches of yellow fluid, the pale belly, the sunken genitals, and the curved toes. For a moment, I felt disgusted by the corpse, not only of the body but of all the yellow spots on the body. The sight of the deceased disturbed me, and the memory of this sight would flare up for a long time in my mind's eye.

I watched as Thomas and his colleague transplanted the corpse from the table into the coffin; one grasped his legs, the other the upper body. As they raised the corpse, his hand fell limply to the floor. In addition, a yellow-greenish secretion came out of his nose, and dark red liquid came out of his mouth. The cemetery clerk explained where these fluids came from. One could close the mouth to prevent it from leaking out. Likewise, one could also clog the nose. But he does not find such practices pious and prefers to accept that the death shirt gets stained; otherwise, he would have to stab the deceased with a large needle through the jaw into the mouth. As they were wrapping the body in the coffin, the two funeral directors picked up scissors and cut the back of the clothes given to them by the bereaved. "So, we do not have to raise the body again and to dirty up the clothing of the deceased with the body fluids," the cemetery employee explained to me. "He will not be burdened anyway." I was doubly shocked—on the one hand because of the escaping body secretions and the associated odor, and on the other because of the cemetery employee's detachment as he cut the clothes the survivors had chosen as the deceased's last outfit and on which—at least in my imagination—many memories and emotions hung.

In the evening, I processed my impressions again in my field diary: the sterile atmosphere of the pathology, the sight of the dead body, the smells and liquids, as well as the fact that I was highly irritated by the utterances of the cemetery employee. These diary entries were also interspersed with my feelings, assumptions, and sometimes also stereotypes that I had internalized so far about the care of the dead. My emotionality, my perception, and my sense of value distorted my recordings. I would later recognize this in the other diary entries written during my early days as a funeral director, especially when I touched a corpse myself for the first time, conducted funeral talks with the bereaved, and held a memorial service. The entries were an expression of my observer's stance in the field of death. Accordingly, I could read in them my emotions and concerns about my job. However, due to these initial experiences, I still could not understand the behavior of funeral professionals. Instead, the observed situations and my emotions and values initially led me to feel that their actions were even more distant, cooler, and more alienating than before.

Part Three

Especially in the early days as a "funeral intern," I needed time to process the encounters with the mourners and the dead. My first few weeks in the funeral home caused me immense emotional trouble. I was severely affected by conversations with the bereaved, the dead bodies imprinted themselves in my memory, and the experiences during the funeral wore on me relentlessly. I had nightmares and daydreams in which I relived my experiences, or in which known persons suddenly stood dead in front of me. This was also reflected in my field diaries; at first glance, the instances that I was able to observe were described objectively and distantly, but on closer inspection I found evidence of an intense emotional struggle. In addition, I was able to trace a change in my attitude toward the professional actors.

While my time at Thomas's funeral home passed, my impression changed regarding funeral directors and cemetery workers and their behavior. When they appeared to me at the beginning as cool, serene, and emotionless, I gradually noticed that things are not as easy as they seem from afar. Among other things, this may have something to do with the fact that I became accustomed to dealing with mourners and the dead. Several times a week I took a corpse from his place of death or pathology, held funerals, and planned and organized funeral services. The tears of the bereaved did not touch me as much after a few weeks as they did during the first funeral interview. Likewise, the sight of the deceased and the work on the corpse became an everyday occurrence for me

My habituation to the dead and mourners also led to a change in my behavior in the funeral system. My funeral activity became increasingly routine. Certain phrases and behaviors toward the mourners as well as dealing with the dead became commonplace. And the individual steps in the planning and execution of funeral ceremonies became to me like a checklist that I was able to methodically complete without much difficulty. However, this does not mean that I was emotionally dulled or that I did not care for the mourners and the deceased. On the contrary, I sympathized with the bereaved, had emphatic and in-depth discussions with them, and treated the dead with great respect. Although I may have seemed aloof and subdued on the outside, I was not. I simply did not allow myself to be overwhelmed by the dead and mourners; instead, I turned my attention to other phenomena: namely, the actions necessary to allow the mourner a proper burial and to ensure a dignified farewell to the dead. Instead of letting myself be severely affected by the events in the field, I came to view them as typical events. Still, the tears and sobs of the bereaved continued to affect me, and there were still some corpses that shocked me. My everyday life in the funeral home (i.e., the totality of the actions, interactions, and observations that I experienced in dealing with the deceased and the mourners) enabled me to have a more differentiated view.

Gradually, I also understood the behavior of professional actors. I could understand why, during their coffee breaks and at the funeral services, they joked with each other, often with a black sense of humor, or, when appropriate, declined to show emotion when they were carrying a coffin or talking to the mourners. All these actions are not initially an expression of factual and emotional coldness toward the dead and mourners but a self-technology for distancing.[17] The pragmatics of staging the funeral and the burial, the rough tone at times, and the indifferent participation in the burial ritual serve as self-protection for the professional actors. The professional role they embody enables them not to get too involved in death and grief.

Finally, I understood the behavior of the professional actors that had initially irritated me. However, this was only possible for me to discover because I got involved in their lifeworld as a funeral director. Only by sharing their daily lives, acquiring their knowledge, and being confronted with the same daily emotional tensions and existential challenges did I succeed in deciphering the emotionlessness that many funeral directors outwardly showed. It was a key skill to be able to endure the funeral events at all.

Part Four

After six months I left the funeral home. At that time I received an offer to work as a research assistant, which enabled me to devote most of my time to my research project. At the end of my six months at a funeral home,

I had collected extensive field records, journal entries, sketches, imagery, and artifacts that were now at the heart of my data analysis. However, I quickly realized that I was bringing something else out of my time in the field that both helped and hindered my cognitive process. In addition to all the data that I had stored on my laptop, I had acquired a habitus in the funeral home that opened my eyes for certain objects of investigation, but it was not always perceptible—as I should soon notice—to other scientists

This was clearly exemplified when I handed my supervisor a text for the first time with a request for feedback. The chapter I had written was one in which I first presented the current state of research and clarified some social and ritualistic considerations based on individual examples.[18] At one point I described that, in rituals, there are always certain structures that normalize a certain action. I wrote that bereaved people may burst into tears during the funeral, suffer a fainting spell, or fail to carry out scheduled activities at the grave. I described these as "deviations" anchored in a fixed framework.

The semantics of the "deviation" made sense to me because as a funeral director it was my job, among other things, to ensure a smooth burial. Disruptions and deviations from the plan could jeopardize the success of the burial ritual.[19] My supervisor, however, was extremely disturbed by this term. "What's the field done to you?" He asked me indignantly. Obviously, he could not understand why I understood tears and fainting as "deviations." Instead, he suggested that I call them "expectable events." My previous formulation seemed "hard" and "unfeeling." He could not understand how I could view the funeral processes in such a way, at least not here.

This unexpected intervention by my supervisor opened my eyes to an important aspect in the exploration of the social handling of death, dying, and bereavement. His question was essential: the field is doing something to the researcher. It touches the explorer inside and changes his view of things. Field research is not just a process in which data is continually being accumulated; it is also, above all, one in which the researcher gathers new experiences, reflects on them, and thus changes their perception of them.[20] In other words, at the beginning of my research process, I had little understanding of the behavior of funeral professionals. But by sharing their lifeworld, experiencing their everyday problems, and thus adapting to them, my way of observing them changed as well. The dead body and the mourners initially affected me very much. But over time, my attitude toward all the actions involved in disposing of the corpse and planning a memorial service changed. The field had done something to me. It changed my observation point. I no longer regarded the funeral system as scientific, instead seeing it from the perspective of the scientifically informed funeral director.

However, this process now leads to the concern that it usually only affects the field researcher alone. Other members of the scientific community and other external actors have not been able to gain the same experience and cannot acquire the prevailing habitus. While I thought I had acquired the capacity to understand the funeral directors' behavior was able to look at funeral processes from their perspective, others were not yet able to do so. In the same way I used to be a scientist who could not understand the professional actors of the funeral system, other scientists could not always understand my perspective after I had spent time in the field.

Another of my mentors put it in a nutshell, telling me that in some places I was still pretty *verbuscht* [in the jungle] and would follow the logic of my research field too far. After all, I had to learn to distance myself from the field again while simultaneously preserving my experiences. It was only through a suitable language that I was able to communicate to others the insights I had gained through my bodily participation in the funeral. I realized that the rough language and the black humor[21] nurtured in the funeral home can be very strange to outsiders. The language that I wanted to find for my scientific texts, therefore, had to be sensitive to the emotions of external field actors. At the same time, this language must also be able to link different worlds of experience. It must link my changed relationship to the dead and the (non)understanding of people unfamiliar with the funeral system.

Conclusion

In this chapter I have tried to show that the subjectivity of the death researcher exerts a great influence on the observation both inside and outside the field of death, dying, and grief. The presuppositions, emotions, moral values, stereotypes, and prejudices that a field researcher has guide his perception in the field. From this arise in some places irritations and amazement about strange actions, while in other places individual events are taken for granted.

Death research is an intense journey that confronts the researcher with his or her own attitude toward death. Sometimes one faces people who have experienced a great loss and make it observable and, above all, noticeable. Similarly, the researcher may see things that shock, disgust, or even sadden him. The field of death challenges the researcher-subjects. It rubs against them, leaving its explicit and implicit traces in the habitus of the researchers. These can be partly reflected in the documentation of the research process. But they can also stay undetected and thus secretly enroll in the field reports that the death researchers make after their field stays.

The results of these inscriptions of field habitus can sometimes be disturbing to readers who are unfamiliar with the field. Consequently, the researcher must reflect his or her language and find a suitable language for others. This language must make it possible to soften the traces of the field within it so that it comes across in an aesthetically and morally adequate form. Only then can the death researcher be enabled to share and discuss his or her findings beyond the field of dying, death, and mourning. It is up to him or her to translate the social view of death into a language that everyone understands.

Ekkehard Coenen (né Knopke) studied cultural scientific media research, media culture, sociology, and musicology in Weimar and Jena (Germany). He is currently a research assistant at the Chair of Media Sociology at the Bauhaus-Universität Weimar. His research foci are qualitative methods of social research; sociology of knowledge, emotions, violence, as well as death; dying and bereavement; and cultural sociology.

Notes

1. Geoffrey Gorer, "The Pornography of Death," *Encounter* 5, no. 4 (1955).
2. Louise Rowling, "Being In, Being Out, Being With: Affect and the Role of the Qualitative Researcher in Loss and Grief Research," *Mortality* 4, no. 2 (1999).
3. Juliet Corbin and Anselm L. Strauss, *Basics of Qualitative Research: Techniques and Procedures for Developing Grounded Theory*, 4th ed. (Los Angeles: SAGE, 2015), 38–52; Günter Mey and Katja Mruck, "Grounded Theory and Reflexivity," in *The SAGE Handbook of Grounded Theory*, eds. Antony Bryant and Kathy Charmaz (London: SAGE, 2007).
4. Valli Kalei Kanuha, "'Being' Native versus 'Going Native': Conducting Social Work Research as an Insider," *Social Work* 45, no. 5 (2000).
5. Ekkehard Knopke, "Touching the Dead: Autoethnographical Reflections about the Researcher's Body in the Field of Death, Dying, and Bereavement," *Death Studies* 42, no. 10 (2018).
6. Ben Anderson, "Affective Atmospheres," *Emotion, Space and Society* 2, no. 2 (2009).
7. Gernot Böhme, "Atmosphere as the Fundamental Concept of a New Aesthetics," *Thesis Eleven* 36, no. 1 (1993).
8. Andreas Witzel, "The Problem-Centered Interview," *Forum Qualitative Sozialforschung/Forum: Qualitative Social Research* 1, no. 1 (2000).
9. For a similar field experience, see Kate Woodthorpe, "My Life after Death: Connecting the Field, the Findings and the Feelings," *Anthropology Matters* 9, no. 1 (2007).
10. Ronny E. Turner and Charles Edgley, "Death as Theater: A Dramaturgical Analysis of the American Funeral," *Sociology and Social Research* 60, no. 4 (1976).
11. Julien Bernard, *Croquemort: Une Anthropologie des émotions* (Paris: Éditions Métailié, 2009), 57–84.
12. David R. Unruh, "Doing Funeral Directing: Managing Sources of Risk in Funeralization," *Urban Life* 8, no. 2 (1979).
13. Philippe Ariès, *Western Attitudes toward Death: From the Middle Ages to the Present*, trans. Patricia M. Ranum (Baltimore: Johns Hopkins University Press, 1974).
14. Ekkehard Knopke, "Fühlbarer Abschied: Zur Produktion von Atmosphären auf Trauerfeiern aus praxistheoretischer Perspektive," Master's thesis, Bauhaus-Universität Weimar, 2015.

15. Thomas Schmidt is a pseudonym.
16. Knopke, "Touching the Dead."
17. James A. Thorson, "A Funny Thing Happened on the Way to the Morgue: Some Thoughts on Humor and Death, and a Taxonomy of the Humor Associated with Death," *Death Studies* 9, nos. 3–4 (1985).
18. Ekkehard Coenen, *Zeitregime des Bestattens: Thanato-, kultur- und arbeitssoziologische Beobachtungen* (Weinheim: Beltz Juventa, 2020).
19. Mary Douglas, *Purity and Danger: An Analysis of Concepts of Pollution and Taboo* (London: Routledge and Kegan Paul, 1966).
20. Franz Breuer, "Subjectivity and Reflexivity in the Social Sciences: Epistemic Windows and Methodical Consequences," *Forum Qualitative Sozialforschung/Forum: Qualitative Social Research* 4, no. 2 (2003).
21. Edwin Rosenberg, "Humor and the Death System: An Investigation of Funeral Directors," in *Humor and Aging*, ed. Lucille Nahemow, Kathleen A. McCluskey-Fawcett, and Paul E. McGhee (Orlando, FL: Academic Press, 1986).

Bibliography

Anderson, Ben. "Affective Atmospheres." *Emotion, Space and Society* 2, no. 2 (2009): 77–81.
Ariès, Philippe. *Western Attitudes toward Death: From the Middle Ages to the Present*. Translated by Patricia M. Ranum. Baltimore: Johns Hopkins University Press, 1974.
Bernard, Julien. *Croquemort: Une Anthropologie des émotions*. Paris: Éditions Métailié, 2009.
Böhme, Gernot. "Atmosphere as the Fundamental Concept of a New Aesthetics." *Thesis Eleven* 36, no. 1 (1993): 113–26.
Breuer, Franz. "Subjectivity and Reflexivity in the Social Sciences: Epistemic Windows and Methodical Consequences." *Forum Qualitative Sozialforschung/Forum: Qualitative Social Research* 4, no. 2 (2003): 1–14.
Coenen, Ekkehard. *Zeitregime des Bestattens: Thanato-, kultur- und arbeitssoziologische Beobachtungen*. Weinheim: Beltz Juventa, 2020.
Corbin, Juliet, and Anselm L. Strauss. *Basics of Qualitative Research: Techniques and Procedures for Developing Grounded Theory*. 4th ed. Los Angeles: SAGE, 2015.
Douglas, Mary. *Purity and Danger: An Analysis of Concepts of Pollution and Taboo*. London: Routledge and Kegan Paul, 1966.
Gorer, Geoffrey. "The Pornography of Death." *Encounter* 5, no. 4 (1955): 49–52.
Hockey, Jenny. "The Acceptable Face of Human Grieving? The Clergy's Role in Managing Emotional Expression During Funerals." In *The Sociology of Death*, edited by David Clark, 129–48. Oxford and Cambridge: Blackwell, 1993.
Kanuha, Valli Kalei. "'Being Native' versus 'Going Native': Conducting Social Work Research as an Insider." *Social Work* 45, no. 5 (2000): 439–47.
Knopke, Ekkehard. "Fühlbarer Abschied: Zur Produktion von Atmosphären auf Trauerfeiern aus praxistheoretischer Perspektive." Master's thesis, Bauhaus-Universität Weimar, 2015.
———. "Touching the Dead: Autoethnographical Reflections about the Researcher's Body in the Field of Death, Dying, and Bereavement." *Death Studies* 42, no. 10 (2018): 640–48.

Mey, Günter, and Katja Mruck. "Grounded Theory and Reflexivity." In *The SAGE Handbook of Grounded Theory*, edited by Antony Bryant and Kathy Charmaz, 515–38. London: SAGE, 2007.

Michels, Christoph. "Researching Affective Atmospheres." *Geographica Helvetica* 70 (2015): 255–63.

Reckwitz, Andreas. "Affective Spaces: A Praxeological Outlook." *Rethinking History* 16, no. 2 (2012): 241–58.

Rosenberg, Edwin. "Humor and the Death System: An Investigation of Funeral Directors." In *Humor and Aging*, edited by Lucille Nahemow, Kathleen A. McCluskey-Fawcett, and Paul E. McGhee, 175–98. Orlando, FL: Academic Press, 1986.

Rowling, Louise. "Being In, Being Out, Being With: Affect and the Role of the Qualitative Researcher in Loss and Grief Research." *Mortality* 4, no. 2 (1999): 167–81.

Thibaud, Jean-Paul. "Urban Ambiances as Common Ground?" *Lebenswelt* 4, no. 1 (2014): 282–95.

Thorson, James A. "A Funny Thing Happened on the Way to the Morgue: Some Thoughts on Humor and Death, and a Taxonomy of the Humor Associated with Death." *Death Studies* 9, nos. 3–4 (1985): 201–16.

Thorson, James A., and F. C. Powell. "Undertakers' Sense of Humor." *Psychological Reports* 89, no. 1 (2001): 175–76.

Turner, Ronny E., and Charles Edgley. "Death as Theater: A Dramaturgical Analysis of the American Funeral." *Sociology and Social Research* 60, no. 4 (1976): 377–92.

Unruh, David R. "Doing Funeral Directing: Managing Sources of Risk in Funeralization." *Urban Life* 8, no. 2 (1979): 247–63.

Witzel, Andreas. "The Problem-Centered Interview." *Forum Qualitative Sozialforschung/Forum: Qualitative Social Research* 1, no. 1 (2000): 1–9.

Woodthorpe, Kate. "My Life after Death: Connecting the Field, the Findings and the Feelings." *Anthropology Matters* 9, no. 1 (2007).

Young, Malcolm. "Black Humor—Making Light of Death." *Policing and Society* 5, no. 2 (1995): 151–67.

CHAPTER 7

The Historical Study of Death and Dying

The Intersection of Familial Stories and Catholic Rituals

Sarah Nytroe

My Catholic religious upbringing and formation as a young adult partly inspired my decision to become a historian of American religion. Rarely, however, did my historical interest in the American religious experience intersect with my familial relationships and interactions. My professional and personal life converged in intimate, complex, and unanticipated ways when I began to research the beliefs, rituals, and prayers that American Catholics could draw upon to attain a "good" death prior to the Second Vatican Council in the first half of the twentieth century.[1] As I dove into the primary sources, I discovered an abundance of religious publications authored primarily by clergy and theologians for instructional, educational, and devotional purposes. Close analysis of these documents revealed that the Catholic Church provided a consistent message to the faithful on how to live with death throughout their lives and particularly at the hour of death. These sources rarely allowed lay Catholics to speak. To supplement these primary sources, I conducted oral history interviews with my maternal grandparents (b. 1928) and my mother (b. 1956) to gather evidence that spoke more directly to how pre-conciliar Catholics may have internalized and integrated beliefs, rituals, and prayers into their lives. As a historian, I deliberately sought to remain objective while asking questions, interacting with the subjects, and analyzing the evidence. The interviews revealed deep truths about how they expressed their Catholic faith, thought about death and dying, and processed painful losses. The interviews, and subsequent analysis of evidence, compelled me to continually think about my identity as a scholar, as a granddaughter and daughter, and as a practicing Catholic. This research project demonstrates how the familial and personal intersect with the professional and historical in a manner that simultaneously provides an avenue to uncover unique evidence and challenges the scholar's ability to objectively practice the historical craft.

What follows is a "critical self-examination," as religious studies scholar Robert Orsi suggests, of how the familial and scholarly have intersected with my historical research and writing on death. I am positioned in three interrelated ways to the topic: as a historian studying death in the American Catholic religious culture; as a Catholic who continues to practice the faith; and as a daughter and granddaughter who shares a faith tradition with her mother and grandparents, albeit one cultivated within different sociocultural contexts.[2] During the interviews with my grandparents and mother, I became more cognizant of how these aspects of my identity consistently overlapped, both deepening my scholarly engagement with the topic and blurring the line between the subjective and objective. Maintaining historical objectivity during the interviews required deliberate attention to gather evidence about how my grandparents and mother encountered death in a way that not only spoke to their personal lives and religious convictions but might also illustrate the broader experiences of the faithful before Vatican II. Their recollections assisted me in examining the association between institutionally prescribed beliefs, rituals, and practices and individually enacted experiences of loss and grief. Conducting the interviews with my grandparents and mother contributed to an acute awareness of my own subjectivity in relationship to the topic. Moreover, the research process led me to recognize more clearly how my Catholic faith shapes my experiences with death. My scholarly attention to the subjective sharpened the lens through which I examined and interpreted the past.

The "Positioned (and Repositioned)" Scholar

From research conducted in archives to the close reading and analysis of primary sources to drafting and revising a manuscript, I have lived with the historical topic of death in the American Catholic religious culture before the Second Vatican Council for nearly ten years. When my primary source evidence base expanded to include oral history interviews with family, I moved beyond merely encountering death intellectually to wrestling with my own mortality. In the essay "Grief and a Headhunter's Rage," anthropologist Renato Rosaldo contemplated how the scholar related to his/her topic through the idea of the "positioned (and repositioned) subject."[3] The "meandering course of ethnographic inquiry," Rosaldo suggested, prompts the scholar to continually reposition oneself to the topic and subjects of one's inquiry. The questions asked, fieldwork conducted, and life experienced influence how one interacts with his/her scholarship.[4] This became most apparent for Rosaldo when he studied headhunting as an expression of grief after acute loss among the Ilongot in northern Luzon in the Philippines. After he completed his research, first in the late 1960s and then again in 1974, Rosaldo found it difficult to arrive at a rationally compelling explanation for this "most salient cultural practice."[5] His scholarly approach to the Ilongot enabled him to maintain objective distance from his subjects but prevented him from being subjectively aware of their intense grief. Rosaldo recognized that he was "not yet in a position to comprehend the force of anger possible in bereavement." His own "devastating loss," first that of his brother in 1970 and then of his research colleague and wife in 1981, prompted him to reposition himself to his scholarly subjects and topic. Only acute personal loss, not extensive professional training, put him in a position to understand and interpret the actions of his subjects. He concluded, "My use of personal experience serves as a vehicle for making the quality and intensity of the rage in Ilongot grief more readily accessible to readers than certain more detached modes of composition."[6] Like Rosaldo when he first conducted his field research, I lived with death largely within the parameters of my disciplinary training and detached observation. Similar to Rosaldo, my limited personal encounters with death leave me without a subjective frame of reference to fully grasp the relevance of religious doctrine, beliefs, and rituals to those who grieve. Through their open and honest recollections of personal loss, my grandparents and mother drew me closer to a subjective awareness of death without compromising the historical integrity of my research. Conducting the interviews with my family required a continual renegotiation of my historical, intellectual, and personal relationship to death.

As my family became subjects of my historical inquiry, I was invited into their lives as a scholar, granddaughter, and daughter as they discussed how they understood and encountered death as Catholics. Historical inquiry led me to a personal appreciation of how they lived with death, and in turn, their personal encounters with death illuminated how I lived with death as a historian. Before beginning my historical study of death, I understood the Catholic faith and religious convictions of my grandparents, Dolores (Lens) and Vincent Madsen, and my mother, Mary (Madsen) Nytroe, through our familial ties. As I became steeped in the historical literature on death and as we informally discussed my initial observations, I increasingly recognized that my grandparents' and mother's lived experiences offered insights that I could not glean from documents. Archival research yielded evidence about institutional expectations, but limited to no sources allowed the laity to directly voice how they lived with death. Extensive formal interviews with my grandparents and mother bore evidence about what lay Catholics believed about death and how they related to religious practices, affirming and challenging conclusions I began to draw from primary source documents.

In the shift from informal conversations to formal interviews, I repositioned myself in relationship to my grandparents and mother, less as family members and more as subjects associated with the topic of my historical research. They were now historical actors who lived in a pre–Vatican II Catholic culture characterized by a distinct religious ethos and specific rituals governing death. They understood this culture of death as lived experience. I inquired into matters of their faith, the meaning of death, and encounters with the dying, seeking to historicize their personal encounters. The nature of these questions could, and did, prompt my grandparents and mother to recall periods of intense grief in their lives. They opened up to my questions, highlighting their vulnerabilities when facing the reality of death as children and adults. I struggled with an internal conflict. As a historian, I sought evidence about how Catholicism informed lay understanding and experiences of death. To do so, I asked probing questions that encouraged my grandparents and mother to reflect on their faith formation and death in explicit and clear terms, perhaps in ways they had not prior to the interview. By approaching the interviews as professionally and objectively as possible, the process could produce evidence about lay experience largely absent from the documentary primary source base. In so doing, I could not help but listen with an acute sense of sympathy for the intensity of their personal loss, even as I posed questions seeking clarity and additional detail.

Although Dolores and Vincent took different paths to their faith, like many other laypersons immersed within the Catholic religious culture before Vatican II, they possessed a clear understanding of the doctrine and rituals governing a good death.[7] The distinct markers of "cultural Catholicism" most evident in urban environments of the Midwest and Northeast also emerged in the small towns and rural areas of the Plains region, like Minnesota, where my grandparents grew up.[8] Dolores was born and brought up in the faith through the decision of her parents, who had also been raised Catholic. As Dolores came of age, she made her own choice to practice the faith, one that permeates her daily routine and sense of identity to this day. As for many Catholics prior to Vatican II, the spaces of the home and neighborhood mutually reinforced my grandmother's religious beliefs, values, and morals from childhood into early adulthood.[9] Dolores testified to the presence of this foundation in her religious upbringing. She indicated that she was "blessed with [a] wonderful Mom and Dad" who gave her a "Catholic upbringing from the start."[10] Her faith formation included the "blessings of a Catholic education," including religious instruction at a school operated by the Sisters of St. Joseph and through *The Baltimore Catechism*. Alongside her parents and siblings, she attended Mass each Sunday, said the rosary, and went to confession on Thursday evenings as part of the First Friday Novena.[11]

Vincent took an alternative route to the Catholic faith, but one no less influential on his adulthood and sense of identity. Unlike my grandmother, my grandfather was largely "unchurched" throughout his childhood. As I interviewed him about his religious upbringing, Vincent stated that his mother encouraged him to attend church in a relaxed manner. She asked him to go to the Presbyterian church, which he did but then became "delinquent." She asked him to attend a Baptist church. He went a few times, but after hearing ideas about submersion in water, he stopped going. He did not recollect "ever being pushed to go to church" during his early childhood.[12] When his older sisters married men of the Catholic and Lutheran faiths, Vincent gained exposure to other religions. Parental guidance and life experiences made Vincent aware of the options available in the American "spiritual marketplace," but he did not avail himself of any particular brand of church at that point in his life. When Vincent met and began dating Dolores, their developing relationship provided another avenue for him to be exposed to the Catholic Church. After they became engaged and Vincent relocated to Sioux Falls, South Dakota, to start a new job, he began formal catechesis to prepare for initiation into the Church, unbeknownst to his fiancée and her family at the time. Upon completing instruction at St. Joseph's Cathedral, Vincent indicated that he "could find no reason why I shouldn't ... join the Church."[13] Becoming a member of the Catholic Church through baptism and confirmation was a more definitive choice for Vincent than for Dolores, but being Catholic was no less comprehensive.[14] In fact, for much of my life, I never knew my grandfather as anything but Catholic and was genuinely surprised when I learned that he was not a "cradle Catholic."

Against the backdrop of economic hardship in the 1930s and the social realities of World War II, Dolores and Vincent both experienced profound personal loss at a young age. Dolores's earliest memory of death occurred when she was seven years old. In 1936, her youngest brother Lawrence died from complications from pneumonia at the age of two months. While only a child at the time, Dolores remembered her mother (Gertrude) cradling her dying brother as she and her siblings sat around a "cookstove" waiting for their father (Frank) to return with medicine.[15] As Catholics, Dolores's parents had Lawrence buried within the Church. Vincent also experienced personal loss in his childhood. In the span of a few short months from the fall of 1941 through the winter of 1942, Vincent's mother (Emma) and father (Oscar) died in their early forties. Emma had undergone surgery to address a medical condition at a hospital in Minneapolis, only a few hours' drive northeast of Russell where they lived. After visiting her at the hospital, Vincent believed she was recovering. The next thing he knew, "Dad came home and told us she had passed away."[16] In February 1942, Vincent's father and the town constable died from unknown causes. In the same months that American society experienced profound dislocation when World War II arrived at the country's doorsteps, my grandfather's personal life "changed immensely."[17] His upbringing and life were fundamentally transformed in light of the absence of his parents. His older sisters, newly married and beginning a new part of their lives, made the arrangements for their parents' funerals and burials. As the closest living relatives of adult age, they also assumed responsibility for the care of their younger siblings, including my grandfather, just thirteen years old at the time. Vincent recalled that he was largely unaware of the minutiae of the decisions being made by his sisters and was not part of those conversations. At his age, he "just did what I was told."[18] Looking back upon this personal loss from the vantage point of nearly eighty years, my grandfather described the death of his parents as "devastating to me." While he did not state so explicitly, their deaths formatively shaped the direction of his life, his attitude toward personal challenges, and his emphasis on self-reliance.[19] While I was aware of their personal loss before interviewing them, I remained uninformed of how they made sense of it at a young age. As I listened to Dolores and Vincent recall their early encounters with death, I was struck by both the sharpness of their memories, as if the deaths transpired recently and not decades ago, and the openness with which they responded to questions that conjured up emotions from the past and in the present.

My mother's religious formation cut across a dynamic period within the life of the American Catholic Church.[20] Mary was born in 1956, a mere six years before members of the Catholic hierarchy from across the world gathered for the first session of the Second Vatican Council.[21] Her religious upbringing and sense of Catholic identity resembles that of her parents in several respects, in part because her early formation occurred within the same religious culture. Like her mother, the mutually reinforcing values of the Catholic home and school permeated Mary's religious formation. In my interview with her, my mother indicated that "Mom and Dad loved their Catholic faith, and they wanted to instill that in their children."[22] Dolores and Vincent nurtured Mary's faith and that of her siblings by maintaining prayer in the household, attending Mass every Sunday, and saying the rosary nearly "every evening."[23] Moreover, my mother and her three siblings received a Catholic education from kindergarten through high school. The religious values and morals taught by their parents at home were reinforced by the Benedictine Sisters at St. Joseph's Cathedral School and later by both religious and lay teachers at O'Gorman High School.[24] For Mary, like Dolores, the home and school were environments in which Catholic beliefs, values, and morals could infuse their daily lives.

Her relationship to death and dying does, however, provide a significant point of contrast. Compared to her parents, my mother had fewer personal encounters with death at a young age. Therefore, the occasions for her to draw upon Catholic doctrine and rituals to frame and process loss in tangible terms was more limited. While Dolores first learned about the Church's expectations for the care of the dead through religious education, Mary did not recall any "formal teaching about what occurs or what happens."[25] Instruction in this area more than likely occurred, but its hold on her memory was not as strong as that of Dolores. The religious instruction about death Mary would have received in elementary and junior high school, moreover, more than likely shifted in both tone and content to reflect statements from the Second Vatican Council guiding the reform of the sacrament of extreme unction and the funeral and burial rite.[26] While her parents faced deep personal loss at a very young age, Mary indicated that her first vivid memory of death was that of her maternal grandfather, Frank Lens, in 1974. Still living at home, Mary accompanied her parents to visit her grandfather as he was dying from lung cancer. She remembers walking into her grandparents' apartment and being "totally shocked, totally shocked because he was a big man and he was down to nothing."[27] Her grandfather's physical deterioration and the realization of his impending death, then and now, triggered a strong emotional response for Mary, as she held back tears recalling the memory. The family drew upon Catholic beliefs and rituals in the postmortem spiritual and physical care of Frank. Mary remembered that a prayer service was held at the funeral home the night before Frank's burial. The service included saying the rosary and reading Bible passages. On the following day, the family "processed" the one block from the funeral home to the entrance of Holy Redeemer Church, where the priest said a blessing before the family walked up the main aisle of the church "with the casket." The concluding ritual offered through the church consisted of a final blessing at his grave, after which family and friends reconvened for a luncheon in the church basement.[28] In the wake of Vatican II, a new funeral and burial rite was instituted in 1971, which would have been used at Frank's death. The "fixed program" of the funeral and burial rite provided a means by which the Church and the faithful could usher the dead out of the earthly realm and into an eternal one.[29] Mary acknowledged more than once in the interview that the rituals and prayers were "beautiful," providing "comfort to the living" in "sending off the loved one."[30] The spiritual ethos and beliefs about death emphasized within the rite and the content of prayers offered consolation for my mother as she made sense of her grandfather's death and grieved his loss.

Born in 1980, I was raised in a post-conciliar Catholic culture, which shaped not only my relationship to the Church but also my encounters with death.[31] Traces of my mother and grandparents' pre-conciliar religious experiences existed in my religious upbringing but were less absolute and all-encompassing as they had been for earlier generations of American Catholics. Like growing numbers of laypersons of her generation, my mother married a non-Catholic. Although my father was raised Lutheran, he practiced his faith minimally by the time I was born. Seeking to instill the same beliefs and values she received as a child and young adult, my mother initiated my religious formation in the Catholic Church. Like my mother, I too received my First Holy Communion when I was in second grade, in 1987. I too went to Catholic school from kindergarten through twelfth grade, attending two of the same schools as my mother and her siblings. By the time I attended St. Joseph's Junior High and O'Gorman High School in the 1990s, the teachers and administrators were predominantly laypersons. After graduating from high school, I chose to attend a small liberal arts college affiliated with the Dutch Reformed Church of America. A Catholic teenager attending college during my grandparents' and even my mother's generation would have more than likely chosen a school affiliated with their own faith tradition, one shaped and formed by the religious values of the pre-conciliar neo-Thomistic approach to intellectual development.[32] The cultural isolation of Catholics and separation from their non-Catholic counterparts in American society began to break down after World War II. Working alongside, living among, and socializing with non-Catholics became increasingly common for my mother's generation, giving way to experiences that were not fundamentally informed by the values of the Catholic Church, including higher education. This was true for me as I became immersed in a university environment shaped by a religious culture theologically and ritualistically different from Catholicism. This college experience led me to think critically about the Catholic tradition, personally and intellectually, which proved both exciting and unsettling.

Juxtaposed with my mother, and especially my grandparents, I have had infrequent and indirect experiences with death, affording fewer opportunities to draw upon Catholic doctrines and rituals to process loss. My historical study of death and dying has been more systematic and in-depth than my personal encounters. The first personal death I can remember occurred when I was a sophomore in high school. In 1995, my maternal great-grandmother, Gertrude Lens, died at the age of ninety-two. While I never knew Gertrude in the same way I knew my grandmother and mother, I often accompanied my grandmother on frequent visits to the nursing home where Gertrude lived in Marshall, Minnesota. When she died, I encountered this loss neither with the naivety of a child nor the full maturity of an adult. By this point in my life, I was aware of mortality, and my great-grandmother's death illuminated my emerging uneasiness with its universality. The postmortem physical and spiritual care of Gertrude, like her husband, occurred with the beliefs and rituals of the Catholic Church. Although they died nearly twenty years apart from one another, the funeral and burial rite of the Church for the great-grandfather I never knew and the great-grandmother I did altered little structurally, but it did significantly in terms of spiritual ethos. In reflecting on Gertrude's death, however, I do not recall whether Catholic rites and prayers provided the same degree of comfort as they did for my mother as she processed Frank's death. While the emotional intensity of the shock my mother recollected at the death of her grandfather was greater than what I remember feeling at the loss of my great-grandmother, the grief and sorrow were still real. Sitting in the front pew of Holy Redeemer Church, surrounded by my parents, grandparents, aunts and uncles, and cousins, I choked back tears while trying to sing hymns and respond to prayers that called to mind the promise and joys of eternal life. Perhaps because of an immature faith or memories dulled over time, I remember little of the religious message at her funeral and burial. In fact, I do not recall receiving any instruction about death, dying, and eternal life in my religious upbringing, a clear divergence from the experience of my grandmother in the 1930s and early 1940s. In my life, this close personal encounter with death, however, is the exception, not the rule.

A number of factors within the Catholic Church and American society have contributed to my infrequent encounters with death and lack of personal awareness of Catholic religious beliefs about death. In the twentieth century, particularly in the first half, infant mortality rates declined, average life spans increased, and the primary causes of death shifted away from communicable diseases. The social circumstances of my personal and professional life have also led to fewer personal encounters with death. Since 2002, I have lived and worked on the East Coast, physically distant from family in South Dakota and the Midwest. I flew home when my paternal grandparents passed away one year apart from one another in 2006 and 2007, but I have not traveled back home when relatives outside of my immediate family have died. Finally, when I have encountered death while living on the East Coast, these experiences have been more remote. When I have mourned, I have done so out of sympathy for friends and colleagues experiencing direct personal loss, not my own. The shift in spiritual ethos of the Catholic Church since the Second Vatican Council has also contributed to my limited awareness of the theological framework to process death. In the wake of the Council, lay Catholics largely "abandoned the sacrament of penance," a concrete rejection of the Church's "preoccupation with what we used to call the 'four last things,'" that of death, judgment, heaven, and hell.[33] The beliefs and sacramental practices that once maintained institutionally determined ideas about death and the afterlife among the laity were perhaps no longer as regularly integrated into the lives and consciousness of all Catholics.[34] This fragmented, and often vague, understanding of Catholic teaching and practices among laypersons is evident in my own life and the historical scholarship. In her study of how purgatory has been imagined within the devotional culture, Diana Walsh Pasulka points to the "problem" of purgatory among contemporary Catholics. Purgatory had once been a central and much talked about feature of Church teaching and belief about the afterlife. Pasulka suggests that "most American Catholics are unsure about its doctrinal status, and many even wonder what it is."[35] Few pre-conciliar Catholics who received religious instruction would have been illiterate or ambivalent about purgatory, as many contemporary Catholics appear to be.

My personal ignorance about purgatory emerged while studying the sacraments for the sick and dying. What is now called the anointing of the sick was known by clergy and laity prior to the Second Vatican Council as extreme unction. Then, and now, the sacrament was intended for both the sick and those in danger of death. From the available documentary evidence, pre-conciliar Catholics commonly believed the sacrament was solely intended for the dying. Authors of instructional and educational publications that outlined the purpose of the sacrament and its administration by a priest continually underscored the importance of preparation. The Catholic family in particular needed to ready the home, the "sick room," and the patient for the occasion in which a priest would visit to administer the sacrament. This preparation included the ownership of a sick call set, which functioned like an emergency spiritual kit containing all the items a priest might need to administer the sacrament in a timely and effective manner.[36] While occupied with my growing base of primary source documents on death and dying during a visit home, my mother revealed that she not only owned one of these sets, which was in the shape of a crucifix, but that it was prominently displayed on the bedroom wall. Her grandmother, Gertrude, gifted the set to her. She also indicated that my grandparents owned a sick call set as well, which had been displayed in each home they lived in since they were married. The ownership and display of the sick call set was a visible manifestation of Catholic beliefs about dying for both my mother and grandparents, of which I was completely ignorant. As my grandmother stated when I interviewed her, "Most homes, as I remember, had a sick call set."[37] Growing up and practicing my Catholic faith in a post-conciliar environment, my religious formation did not cultivate in-depth knowledge of Catholic teaching on rites for the sick and dying let alone an awareness of tools used in the administration of the sacrament. To this point in my research, I understood the role of the sick call set in the homes of pre-conciliar lay Catholics from an intellectual and objective perspective, one removed from the realities of my religious instruction and personal experience in the Church. The deliberate choices made by my family, gifting and displaying the set, demonstrates an affirmation of Catholic doctrine about death and an implicit agreement to observe institutional expectations to receive the sacraments. Although anecdotal, this experience points to a generational divide among pre-conciliar and post-conciliar Catholics, specifically in knowledge of sacramental rites to care for the sick and dying. I first became aware of the sick call set and its purpose in the Catholic religious culture through historical inquiry, mainly via documents highlighting institutional expectations on achieving a good death. Observations made by mother and grandparents offered personal insight into how they internalized Church teaching and sought to avail themselves of all rites at the end of life. While my mother, grandparents, and I share the same faith tradition, their religious formation as Catholics prior to the Second Vatican Council occurred in a "vastly different structure" and with different "emphases and surrounding contexts" than of my own.[38]

The "Intersubjective" History

Personal experience as a practicing Catholic who has witnessed death subjectively ties me to the topic of my historical study, while disciplinary expectations and training call for objective inquiry. The historical discipline generally views the interference of the personal, the subjective, negatively. Robert Orsi suggests the discipline's "deep reticence" toward a scholar's engagement or identification with his or her own religious stories is neither healthy nor obtainable.[39] He appeals for a deliberate acknowledgment of the "intersubjective" nature of scholarly choices, research, and writing. The "intersubjective" study of religion presents a "paradox of understanding," as the subjects of a scholar's inquiry can "become at once both closer and more distinct in their separateness and difference."[40] The scholar, Orsi indicates, must seek to "balance carefully and self-reflectively on the border between familiarity and difference, strangeness and recognizability."[41] Orsi himself integrated familial stories into his study of human relationships with the "holy," providing a clear model of how scholars can engage the "intersubjective."[42]

Recent publications indicate that scholars of American religion have heeded Orsi's call. They have applied the "intersubjective" as they uphold the standards of the historical discipline and demonstrate the insight that can be gained from including familial stories in their histories. Colleen

McDannell and Mary Ellen O'Donnell have written histories that seamlessly incorporate familial stories and personal anecdotes to address the broader issues, themes, or patterns present in the mid-twentieth-century American Catholic religious culture and experience. Both McDannell's study of the social and cultural history of the Second Vatican Council and O'Donnell's examination of the intertwined experience of church, home, and neighborhood bring the personal to the historical.[43] In *The Spirit of Vatican II*, McDannell leaned on the story of her mother's religious experience before, during, and after Vatican II to illuminate the relationship between the Council's reforms and lay Catholics. She indicated that her mother's relationship to the Catholic Church illustrated the dominant themes of American Catholicism, arguing that her religious biography is "typical" of lay Catholics and "mirrors" much of the change that occurred across the country.[44] O'Donnell frequently made references to the similarities and differences between her religious upbringing and that of her own daughter to demonstrate the continuity and change experienced by generations of American Catholics in *Ingrained Habits*. She drew upon her own biography to highlight what it meant to grow up Catholic as part of the "bridge generation," in which her religious formation included "vestiges" of an earlier period from the 1940s through the early 1960s, but also features of a decidedly post-conciliar Church.[45] In telling these historical stories through the lens of familial experience, both McDannell and O'Donnell positioned themselves openly to the topic, employing the first-person narrative to identify their personal relationship to their historical study and the reasons why they incorporated the familial in their histories.[46] They also seamlessly wove together evidence gathered about their family with that collected from textual-based primary sources to craft narratives and advance historical interpretation. They effortlessly move back and forth between the subjective first-person and the objective third-person narrative, from the micro-level of the family to the macro-level of the religious culture and institutional development at a critical juncture in mid-twentieth-century American Catholicism.

The account that follows seeks to model the "intersubjective" way of doing history called for by Orsi and employed by McDannell and O'Donnell. The narrative tells the story of my grandparents' encounter with death and personal loss—that of their fifth and last child, Vincent Frank Madsen, at birth—within the larger context of the religious culture of American Catholicism in the late 1950s. The micro- and macro-narratives inform each other in ways that could not be achieved if they were not placed in historical conversation with one another. My grandparents' recollections highlight how laypersons could internalize Catholic teaching and the degree to which they could draw upon a rich font of beliefs and rituals when they encountered death and grieved loss.

By 1958 Dolores and Vincent Madsen were thirty years old. They had been married for ten years, and their family was growing as they raised four young children between the ages of two and ten. Their Catholic faith permeated their daily lives as a married couple and parents as they brought their children up in the Church. Like McDannell's mother and the main subjects of O'Donnell's study, the structures, expectations, and "clear guidelines" established by the Catholic Church for living profoundly shaped my grandparents' religious identity and faith.[47] Through religious formation, the example of family, and personal choice, Vincent and Dolores practiced their faith in alignment with Catholic doctrine and teaching. When my grandmother recalled her religious upbringing in her parents' household and religious instruction through the omnipresent *Baltimore Catechism*, Dolores distinctively remembered how Catholic images and practices permeated the home and the day. As she stated, they were "just part of our life."[48] Throughout the interviews, moreover, my grandparents employed language that reflected the pre-conciliar ethos of obedience to institutional "rules."[49] The beliefs and rituals of the Church were "just always expected," "what was required," and what they "just knew."[50] The observation of Catholic beliefs and practices also applied to their experiences with death. At this point in their lives, and to this day, my grandparents possessed a sincere and deep faith. It was perhaps a natural response for them to physically and spiritually care for their deceased son through Church rituals and grieve his loss drawing upon their Catholic faith.

In 1958 Vincent and Dolores also eagerly awaited the arrival of their fifth child. Rather than welcoming Vincent Frank into the world and into the Catholic Church, they drew upon the doctrines and rituals of the tradition as they faced his death. One Sunday morning as their family got ready for Mass, Dolores fell sick eight months into her pregnancy. As she returned to that day in her memory, Dolores remembered "hurting so bad."[51] Alarmed, Vincent took his wife to McKennan Hospital, a Catholic healthcare facility founded in 1906 and operated by the Presentation Sisters of Aberdeen. The doctors and nurses, my grandfather recalled, "took over" as he paced the floor of the waiting room. Waiting to receive an update about Dolores and their unborn child, Vincent had no frame of reference other than the births of their four other children. He had no knowledge of "how she felt ... I had no idea."[52] Their religious formation equipped them with knowledge about Catholic teaching about death. As the severity of Dolores's medical condition became apparent and Vincent Frank's stillbirth became real, they now enacted and lived out that teaching. A reservoir of deep faith and available religious rites more than likely provided Vincent and Dolores with the means to process what could only have been an uncertain experience.

During their religious formation, Vincent and Dolores learned about the sacrament of extreme unction, the rite for the spiritual care of the sick and those in danger of death, particularly at the hour of death. Dolores identified spiritual lessons she learned in grade school about extreme unction. She recalled that "we wanted them [the dying] to receive" the sacrament, as a means of "preparing to enter our eternal home and have our sins forgiven."[53] As emphasized within their religious instruction, their "first thought" in 1958, and at other moments of sickness in their lives, was to call the priest.[54] The abundance of instructional literature created for lay consumption in the first half of the mid-twentieth century reinforced the spiritual value of the sacrament and the need to call a priest in a timely manner when faced with sickness or the prospect of death.[55] At this critical moment, my grandparents knew that by obtaining medical assistance at a Catholic healthcare institution, the "Catholic people present" would "apply the proper procedures" for not only the physical but also the spiritual well-being of the patient. The Presentation Sisters who staffed the hospital, the Catholic priest assigned to the hospital, and many doctors, including my grandmother's, were Catholic. For Dolores the "proper" treatment available to her through the Catholic tradition also included receiving extreme unction. The pain she had experienced at home was caused by a ruptured uterus, leading to a life-threatening loss of blood when she gave birth to Vincent, who was stillborn at delivery. As my mother recalled, the doctor informed Dolores that she was lucky to be alive.[56] The priest assigned to the hospital administered extreme unction to Dolores, seeking to ensure that her soul was spiritually prepared if she were to die. Firm in their faith and understanding of Catholic teaching, there was little doubt that either Vincent or Dolores would be recipient of Catholic rites to care for the sick and the dead.

Vincent and Dolores also ensured that Vincent Frank's body and spirit were cared for in a manner that reflected Church teaching and their Catholic beliefs. When Vincent Frank was stillborn in 1958, the administration of Catholic sacraments and rituals was governed through the Code of Canon Law of 1917. Comprising a "compilation of natural law, Scriptural imperatives, custom, tradition, and doctrine," the Code included regulations for how Catholics, practicing or non-practicing, adult or infant, should receive the rites of the Church.[57] Canon law distinguished between adults and infants, those with and without the "use of reason," in relationship to sin, the afterlife, and the conferral of sacraments.[58] Within Catholic teaching, all persons are born with original sin, for which the rite of baptism provides remission. Persons who reach the age of reason, arrived at after infancy, possess the capacity to commit actual sin. Infants born with original sin but who die before reaching the age of reason could not commit actual sin. An adult or infant's relationship to sin also had direct bearing on eternity. For those persons who reached the age of reason and the ability to commit actual sin, eternal options included heaven, hell, or purgatory. Catholic tradition assigned unbaptized infants, those free from actual sin but still in a state of original sin, to limbo.[59] While canon law outlined circumstances for the conditional baptism of infants in "imminent danger of death," for those "exposed and discovered" and for "deformed and abnormal fetuses," the law did not specifically address stillborn infants.[60] Based on these distinctions, the Church provided for the administration of sacraments in alternative contexts and to differing degrees.

Canon law guided the Catholic hospital and my grandparents in the postmortem care of Vincent, including his baptism and burial. Because he was stillborn, Vincent Frank's relationship to original sin is not entirely clear, but his relationship to actual sin is. He was baptized, more than likely conditionally in light of the circumstances of his birth, at the hospital and not in the parish church. My grandparents recalled that a religious sister rather than a priest administered the rites of baptism. In these kinds of "emergency" situations, the Church allowed (and continues to allow) for baptism to be administered by an individual other than a priest.[61] Like those of adult Catholics buried out of the Church, Vincent Frank's body was taken to a funeral home where it was prepared and laid out in a casket. Unlike adult Catholics, however, there was no funeral Mass said for him. While his baptism gave Vincent Frank the right to be buried out of the Catholic Church, canon law also imposed certain restrictions on burials. Full canonical rights included "transfer of the body to the church, funeral Mass, and interment."[62] In Vincent Frank's case, in accordance with canon law and as my grandparents recalled, he was neither transferred to the parish church nor given a funeral Mass. In lieu of the administration of these ecclesiastical rights, however, a "service" was conducted at the funeral home at which my grandfather and his four children were present. As Vincent remembers, "it wasn't a normal funeral."[63] After the service, Vincent Frank was interred in a section designated solely for infants, once again in accordance with canon law, at St. Michael's Cemetery, the burial ground established by the diocese.[64] Neither Dolores nor Vincent made any comments about the Church regulations governing the postmortem care of their son, at the time or since. Just as they observed Church teaching in other expressions of their faith, so too did they in the care of their son at his death.

Reflecting the pre-conciliar Catholic culture's emphasis on the "four last things," the Church guided and encouraged the faithful to maintain the spiritual connection between the living and the dead, specifically the responsibility of the living to spiritually care for the deceased. Prior to Vatican II, the Church regularly conveyed to Catholics the importance of the spiritual bonds between the living and the dead, particularly those souls in purgatory in need of the living's prayers to obtain their release into heaven. As she recalled her religious instruction, Dolores affirmed that, "yes, ... we always pray for the poor souls. ... It's the belief of the Catholic faith."[65] Moreover, she indicated that it was "just always expected that we were going to have ... a Catholic funeral ... you know, follow the rules of the Church."[66] Dolores and Vincent naturally and purposefully participated in the burial of the dead, a "corporal work of mercy," and prayed for the dead, not just for their son but also for other deceased members of their parish. Participating in these religious practices served as living expressions of Catholic teaching about the afterlife and demonstrated how it permeated their lives. Not only did they have their son buried at St. Michael's Cemetery, they also regularly recited prayers for his soul. They visited his grave, a practice not required of the Church, but one that functioned as an additional enactment of their grief. In the immediate days, weeks, and months following Vincent's death, my grandmother "wanted to go quite frequently" to visit his grave, perhaps motivated in part by her inability to attend his burial as she still remained hospitalized. After all, she lovingly and thoughtfully said, "he was ours, and [we] just wanted to be there with him."[67]

This spiritual attention to the dead was not solely reserved for their infant son, however, but also pertained to their parish community. Dolores indicated that they could arrange for a Mass to be said for any deceased member of the parish, and she explicitly identified the prayers said for the dead at each Mass.[68] In addition to these individual actions, Dolores and Vincent participated in the burial of the dead through their membership in Catholic organizations. As a member of Catholic Daughters, Dolores prepared food for the social gathering after the burial of a deceased member of their parish, which she continues to do to this day. When he was a member of the Knights of Columbus, Vincent participated in saying the rosary at the prayer service of fellow members, even leading the rosary in his capacity as Grand Knight if the priest was unavailable.[69] Vincent and Dolores lived with death through the lens of their faith in a manner indicative of a total immersion in the Catholic beliefs and rites available to and expected of the faithful prior to Vatican II.

Engaging in "intersubjective" historical inquiry proved to be challenging, both methodologically and personally. My personal relationship with my grandparents and sympathy for their loss intersected with and challenged my ability to uphold the standards of objective inquiry during the interviews. My grandparents and mother responded to questions about their religious beliefs and personal loss with thoughtfulness, honesty, and transparency, but doing so was clearly difficult and painful, evident in tears and pauses in the interviews. What were once sharp memories may have dulled with time, but the grief they first felt decades earlier seemed quite acute in the contemporary moment. While I knew that my grandparents lost their son at birth, I had limited personal knowledge of the circumstances of Vincent Frank's death and the ways my grandparents processed his loss. The death of their child was a key moment in their lives as parents and a married couple. To complete my historical research, I—as a scholar but also their granddaughter—asked them questions that directed their attention back to this experience. My close relationship with my grandparents contributed to my reluctance to pose questions that required them to emotionally and psychologically dig into the memory bank of his death. I wrestled with the potentially intrusive quality of my inquiries. Yet, when I approached the topic of Vincent Frank's death, my grandparents graciously drew me into a personal past of acute loss, one they experienced within the holistic framework of Catholic doctrine, beliefs, and rituals. Vincent Frank's death was neither the first nor the last they would encounter, process, and grieve through their Catholic faith, but it would probably be one of the most intense. During the interviews and while writing about their past, I sought to respect their personal loss while also maintaining the critical eye of the historian. As a granddaughter, I came to more fully understand and greatly admire the marriage, family, and faith my grandparents had nourished and sustained. As a scholar, I arrived at a more complete understanding of how the laity might encounter death through the Catholic faith and gained a greater appreciation of how the beliefs and rites of the Church served as a source of comfort amid intense personal loss.

Conclusion

Historians are trained to maintain objective distance from the topic and subjects of their inquiry. The universality of death presents a challenge to the scholar who seeks to study what is a highly personal experience through disciplinary standards. Each of us has, and will, witness the deaths of family members, close friends, and acquaintances, prompting us to draw upon ideas, beliefs, and rituals (or lack thereof) to process loss and grief. And each of us will die shaped by ideas and beliefs about the meaning of death and the afterlife (or lack thereof). Over the past several years, my intellectual engagement with an American Catholic culture of death in the first half of the twentieth century has intersected in unexpected and insightful ways. Like Renato Rosaldo, I continually repositioned myself as a scholar, granddaughter, and daughter to a topic of not only intellectual interest and objective inquiry but also personal meaning and familial significance.

For my grandparents, my mother, and myself, our common Catholic faith has informed how we respond to death. The social, religious, and cultural environments in which we received our religious formation in the Catholic Church and embraced the faith, however, have dynamically changed over the course of three generations. Growing up in a definitively post-conciliar Church, I know the religious culture of American Catholicism prior to the Second Vatican Council through a critical study of the past. Once a living reality for my grandparents, and to a degree my mother, they have personal knowledge of this religious culture. My encounters with death at a personal and intimate level have been infrequent. Catholic beliefs about death and the rites that govern the care of the sick, the dying, and the deceased have shaped these encounters in a fragmented way. My mother and particularly my grandparents' encounters with death have been more profound and intimate than my own. They have managed personal loss through the ideas, beliefs, and rituals provided by the Catholic Church more holistically and thoroughly than I have. The rigor of their religious education, the institutional attentiveness to the "four last things," and their own choices in a pre-conciliar American Catholic religious culture equipped them with the tools to make meaning out of death.

In doing "intersubjective" history I also engaged in a "self-reflective" process, first as a historian seeking to study an American Catholic culture of death, and second as a granddaughter and daughter seeking to understand the personal loss of my grandparents and mother. The traditional examination of textual primary sources provides the historian with a firm foundation to study, craft a compelling narrative about, and speak to the truth of the past. Within the past two decades, scholars of American religious history have increasingly turned to the personal and the subjective as a means not only of illuminating how the laity enacted their beliefs but also of understanding themselves and familial histories. While traditional primary sources supply a means by which I could examine Church teaching and institutional expectations, interviews with my grandparents and mother offered insight into how laypersons lived with death through Catholic beliefs and rituals. They invited me into their personal experience of acute loss, opening their lives to me as a historian. As a historian, I have sought to open their lives "out to history," examining how their experiences have been both typical of and yet unique from the broader pre-conciliar Catholic religious culture.[70]

Sarah Nytroe completed her doctorate degree at Boston College in 2009. In 2010 she began teaching at DeSales University, a liberal arts institution of higher education in the Catholic Salesian tradition, where she is currently an associate professor of history. She is completing a manuscript that examines the religious literature that supported and sustained institutional values, beliefs, and practices about death and dying within American Catholicism in the first half of the twentieth century.

Notes

1. Guidelines for what it meant to be a "good" Catholic were clearly outlined by the institution and understood by the laity in the American Catholic religious culture prior to the Second Vatican Council; for American Catholics adhering to church teaching "was a given." Chester Gillis, *Roman Catholicism in America* (New York: Columbia University Press, 1999), 18. Also see William D'Antonio, James D. Davidson, Dean R. Hoge, and Mary L. Gautier, *American Catholics Today: New Realities of Their Faith and Their Church* (Lanham, MD: Rowman & Littlefield, 2007), 17–18; and chapter 3, "A Brief History of Catholics in America: 1900 to the Second Vatican Council," in Gillis, *Roman Catholicism in America*, 68–94.
2. Robert Orsi, *Between Heaven and Earth: The Religious Worlds People Make and the Scholars Who Study Them* (Princeton, NJ: Princeton University Press, 2005), 14.
3. Renato Rosaldo, *Culture and Truth: The Remaking of Social Analysis* (Boston: Beacon Press, 1989), 7.
4. Ibid.
5. Ibid., 3.
6. Ibid., 11.
7. In contemporary studies of American Catholics, those defined as pre–Vatican II Catholics were born in 1940 or earlier; see D'Antonio et al., *American Catholics in Transition*, 19.
8. For a history of the Catholic Church in South Dakota, see Sister M. Claudia Duratschek, OSB, *Builders of the Kingdom of God: The History of the Catholic Church in South Dakota* (Yankton, SD: Sacred Heart Convent, 1985); also see Mary Ellen O'Donnell, *Ingrained Habits: Growing Up Catholic in Mid-twentieth Century America* (Washington, DC: The Catholic University of America Press, 2018), xvii–xviii.
9. O'Donnell, *Ingrained Habits*, 12–13.
10. Dolores (Lens) Madsen, interviewed by Sarah K. Nytroe, 20 July 2016, Sioux Falls, SD.
11. Ibid.
12. Vincent's parents were Presbyterian, and his maternal grandparents were Lutheran.
13. Vincent Madsen, interviewed by Sarah K. Nytroe, 20 July 2016, Sioux Falls, SD.
14. Adult initiation into the Catholic Church usually includes one's First Communion and confirmation, but in my grandfather's case no records of his baptism could be located, so he was also baptized.
15. Dolores (Lens) Madsen, interviewed by Sarah K. Nytroe, 22 July 2016.
16. Ibid.
17. Vincent Madsen, interviewed by Sarah K. Nytroe, 25 July 2016.
18. Vincent Madsen, interviewed by Sarah K. Nytroe, 19 July 2016.
19. Ibid. Upon the death of his parents, Vincent worked as a "hired hand" at a farm south of his hometown for the remainder of the school year and through the summer before taking the train to Pontiac, Michigan, where he would then live with his older sister and her husband. At the end of his first year in Pontiac, Vincent told his sister he was moving back to Minnesota, which he did, returning to work on the same farm while he finished high school.
20. James O'Toole, *The Faithful: A History of Catholics in America* (Cambridge, MA: Belknap Press of Harvard University Press, 2010).
21. Those persons, like my mother, born between 1940 and 1960 are known as Vatican II Catholics; see D'Antonio et al., *American Catholics in Transition*, 37.
22. Mary (Madsen) Nytroe, interviewed by Sarah K. Nytroe, 19 July 2016, Sioux Falls, SD.
23. Ibid.
24. For explorations of American Catholic schools, see Timothy Walch, *Parish School: American Catholic Parochial Education from Colonial Time to the Present* (Washington, DC: National Catholic Educational Association, 2003); and chapter 2, "Like an Owner's Manual for a Very Complicated Vehicle: Learning the Rules in the Classroom and the Confessional," in O'Donnell, *Ingrained Habits*, 35–74.
25. Mary (Madsen) Nytroe, interviewed by Sarah K. Nytroe, 19 July 2016.

26. Issued in December of 1963, "The Constitution on the Sacred Liturgy" established principles to guide the reform of the liturgy of the Mass, the sacrament of extreme unction, and the funeral and burial rite. See "The Constitution on the Sacred Liturgy" in International Commission on English in the Liturgy, *Documents on the Liturgy, 1963–1979, Conciliar, Papal, and Curial Texts* (Collegeville, MN: The Liturgical Press, 1982), 16–19.
27. Mary (Madsen) Nytroe, interviewed by Sarah K. Nytroe, 21 July 2016, Sioux Falls, SD.
28. Ibid. By 1974, Catholic funerals were governed by the *Ordo Exsequiarum*, or Order of Funerals, a rite that went into effect in 1970; see Annibale Bugnini, *The Reform of the Liturgy, 1948–1975*, trans. Matthew J. O'Connell (Collegeville, MN: The Liturgical Press, 1990), 771–77.
29. Rosaldo, *Culture and Truth*, 12.
30. Mary (Madsen) Nytroe, interviewed by Sarah K. Nytroe, 21 July 2016, Sioux Falls, SD.
31. Those persons born between 1961 and 1978 are considered post–Vatican II Catholics; those born between 1979 and 1993 are identified as Millennials; D'Antonio et al., *American Catholics in Transition*, 37.
32. For studies on the development of American Catholic higher education, see David J. O'Brien, *From the Heart of the American Church: Catholic Higher Education and American Culture* (Maryknoll, NY: Orbis Books, 1994); and Philip Gleason, *Contending with Modernity: Catholic Higher Education in the Twentieth Century* (New York: Oxford University Press, 1995).
33. Leslie Woodcock Tentler, "The American Reception and Legacy of the Second Vatican Council," in *The Long Shadow of Vatican II: Living Faith and Negotiating Authority since the Second Vatican Council*, ed. Lucas Van Rompay, Sam Miglarese, and David Morgan (Chapel Hill: University of North Carolina Press, 2015), 37–38.
34. For studies of the sacrament of confession in American Catholicism, see Patrick Carey, *Confession: Catholics, Repentance, and Forgiveness in America* (New York: Oxford University Press, 2018); Maria C. Morrow, *Sin in the Sixties: Catholics and Confession, 1955–1975* (Washington, DC: The Catholic University of American Press, 2018); and James M. O'Toole, "In the Court of Conscience: American Catholics and Confession, 1900–1975," in *Habits of Devotion: Catholic Religious Practice in Twentieth Century America*, ed. James M. O'Toole (Ithaca, NY: Cornell University Press, 2004), 131–86.
35. Diana Walsh Pasulka, *Heaven Can Wait: Purgatory in Catholic Devotional and Popular Culture* (New York: Oxford University Press, 2015), 3–4.
36. See Sarah K. Nytroe, "Sick Call Sets: Material Culture and the Sacraments of the Sick and Dying," *U.S. Catholic Historian* 36, no. 1 (Winter 2018): 27–51.
37. Dolores (Lens) Madsen, interviewed by Sarah K. Nytroe, 22 July 2016.
38. O'Donnell, *Ingrained Habits*, 14.
39. Orsi, *Between Heaven and Earth*, 14.
40. Ibid., 3.
41. Ibid. Rosaldo also recognizes the tension between the familiar and the different, the self and the other.
42. This was perhaps most poignantly revealed in chapter 4; here—in the "mirroring of the two lives," that of Saint Gemma Gulguini and his Italian-American grandmother—Orsi entered into the "intersubjective," enabling him to make observations not only about the complex dynamics of the sacred and ideas of suffering in mid-twentieth-century American Catholicism but also about his own family. See Orsi, *Between Heaven and Earth*, 111–45.
43. Colleen McDannell, *The Spirit of Vatican II: A History of Catholic Reform in America* (Basic Books, 2011), and O'Donnell, *Ingrained Habits*.
44. McDannell, *Spirit of Vatican II*, xii.
45. O'Donnell, *Ingrained Habits*, 1, 4.
46. McDannell opened with a story about the experience of her First Communion in 1962, and O'Donnell recalled her sixth-grade fear of the "strict, calculated, and strict" Sister Daria; see McDannell, *Spirit of Vatican II*, ix, and O'Donnell, *Ingrained Habits*, 1–2.

47. O'Donnell, *Ingrained Habits*, 14.
48. Dolores (Lens) Madsen, interviewed by Sarah K. Nytroe, 20 July 2016, Sioux Falls, SD.
49. See Andrew Greeley's discussion of the "rule"-oriented ethos of the American Catholic Church prior to the Second Vatican Council in *The Catholic Revolution*, 27.
50. Dolores (Lens) Madsen, interviewed by Sarah K. Nytroe, 25 July 2016, Sioux Falls, SD.
51. Dolores (Lens) Madsen, interviewed by Sarah K. Nytroe, 23 July 2016, Sioux Falls, SD.
52. Vincent Madsen, interviewed by Sarah K. Nytroe, 22–23 July 2016, Sioux Falls, SD.
53. Dolores (Lens) Madsen, interviewed by Sarah K. Nytroe, 22 July 2016, Sioux Falls, SD.
54. Dolores (Lens) Madsen, interviewed by Sarah K. Nytroe, 22–23 July 2016, Sioux Falls, SD.
55. For examples of this literature, see Walter W. Curtis, *Call the Priest!* (New York: Catholic Information Society, 1947); Andrew Wynn, *Sick Call Ritual: Comfort and Consolation for the Sick* (Boston, MA: Mission Church Press, 1910); D. F. Miller, *Sick Room Guide: Instructions on the Spiritual Care of the Sick and Dying* (Liguori, MO: The Liguorian Pamphlet Office, 1945); Louis Laravoire Morrow, *My Last Sacraments* (Kenosha, WI: My Mission House, 1949); and D. F. Miller, *Guide for Sick Calls* (Liguori, MO: Liguorian Pamphlet Office, 1959).
56. Mary (Madsen) Nytroe, interviewed by Sarah K. Nytroe, 23 July 2016, Sioux Falls, SD.
57. Rev. Joseph N. Perry, "The Right of Ecclesiastical Burial," *Catholic Lawyer* 28, no. 4 (Autumn 1983): 331. The 1917 Code of Canon Law was superseded by the 1983 Code of Canon Law, the work for which was initiated in 1963 along with the establishment of the Pontifical Commission for the Revision of the Code.
58. See Canon 88 and 745 in Edward N. Peters, curator, *The 1917, or Pio-Benedictine Code of Canon Law* (San Francisco: Ignatius Press, 1918), 53 and 276.
59. Pasulka, *Heaven Can Wait*, 3, 176.
60. See Canon 746, 748, and 749 in Peters, *The 1917*, 276–77.
61. See Canon 743, which indicates that the "faithful," particularly "obstetricians, doctors, and surgeons, are carefully taught the correct manner of baptizing in case of necessity"; see Peters, *The 1917*, 276. For additional laws on infant baptism, see Canons 746–51 and 770 in Peters, *The 1917*, 276–78, 281.
62. Perry, "Right of Ecclesiastical Burial," 317.
63. Dolores (Lens) Madsen, interviewed by Sarah K. Nytroe, 23 July 2016, Sioux Falls, SD; Vincent Madsen, interviewed by Sarah K. Nytroe, 23 July 2016, Sioux Falls, SD.
64. See Canon 1209 in Peters, *The 1917*, 411; for additional laws regarding ecclesiastical burial see Canons 1203–42 in Peters, *The 1917*, 409–22. Even with revisions to canon law, anecdotal evidence suggests that there may be continued confusion or uncertainty among laypersons today regarding whether the rites of the Church are available to deceased infants or stillborn babies who have been baptized. The Archdiocese of Boston's website contains a page titled "Pastoral Notes on the Celebration of Liturgical Rites for Deceased Infants and Stillborn or Miscarried Infants"; see https://www.bostoncatholic.org/Offices-And-Services/Office-Detail.aspx?id=12540&pid=464.
65. Dolores (Lens) Madsen, interviewed by Sarah K. Nytroe, 25 July 2016, Sioux Falls, SD.
66. Ibid.
67. Dolores (Lens) Madsen, interviewed by Sarah K. Nytroe, 23 July 2016, Sioux Falls, SD.
68. Dolores (Lens) Madsen, interviewed by Sarah K. Nytroe, 25–26 July 2016, Sioux Falls, SD.
69. Dolores (Lens) Madsen, interviewed by Sarah K. Nytroe, 25 July 2016, Sioux Falls, SD; Vincent Madsen, interviewed by Sarah K. Nytroe, 25 July 2016, Sioux Falls, SD.
70. Orsi, *Between Heaven and Earth*, 142.

Bibliography

Bugnini, Annibale. *The Reform of the Liturgy, 1948–1975*. Translated by Matthew J. O'Connell. Collegeville, MN: The Liturgical Press, 1990.

Carey, Patrick. *Confession: Catholics, Repentance, and Forgiveness in America*. New York: Oxford University Press, 2018.

Curtis, Walter W. *Call the Priest!* New York: Catholic Information Society, 1947.

D'Antonio, William, James D. Davidson, Dean R. Hoge, and Mary L. Gautier. *American Catholics Today: New Realities of Their Faith and Their Church*. Lanham, MD: Rowman & Littlefield, 2007.

Duratschek, Sister M. Claudia, OSB. *Builders of the Kingdom of God: The History of the Catholic Church in South Dakota*. Yankton, SD: Sacred Heart Convent, 1985.

Gillis, Chester. *Roman Catholicism in America*. New York: Columbia University Press, 1999.

Gleason, Philip. *Contending with Modernity: Catholic Higher Education in the Twentieth Century*. New York: Oxford University Press, 1995.

Greeley, Andrew. *The Catholic Revolution: New Wine, Old Wineskins, and the Second Vatican Council*. Berkeley: University of California Press, 2004.

International Commission on English in the Liturgy. *Documents on the Liturgy, 1963–1979, Conciliar, Papal, and Curial Texts*. Collegeville, MN: The Liturgical Press, 1982.

Madsen, Dolores (Lens). Interviewed by Sarah K. Nytroe. Oral history interview. Sioux Falls, SD. 20–25 July 2016.

Madsen, Vincent. Interviewed by Sarah K. Nytroe. Oral history interview. Sioux Falls, SD. 19–25 July 2016.

Massa, Mark, SJ. *The American Catholic Revolution: How the Sixties Changed the Church Forever*. New York: Oxford University Press, 2010.

McDannell, Colleen. *The Spirit of Vatican II: A History of Catholic Reform in America*. New York: Basic Books, 2011.

Miller, Donald F. *Sick Room Guide: Instructions on the Spiritual Care of the Sick and Dying*. Liguori, MO: The Liguorian Pamphlet Office, 1945.

———. *Guide for Sick Calls*. Liguori, MO: Liguorian Pamphlets Redemptorist Fathers, 1959.

Morrow, Louis Laravoire. *My Last Sacraments*. Kenosha, WI: My Mission House, 1949.

Morrow, Maria C. *Sin in the Sixties: Catholics and Confession, 1955–1975*. Washington, DC: The Catholic University of America Press, 2018.

Nytroe, Mary (Madsen). Interviewed by Sarah K. Nytroe. Oral history interview. Sioux Falls, SD. 19–26 July 2016.

Nytroe, Sarah K. "Sick Call Sets: Material Culture and the Sacraments of the Sick and Dying." *U.S. Catholic Historian* 36, no. 1 (Winter 2018): 27–51.

O'Brien, David J. *From the Heart of the American Church: Catholic Higher Education and American Culture*. Maryknoll, NY: Orbis Books, 1994.

O'Donnell, Mary Ellen. *Ingrained Habits: Growing Up Catholic in Mid-twentieth Century America*. Washington, DC: The Catholic University of America Press, 2018.

O'Malley, John. *What Happened at Vatican II*. Cambridge, MA: The Belknap Press of Harvard University Press, 2008.

Orsi, Robert. *Between Heaven and Earth: The Religious Worlds People Make and the Scholars Who Study Them*. Princeton, NJ: Princeton University Press, 2005.

O'Toole, James M. *The Faithful: A History of Catholics in America*. Cambridge, MA: The Belknap Press of Harvard University Press, 2008.

———. "In the Court of Conscience: American Catholics and Confession, 1900–1975." In *Habits of Devotion: Catholic Religious Practice in Twentieth Century America*, edited by James M. O'Toole, 131–86. Ithaca, NY: Cornell University Press, 2004.

Pasulka, Diana Walsh. *Heaven Can Wait: Purgatory in Catholic Devotional and Popular Culture*. New York: Oxford University Press, 2015.

Perry, Joseph N. "The Right of Ecclesiastical Burial." *Catholic Lawyer* 28, no. 4 (Autumn 1983): 315–35.

Peters, Edward N., curator. *The 1917 or Pio-Benedictine Code of Canon Law*. San Francisco: St. Ignatius Press, 2001.

Rosaldo, Renato. *Culture and Truth: The Remaking of Social Analysis*. Boston: Beacon Press, 1993.

Tentler, Leslie Woodcock. "The American Reception and Legacy of the Second Vatican Council." In *The Long Shadow of Vatican II: Living Faith and Negotiating Authority since the Second Vatican Council*, edited by Lucas Van Rompay, Sam Miglarese, and David Morgan, 37–57. Chapel Hill: University of North Carolina Press, 2015.

Walch, Timothy. *Parish School: American Catholic Parochial Education from Colonial Time to the Present*. Washington, DC: National Catholic Educational Association, 2003.

Wynn, Andrew. *Sick Call: Comfort and Consolation for the Sick*. Boston: Mission Church Press, 1910.

Part IV

Memorialization

CHAPTER 8

Touch 'Em All
Memorializing Harmon Killebrew

Debbie A. Hanson

When Minnesota Twins Hall of Fame player Harmon Killebrew died of esophageal cancer on 17 May 2011, it was clear that the connections made between him and the state in which he played fourteen of his twenty-two seasons were many and immediate. Though I had not lived in the state for over twenty years, as a native Minnesotan, I had friends checking in to see if I was okay, including a colleague who told me I was the first person he had thought of when he heard the news. Of course, most people were more concerned with the reactions of those more closely connected to Killebrew, such as former teammates Rod Carew and Tony Oliva, who called him the eternal face of the Twins[1] and Mr. Minnesota respectively,[2] and Kent Hrbek[3] and National Hall of Fame president Jeff Idelson, both of whom compared him to Paul Bunyan, a Minnesota icon.[4] Reporter Vance Barker, on the other hand, stated that Killebrew was not just the face of the Twins but also that of the entire state.[5] Minnesotans responded in kind, not only by attending the formal service held at Target Field but also by constructing spontaneous shrines and cybershrines in Killebrew's honor. All of these commemorations served to pay homage both to Killebrew and to the memory of the times in which he played while simultaneously offering an opportunity to discuss how to perpetuate the best of his legacy in a changing sport and culture.

Elected to the Major League Baseball Hall of Fame in 1984, Harmon Killebrew amassed an impressive record at the plate over more than two decades of play. He led the American League in home runs six times and hit 573 overall, making him fifth on the list of all-time home run hitters at the time of his retirement in 1976 and third in home run frequency, behind only Ralph Kiner and Babe Ruth.[6] In the 1960s alone, Killebrew hit 393 home runs, the most in that decade, a decade in which he also had 1,031 RBI.[7] In addition, he had eight seasons in which he hit forty or more home runs[8] and nine seasons during which he drove in more than one hundred runs.[9] He was also an eleven-time All-Star and the American League's Most Valuable Player (MVP) in 1969.[10] Moreover, Killebrew played in 2,935 games without being ejected from a game even once—or laying down a single bunt.[11] Given these statistics, it is not surprising that pitcher Tommy John called Killebrew "the single most dangerous hitter in our league," adding that he had "the perfect batting stance. You look down at him, and there's no place to throw the ball."[12] When asked about his strategy for pitching to Killebrew, pitcher Denny McClain, 1968 American League Cy Young Award winner and MVP, simply replied, "Prayer, for the most part."[13]

As fine as his batting statistics were, though, Killebrew's personal story was even better; in some respects, it is almost legendary. He was the grandson of Culver Killebrew, the Union Army's heavyweight wrestling champion, a feat that earned him the title of the strongest man in the Union Army.[14] Culver Killebrew was also rumored to be able to "stand flat-footed and jump over a horse."[15] Killebrew's father, Clayton Killebrew, was an Idaho housepainter who read Homer, Socrates, Plato, and Cicero and taught his sons both sports and sportsmanship.[16] He also famously told his wife Katie, who objected to the way their sons' games were destroying the lawn, "We're raising boys, not grass."[17] As for Katie herself, Killebrew said that the most significant piece of advice his mother ever gave him was that the most important reason we are here on earth is to love and help each other.[18]

Killebrew grew up throwing around ten-gallon milk cans for the local dairy and bucking bags of onions and potatoes onto trucks for area farmers. As a result of this kind of physical labor and his own natural talents, he excelled at sports, particularly baseball, to the point that by 1954, at the age of seventeen, Killebrew was already hitting better than .600 for the Payette Packers, a semipro team, having been previously banned from American Legion ball because its area organizers felt he hit the ball so hard one of his line drives might actually kill a third baseman.[19] While playing for the Packers, Killebrew was scouted by Ossie Bluege of the Washington Senators after Senator Herman Welker of Idaho convinced owner Calvin Griffith that there was a kid back home who could help his struggling team. Over the course of three games, Bluege watched the teenaged Killebrew go eleven for thirteen, including a double, two triples, and four home runs, one of which Bluege paced out at approximately 435 feet.[20] After that performance, Killebrew was signed as the Senators' first bonus baby, and he saw his first-ever Major League Baseball game as a player.[21] Killebrew continued his affinity for the long ball in the majors, hitting balls so high and so far that they were affectionately called "moonshots."[22] In 1960 Killebrew hit the first homer onto the roof of the double-decker left field stands of Tiger Stadium, and in 1962 he hit one that cleared the roof of that same stadium.[23] Killebrew also hit homers onto and over the roof in Chicago and over the hedge in Baltimore,[24] as well as smashing the longest home run in the history of Minnesota's own Metropolitan Stadium, one that allegedly cracked a seat in the upper deck approximately 520 feet from home plate.[25] Killebrew's ability to hit such shots led Baltimore manager Paul Richards to quip, "The homers he hit against us would be homers in any park—including Yellowstone."[26]

When the Senators became the Minnesota Twins in 1961—in the same month and year in which I was born—Killebrew was not immediately thrilled with the idea. He worried particularly about the cold but said that once he arrived in the state, he found Minnesotans much warmer than their weather. Killebrew stated, "I loved the fans because they were down-to-earth Midwestern people. ... The people in the Upper Midwest were the same kind of people I grew up around in Idaho."[27] As one reporter put it, "Harmon was never flashy, never cocky, never sexy. He and Minnesota were a perfect fit."[28]

It was hard for Twins fans not to respond enthusiastically to Killebrew's presence on their team and in their state, not only for what he did on the field but off it as well. Pitcher Mudcat Grant said, "He was a star but he thought the fans were stars. ... Harmon genuinely thought about the fans and signing autographs."[29] Killebrew brought the same sincere concern to his extensive work on behalf of a wide variety of charities. He established the Danny Thompson Golf Tournament in honor of Twins shortstop Danny Thompson, who died at twenty-nine of leukemia; the tournament has raised $9 million plus $20 million worth of matching grants for leukemia research at hospitals in Idaho and Minnesota.[30] In 1998, he and his wife Nita founded the Harmon Killebrew Foundation, which has contributed to many organizations, including Healing Hands for Haiti and Hospice End of Life Care, and he used his sixty-fifth birthday as a fundraiser for Gillette's Children's Specialty Health Care, a St. Paul hospital that treats children with disabilities.[31] Near the end of his life, Killebrew also personally raised more than $350,000 for the Minnesota Twins Community Fund, which builds diamonds in inner-city neighborhoods, and the Miracle League, which builds diamonds that are handicapped accessible so that children with disabilities may play baseball. Seven such fields now exist in Minnesota.[32] As a result of the scope of his philanthropic endeavors, Killebrew was elected to the World Sports Humanitarian Hall of Fame in 2006.[33] Though Killebrew was unassuming about all he did as a Twin and as a private citizen, his sincerity and dedication did not escape the notice of Twins fans, one of whom wrote that Killebrew was the "'bashful basher from power alley.' The menacing foe with the kind demeanor; an icon, Babe Ruth dressed in Minnesota nice. Always and forever, the face of the Minnesota Twins. ... He should be the face of baseball because he epitomizes what all baseball players should embrace. Walk softly and carry a big stick."[34]

Because of the depth of feeling about Killebrew's death in Minnesota and throughout the upper Midwest, it was inevitable, even essential, that the Twins organization host a public commemoration of Killebrew's life. The need for such an event was apparent in the public reaction to the news of his death and in the comments voiced by current and former Twins players in the local and national media. Catcher Joe Mauer said, "When I learned the news about Harmon today, I felt like I lost a family member. He treated me like one of his own."[35] Jim Kaat, who was a teammate of Killebrew's for longer than anyone else, stressed that Killebrew "really is the face of the Twins franchise. ... I think he's the main reason the Twins have a reputation for being a gentlemanly organization."[36] Tim Laudner, who spent nine years with the Twins, was "awestruck" at getting a text message from a friend who worked as a Japanese translator indicating that Sadaharu Oh, the Babe Ruth of Japan, was desperate to get ahold of Twins president Dave St. Peter so that he could ask where to send flowers.[37] But perhaps the most overwhelming reaction came from Jack Morris, World Series MVP of the 1991 champion Minnesota Twins. Morris, who allegedly convinced Twins manager Tom Kelly that it would be a bad idea to remove him from the mound in the seventh and deciding game of the World Series simply by staring him down, and whom Detroit Tigers manager Sparky Anderson called "one of the nastiest, meanest, most self-centered, and highest strung people I've ever met,"[38] wept openly, wiping tears out of his eyes repeatedly as he said, "I lost a hero. ... But as a grown man ... I look back at him now not as that guy but as the guy who tried to show me that you don't have to be angry, you don't have to be mad. You can love and share love."[39] If Black Jack Morris could be brought to a state of public tears by the death of Harmon Killebrew, it was a foregone conclusion that fans would have an equal need to express their grief and expect that the Minnesota Twins would provide one such avenue to do so.

On 26 May 2011, nine days after Killebrew's death, following a memorial in Arizona where he had been living and a funeral in his hometown of Payette, Idaho, where he was buried, the Minnesota Twins hosted a tribute they called "Remembering Harmon" at Target Field. "Remembering Harmon" began with a light rail train ride that Fox Sports North, which devoted three and a half hours of prime time coverage to the event, called "the train ride from the past to the present."[40] Starting at Bloomington's Mall of America, the former site of Metropolitan Stadium, Lightrail Train Three, emblazoned with a reproduction of Killebrew's elegant autograph and a Twins number three, picked up former Twins players both there and at the Metrodome in Minneapolis. Then the train proceeded to Target

Field, where the passengers entered the ballpark through gate three, the Killebrew gate. At the stadium, the former players joined current players, personnel, and special guests, including Hank Aaron, who had called and asked if he could attend, as well as an estimated four to five thousand fans, the majority of them wearing Twins gear and various types of improvised threes or displaying Killebrew's number on homemade signs. Threes were much in evidence, from the three drawn into the diamond behind second base to the giant three on the newly pinstripe-painted water tower atop the Carmichael Lynch building that could be seen from Target Field and throughout most of the city. Just as it had been on Lightrail Train Three, Killebrew's signature also covered most of an outfield wall, and at one point in the evening, one of Killebrew's game-used jerseys was held aloft by Jim Thome, who was positioned in the only seat in Target field that is 520 feet from home plate, the distance of Killebrew's record-breaking home run in Metropolitan Stadium.[41] As for the ceremony itself, music was provided by local gospel singer Robert Robinson; the Minnesota Chorale; Mudcat Grant and Rick Oliva, Tony Oliva's son, who sang and played Killebrew's favorite song, "What a Wonderful World"; and folk singers Jeff Arundel and Jeff Victor, who sang "Harmon Killebrew," which Arundel had released in 1995. Arundel's song evoked such strong emotions for fans that at least one man in attendance at the memorial stood and held his cap over his heart while it was played, as if it were the Twins version of the national anthem.[42] Many others simply wept as the song was played, including me, while initially watching the memorial in South Dakota and then again while having to transcribe portions of it later, trying to treat it as research but unable to keep from repeatedly breaking down in tears. Speakers at the memorial included Jim Kaat, Michael Cuddyer, Rod Carew, and Paul Molitor, all current or former Twins players, and Nita Killebrew, Harmon Killebrew's widow, who attended the tribute along with over thirty members of the Killebrew family. The memorial concluded with the "gift of a home run" as four Miracle League players, with the help of Killebrew children and grandchildren, each ran one portion of the base path while recordings of announcers calling particularly significant Killebrew homers played over the loudspeaker system.[43]

Even prior to the public memorial, a smaller, more private tribute was paid to Killebrew by the grounds crew at Target Field, who carefully encased a black-and-white photo of Killebrew at the plate in plastic and placed it beneath home plate, where it remained for the rest of the 2011 season. While this decision was later claimed as an officially sanctioned act, approved by the Twins front office, original reports indicated that the grounds crew chose to do it first and report that they had done it later, at which point the Twins management agreed that it was a good idea. That the grounds crew would choose, on their own, to do such a thing underscores Rod Carew's comment that Killebrew treated "everyone from the brashest of rookies to the groundskeepers to the ushers in the stadium with the utmost respect."[44] Carew might have added fans to that list, as Killebrew was known for being particularly considerate of, and attentive to, his fans, who, like the grounds crew, felt a need to do something on their own, beyond the strictures of the memorial organized by the franchise. A spontaneous shrine was begun at the foot of Killebrew's statue outside Target Field almost as soon as the news of his death became public. Commemorative shrines or performative commemoratives invite participation,[45] and the one at the Killebrew statue exhibited what Sylvia Grider has called the "basic vocabulary" of such assemblages, including "flowers, votive candles and a wide range of popular and material culture items appropriate to the event."[46] Posters, bouquets of carefully arranged roses and bunches of backyard lilacs, balloons, a rosary, candy, teddy bears, a cap from the first game at Target Field, baseball cards, cans of Killebrew Root Beer, baseballs, photos, and folded bits of paper with personal notes written on them all appeared near the statue,[47] and after the conclusion of the formal memorial service, fans placed lit candles there as well.[48] Many of these items would qualify as *beau geste*, a term defined by Erica Brady as "objects of personal significance used to mourn the death of loved ones."[49] In particular, objects bearing messages from fans spoke of what Killebrew had meant to them. One hand-lettered sign read, "Harmon Our Humble Hero, A Class Act and Model of a Man, You're a Treasure to Minnesota," and near it was a worn baseball inscribed simply "Thanks, Harmon."[50] Comments from fans interviewed at the shrine bore out what the material items suggested. Amy Capitola, who was one of the first to bring a contribution to the spontaneous shrine, said, "He's an athlete that personified a true hero for sports fans. He was so giving. It's our turn to give back to him."[51] Harry Stofferahn, who made the decision to buy a Killebrew jersey at the clubhouse store when he came to the stadium, said, "All these years, I'd never gotten one. This seemed like the time to do it. He was a gentleman. All baseball players should be like him."[52] Keith Schafer stressed Killebrew's approachability, saying, "I had a chance to meet him, and he was friendly to everyone, just a great guy,"[53] an assessment with which another fan, identified simply as Astrid from Shakopee, Minnesota, readily agreed. Astrid told a Fox Sports North broadcaster,

> A few years ago, I met Harmon outside of the Metrodome, and he was such a nice person. He came walking up to me, shook my hand, he just looked at me and said, "Astrid, how ya doing?" He was just so sincere and honest, just to know that he meant what he was saying, and he will be missed, and I don't think anyone can replace him. He was such a nice person, and he really, truly cared. And I'm glad I was out there that day and met him, it was one of those Minnesota cold days, and we were just standing out there having some coffee and talking and it was just so nice.[54]

Astrid feeling a connectedness to Killebrew, even though she had met him only once, was echoed by those who had never met him at all but for whom he was a significant part of their lives. Kevin Lindquist lamented, "It kind of makes you feel like your childhood years are gone—like a part of your life is taken away. ... I know it sounds stupid ... but I've never been so sad about someone I didn't know."[55] While I had once met Killebrew at an autograph session and had had an extended conversation with him about the then recently released Twins cookbook, which included a number of Killebrew's own recipes, I understood entirely what Lindquist meant. Killebrew seemed like such a part of my childhood, too. My fourth-grade teacher, Miss Esmer Johnson, had placed a Killebrew biography in my best friend Jennifer's desk, knowing we would both eventually read it, and it unleashed in me a lifelong interest in baseball biographies as a result. I was also among many that evening at the Winnebago Avenue softball diamonds in my hometown of Fairmont, Minnesota, who heard, via someone's car radio, that Killebrew had finally hit his 500th home run. Like the rest of the crowd that night, I reacted with both happiness and relief, as it had been an uncharacteristically long time since his 499th home run, and it had felt a bit like the team's, if not the entire state's, pride was on the line. Killebrew was Minnesota's big-name player, a large fish in a small, secondary market pond, and it seemed to matter desperately that he and the Twins get the national attention rarely afforded them. That moment was so significant that I even remember what I was wearing—a white t-shirt and tie-dyed brown jeans. It was, after all, 1971, so to my ten-year-old self, my outfit seemed as appropriate as the fact that I would be at a diamond when I heard about Killebrew's 500th homer.

For all those who were able to make it to the official tribute or Killebrew's statue, there were many more, like me, who were unable to do so but still felt a need to participate in memorializing Killebrew. Hundreds created or sought out cybershrines, "webpages containing photographs of material shrines, photo montages, and other associated images as well as websites for lighting virtual candles and virtual condolence books."[56] Videos popped up on YouTube, some of them simply portions of press conferences, news reports, interviews, or the Twins memorial, but others were produced by fans themselves, including numerous montages set to a wide array of songs, such as "Finger Popping Time," "Buffalo Shuffle," "Gathering Crowds," and Jeff Arundel's "Harmon Killebrew," by far the single most popular choice. One astrologist even presented Killebrew's star chart set to music. Legacy.com and twinsguestbook.com also offered online condolence books, the former being linked to newspapers across the country, including the *Cleveland Plain Dealer*, the *Arizona Republic*, and the *Minneapolis Star-Tribune*. The legacy.com site received 568 posts from 40 states and 3 foreign countries, while twinsguestbook.com, which does not record the geographical origins of its posts, had 345 contributions. As would be expected, many posts were from lifelong displaced Twins fans who had moved far from Minnesota, but a surprising number were also from self-professed fans of other teams, such as the Red Sox, the Yankees, the White Sox, the Cardinals, the Dodgers, the Athletics, the Orioles, the Cubs, and the Braves, who admired Killebrew enough to offer their memories, condolences, and comparisons to their own teams' iconic figures, including Babe Ruth, Lou Gehrig, Roger Maris, Stan Musial, Ernie Banks, and Hank Aaron. Across both sites, certain descriptors cropped up consistently. At legacy.com, the most commonly used terms were "hero," "class," "gentleman," "role model," "kind," "humble," "gentle," and "idol," while at twinsguestbook.com, the most popular terms were "class," "gentleman," "kind," "hero," "gracious," "generous," "idol," and "genuine." While "hero" and "idol," and perhaps even "role model," might be expected ways of describing successful athletes, the rest of the words had little to do with Killebrew's skill on the baseball field. Few individual posts stuck strictly to Killebrew's athletic prowess either, and when it was mentioned, it was frequently linked to his personal qualities, as in a description of Killebrew turning to the opposing team's catcher and laughing after a pitcher deliberately attempted to beanball him and then smacking out a home run on the next pitch,[57] or a recollection of Bill White telling Harry Caray that "Harmon was the only guy who had muscles in his toes and managed to get their power in his swing," only to have Caray reply, "Harmon doesn't have toes or fingers or arms or legs, he's just one gigantic heart that loves baseball and gets all that love in his swing."[58] Many more posts involved detailed, sometimes quite lengthy, descriptions of personal encounters with Killebrew that illustrated what the poster thought were his most distinctive characteristics, much as character principle narratives seek to illuminate an individual's personality via a single story. A legacy.com poster recalled Killebrew stopping in the poster's Georgia hometown on his way to spring training, not because he had an event to attend but because he saw the poster, then a child, playing catch by himself. Killebrew played catch with him for a while, offered him tips on how to improve his game, and gave him some baseball equipment from the trunk of his car before going on his way.[59] Another poster on twinsguestbook.com remembered his brother receiving a handwritten letter from Killebrew after he wrote to let him know that he had lost a bet to their father when Killebrew struck out rather than hitting a game-winning home run on his last at bat. Killebrew not only apologized and promised to do better but also taped a dime to the letter to cover the boy's gambling losses.[60] In addition, other tributes offered on twinsguestbook.com marveled at Killebrew's careful attention to all the Miracle League players with whom he interacted[61] or mentioned his offer of a ride home from the airport to a fan he had just met on the plane.[62] I suppose I could have added to these posts, even though I did not know about the online guestbooks until well after his death, but I did not, partially because I was not sure I should contribute to a source I was using for research and partially because I felt uncomfortable doing so, as I was not yet certain I wanted to be quite so public with my personal stories about Killebrew or my grief over losing both him and the portion of my past with which his memory was so intertwined.

A number of contributions on both legacy.com and twinsguestbook.com linked these sorts of personal reminiscences to a more general longing for the better times of the past that Killebrew represented for them too. During the memorial at Target Field, an announcer said that Harmon "stood in stark contrast to a nation in turmoil. Minnesota nice, he was humble, hardworking, and at the top of his game, hitting more home runs than anyone else in the 1960s."[63] Erin Schmidt indicated much the same sentiment when she wrote at twinsguestbook.com, "you [Killebrew] have left behind a legacy that not only celebrates Minnesota sports but encompasses the kindness and compassion of the human spirit not often found in this day and age."[64] A contributor identified only as "one of your many friends in Cleveland" agreed with Schmidt's assessment, writing that Harmon represented "'good baseball' … the days when people stood with their hands over their hearts and sang the National Anthem, could afford to bring the whole family to a game where the players really gave their all—and when they heard the name, 'Harmon Killebrew'—knew they were in for a REALLY good game."[65] Others, like Judy Chucker, described the connection between Killebrew and the era in which he played in more personal terms that eerily echoed my own experiences. She wrote, "Harmon was summer with my dad at Met Stadium: a Frosty Malt in my hand, my dad dropping peanut shells on my lap to tease me, and Harmon hitting a home run on the first time up to bat after a long time out on the injury list. Nothing but smiles at the mere mention of his name. You can't buy memories like that."[66] While such posts might seem overly sentimental, they also reflect to a degree the way people who knew Killebrew felt, even someone like Mudcat Grant, who, as an African American player married to a white woman, remembers the 1960s differently. According to Grant, Killebrew "didn't say a whole lot, but sometimes he would come sit by you on the bench and if you wanted to say something, you could … a lot of people forget those days, but they were rugged days, but it was the other guys, sometimes, like Harmon, that were sorta smooth that would kind of cool you down some days. … You knew that he knew what was going on, you know?"[67]

Posters at both guestbooks were not content to link Killebrew simply to the past, however. They also proclaimed him as an example of what today's athletes ought to be and so often are not, insisting that "players of all sports should stop, listen and learn something from this great man. He gave back so much more to the world than he ever took from it."[68] Some posters took it a step further, using Killebrew's death as a moment to chastise those currently playing the game and call upon them to do better, claiming that the "ballplayers today need to take a huge step back and play baseball because of the game. The money these so-called athletes get paid ... [has] tainted the game. Give me the 1960s Twins and Harmon Killebrew. He was a class act and others should follow his example."[69] The most anger was reserved for those players regarded as violating the Killebrew legacy by using performance-enhancing drugs, something Killebrew believed terribly damaged baseball. A poster identified only as David in Connecticut referred to Killebrew as "a great slugger who played by the rules and holds real records," quietly condemning by comparison those who did not,[70] while Jon, a poster on twinsguestbook.com, put it much more bluntly, writing, "Harmon, in my mind, is or should be about 6th on the all-time home run list as he did it the old fashioned way with skill, diligence towards his craft and God given talent. The steroid era users should have their records wiped. Sosa, Bonds, Mcguire [sic] and the rest. I hope MLB will correct this wrong."[71]

Fans, of course, have no real control over what Major League Baseball will do, but in the wake of Killebrew's death, a real need to do something concrete in his honor arose. At the Twins memorial, Nita Killebrew asked everyone to take a moment to "stand up to cancer" after describing the charity of the same name, and the Killebrew Foundation and its many causes were also mentioned, providing fans with options if they wished to make donations in Killebrew's memory.[72] In a panel discussion following the memorial, Kent Hrbek stressed that the current players who knew him would probably be those best suited to make sure his legacy continued, and some players did make efforts in that regard. Torii Hunter told a reporter that he always reminds new players to write their autographs legibly because Killebrew told him that to be remembered, you need a signature people can recognize. Similarly, when Michael Cuddyer signed as a free agent with the Colorado Rockies, he requested the number three in Killebrew's honor.[73] In the same panel discussion, Mudcat Grant suggested that the new technologies might help keep Killebrew's reputation alive too, and certainly the posts on cybershrines reflected that possibility. For instance, posters on cybershrines used that opportunity to share their own ideas for personal Killebrew memorials, including small shrines in their own homes and offices,[74] shadowboxes of memorabilia,[75] and autographed baseballs turned into Christmas tree ornaments.[76] Others mentioned naming dogs,[77] and in one case a son, after him.[78] In terms of what actions could be taken, Jason Humphrey recommended that those who could should take a trip to the Mall of America, find Metropolitan Stadium's home plate, and bow their heads in a moment of silence; this reminded me of the time, years before, when I had wondered aloud how to have a friend take my photo at that very location.[79] An older woman, a complete stranger, who was passing by advised, "You need to kneel if you want to be in the photo with the plate—and you should anyway because you're standing on hallowed ground!" Perhaps the most common online suggestion, though, was for posters to pass on their Killebrew memories to the next generation by sharing stories with children,[80] grandchildren,[81] and students.[82] One Little League coach even wrote that he required his team to do reports on Killebrew and was encouraged that the facts they came back with had much more to do with his character than his statistics.[83] That this coach was so heartened by his team's interest in Killebrew as a person reflected the overwhelming urge by the posters at both legacy.com and twinsguestbook.com to honor Killebrew's unassuming, generous nature as opposed to simply his career with the Twins.

The last chorus of Jeff Arundel's 1995 song "Harmon Killebrew" laments the loss of the times Killebrew represented as well as the man himself:

> Harmon Killebrew
> Did you ever get my letter?
> Ten pages of clear blue sky
> Harmon Killebrew
> I need things to get better
> Those days are going, going, gone, gone, gone, gone, gone.[84]

That refrain echoes the sense of loss fans felt at Killebrew's death but not the creativity and determination to make things better reflected by the tributes fans left at spontaneous shrines and cybershrines. Though their offerings might be seen as perhaps insignificant by those who did not share their veneration of Killebrew, fans themselves appear to have seen them as a way to honor Killebrew and his embodiment of the idea that great good can be done even in small ways. By doing what they could, they acknowledged that they might not be able to "touch 'em all" as Killebrew had, but that everyone could at least do something to honor him and the inherent modesty, good character, and habitual generosity he represented, qualities Minnesotans generally like to believe continue to be reflected by the Twins organization, Twins players, and the state itself. Perhaps this chapter, then, is, finally, my letter to Harmon Killebrew, my own "ten pages of clear blue sky,"[85] a tribute dressed up in academic regalia to Harmon Killebrew but also to my fourth grade teacher, Miss

Esmer Johnson; my baseball-loving parents, Elsie Hanson and Russell Hanson, a small town umpire and devotee of the game; and those rare but very special Sundays of my Minnesota childhood that were spent at Metropolitan Stadium with a Frosty Malt in one hand and a strike counter in the other—all things gone but never, ever forgotten.

Debbie A. Hanson received her PhD in English from the University of Illinois at Urbana-Champaign and teaches in the English Department at Augustana University in Sioux Falls, South Dakota. She presents papers regularly at the annual conferences of the American Folklore Society and has published articles and reviews in *Southern Folklore*, *Western Folklore*, and the *Journal of American Folklore*. She also served as the guest editor of *The Willa Cather Yearbook* and was a contributor to *Interior Borderlands: Where Does the Midwest End and the Great Plains Begin?* In 2017, she received the Dakota Conference on the Northern Plains' Herbert W. Blakely Professional Award for her paper "Lending a Feminine Touch to the B-29: Depictions of Women Workers in WWII Aircraft Industry Publications." She is a lifelong Minnesota Twins fan and made a point of thanking the 1987 World Championship Minnesota Twins for proving that all things are indeed possible in her dissertation's dedication.

Notes

1. Vance Barker, "The Minnesota Twins Public Memorial Service for Harmon Killebrew," *Minneapolis Events Examiner*, 27 May 2011, 1–7, retrieved 17 August 2012 from http://www.examiner.com/events-in-minneapolis/the-minnesota-twins-public-memorial-service-for-harmon-killebrew-1.
2. Larry Hurrie, "Payette's Gentle Giant: Remembering the Man They Called 'The Killer,'" *Payette Argus-Observer*, 26 May 2011, retrieved 24 January 2020 from http://www.argusobserver.com.
3. Dave Campbell, "Passing of a Legend: 'Pride of Payette' Killebrew Succumbs to Cancer," *Payette Argus-Observer*, 18 May 2011, retrieved 24 January 2020 from http://www.argusobserver.com.
4. Hurrie, "Payette's Gentle Giant."
5. Barker, "Minnesota Twins Public Memorial Service."
6. Steve Aschenburner, *The Good, the Bad, and the Ugly Minnesota Twins: Heart-Pounding, Jaw-Dropping, and Gut-Wrenching Moments from Minnesota Twins History* (Chicago: Triumph Books, 2008), Nook Edition, 94.
7. "Top 10 Sluggers of the 1960s," 1960s Baseball, n.d., retrieved 24 January 2020 from http://www.1960sbaseball.com.
8. Campbell, "Passing of a Legend."
9. "Top 10 Sluggers of the 1960s," n.d.
10. Steve Aschenburner, *Harmon Killebrew: Ultimate Slugger* (Chicago: Triumph Books, 2011), Nook Edition, 15.
11. Ibid., 143.
12. Ibid., 122.

13. Ibid., 108.
14. Ibid., 28.
15. Ibid., 30.
16. Aschenburner, *The Good*, 31–33.
17. Aschenburner, *Harmon*, 33.
18. *Remembering Harmon*, Fox Sports North, 26 May 2011.
19. Aschenburner, *Harmon*, 38.
20. Ibid., 44.
21. Aschenburner, *The Good*, 94.
22. *Remembering Harmon*.
23. Aschenburner, *The Good*, 96.
24. Aschenburner, *Harmon*, 125.
25. Aschenburner, *The Good*, 96.
26. Ibid., 96.
27. Neal La Velle, "Killebrew was 'Paul Bunyan with a Uniform On,'" *Minneapolis Star-Tribune*, 18 May 2011, retrieved 18 August 2012 from http://www.startribune.com/sports/twins/12 2004519html?page=all&prepage=3&c=y#continue.
28. Steve Date, "Never Flashy, Harmon Killebrew Was the Perfect Role Model for a Minnesota 8-Year-Old," *MINNPOST*, 18 May 2011, retrieved 24 January 2020 from http://www.minnpost.com/viewfinder/2011/05/never-flashy-harmon-Killebrew-was-perfect-role-model-Minnesota-8-year-old.
29. *Remembering Harmon*.
30. Ibid.
31. Ibid.
32. Ibid.
33. Ibid.
34. Bill Huff to Official Twins Guestbook, 21 May 2011, retrieved 23 July 2012 from http://twinsguestbook.mlblogs.com/2011/05/17/twins-fans-remember-harmon-killebrew/#comments.
35. Aschenburner, *Harmon*, 200.
36. Rhett Bollinger, "Killebrew Lauded as Class Act by Ex-Teammates," *Minnesota Twins Daily Clips: Wednesday*, 18 May 2011, retrieved 24 January 2020 from http://www.pressbox.athletics.com.
37. *Remembering Harmon*.
38. Aschenburner, *Good*, 109.
39. Aschenburner, *Harmon*, 200.
40. *Remembering Harmon*.
41. Ibid.
42. Ibid.
43. Ibid.
44. Keith Thursby, "Harmon Killebrew Dies at 74; Hall of Famer Was One of Baseball's Premiere Home-Run Hitters," *Los Angeles Times*, 18 May 2011, retrieved 17 August 2012 from https://www.latimes.com/archives/la-xpm-2011-may-18-la-me-harmon-killebrew-2011 0518-story.html.
45. Jack Santino, "Performative Commemoratives, the Personal, and the Public: Spontaneous Shrines, Emergent Ritual, and the Field of Folklore," *Journal of American Folklore* 117 (2004): 6.
46. Sylvia Grider, "Spontaneous Shrines: A Modern Response to Tragedy and Disaster," *New Directions in Folklore* (2001): 6, retrieved 24 January 2020 from http://www.scholarworks.iu.edu.
47. Rachel Blount, "By Arriving in a Sea of No. 3s, Fans Show Killebrew Was No. 1." *Minneapolis Star-Tribune*, 24 May 2011, retrieved 18 August 2012 from http://www.startribune.com/blount-by-arriving-in-a-sea-of-no-3s-fans-show-killebrew-was-no-1/122482274/.
48. *Remembering Harmon*.

49. Linda Pershing and Nishelle Y. Bellinger, "From Sorrow to Activism: A Father's Memorial to His Son Alexander Arredondo, Killed in the US Occupation of Iraq," *Journal of American Folklore* 123 (2010): 18.
50. Blount, "By Arriving."
51. Ibid.
52. Ibid.
53. Ibid.
54. *Remembering Harmon*.
55. Aschenburner, *Harmon*, 203.
56. Grider, "Spontaneous Shrines," 5.
57. Ken in Denver to Official Twins Guestbook, 20 May 2011, retrieved 23 July 2012 from http://twinsguestbook.mlblogs.com/2011/05/17/twins-fans-remember-harmon-killebrew/#comments.
58. sinkfistulaminniminoeoerniebroglio to Official Twins Guestbook, 17 May 2011, retrieved 23 July 2012 from http://twinsguestbook.mlblogs.com/2011/05/17/twins-fans-remember-harmon-killebrew/#comments.
59. Anonymous poster to Legacy.com, 17 May 2011, retrieved 28 July 2012 from http://www.legacy.com/guestbook/huntsville/guestbook-entry-print.aspx?n=harmon-killebrew&pid=151107856.
60. Lee Raiter to Official Twins Guestbook, 21 May 2011, retrieved 23 July 2012 from http://twinsguestbook.mlblogs.com/2011/05/17/twings-fans-remember-harmon-killebrew/#comments.
61. Scott Price to Official Twins Guestbook, 30 May 2011, retrieved 23 July 2012 from http://twinsguestbook.mlblogs.com/2011/05/17/twins-fans-remember-harmon-killebrew/#comments.
62. Tony Andrews to Official Twins Guestbook, 20 May 2011, retrieved 23 July 2012 from http://twinsguestbook.mlblogs.com/2011/05/17/twins-fans-remember-harmon-killebrew/#comments.
63. *Remembering Harmon*.
64. Erin Schmidt to Official Twins Guestbook, 17 May 2011, retrieved 23 July 2012 from http://twinsguestbook.mlblogs.com/2011/05/17/twins-fans-remember-harmon-killebrew/#comments.
65. One of your many fans in Cleveland to Legacy.com, 17 May 2011, retrieved 28 July 2012 from http://www.legacy.com/guestbook/huntsville/guestbook-entry-print.aspn=killebrew&pid=151107856.
66. Judy Chucker to Legacy.com, 17 May 2011, retrieved 28 July 2012 from http://www.legacy.com/guestbook/huntsville/guestbook-entry-print.aspxn=killebrew&pid=151107856.
67. *Remembering Harmon*.
68. Laurie Jensen to Official Twins Guestbook, 20 May 2011, retrieved 23 July 2012 from http://twinsguestbook.mlblogs.com/2011/05/17/twins-fans-remember-harmon-killebrew/#comments.
69. Sue Trock to Official Twins Guestbook, 17 May 2011, retrieved 23 July 2012 from http://twinsguestbook.mlblogs.com/2011/05/17/twins-fans-remember-harmon-killebrew/#comments.
70. David in Connecticut to Legacy.com, 17 May 2011, retrieved 28 July 2012 from http://www.legacy.com/guestbook/huntsville/guestbook-entry-print.aspxn=killebrew&pid=151107856.
71. Jon to Official Twins Guestbook, 17 May 2011, retrieved 23 July 2012 from http://twins-guestbook.mlblogs.com/2011/05/17/twins-fans-remember-harmon-killebrew/#comments.
72. *Remembering Harmon*.
73. *Remembering Harmon*.
74. Kathy Demers to Official Twins Guest Book, 31 May 2011, retrieved 23 July 2012 from http://twinsguestbook.mlblogs.com/2011/05/17/twins-fans-remember-harmon-killebrew/#comments; Jim Vinz to Legacy.com, 17 May 2011, retrieved 28 July 2012 from http://

www.legacy.com/guestbook/huntsville/guestbook-entry-print-aspxn=killebrew&pid=1511-7856.
75. Bob J to Official Twins Guest Book, 21 May 2011, retrieved 23 July 2012 from http://twinsguestbook.mlblogs.com/2011/05/17/twins-fans-remember-harmon-killebrew/#comments.
76. Jeff Allen to Legacy.com, 17 May 2011, retrieved 28 July 2012 from http://www.legacy.com/guestbook/huntsville/guestbook-entry-print-aspxn=killebrew&pid=151107856.
77. Michael Vopatti to Legacy.com, 17 May 2011, retrieved 28 July 2012 from http://www.legacy.com/guestbook/huntsville/guestbook-entry-print.aspxn=killebrew&pid=151107856.; Jean Hughes to Legacy.com, 17 May 2011, retrieved 28 July 2012 from http://www.legacy.com/guestbook/huntsville/guestbook-entry-print.aspxn=killebrew&pid=151107856; sd twins fan to Official Twins Guestbook, 8 June 2011, retrieved 23 July 2012 from http://twinsguestbook.mlblogs.com/2011/05/17/twins-fans-remember-harmon-killebrew/#comments.
78. Dores Sorenson to Official Twins Guestbook, 18 May 2011, retrieved 23 July 2012 from http://twinsguestbook.mlblogs.com/2011/05/17/twins-fans-remember-harmon-killebrew/#comments.
79. Jason Humphrey to Official Twins Guestbook, 17 May 2011, retrieved 23 July 2012 from http://twinsguestbook.mlblogs.com/011/05/17/twins-fans-remember-harmon-killebrew/#comments.
80. Gail Anderson and family to Legacy.com, 17 May 2011, retrieved 28 July 2012 from http://www.legacy.com/guestbook/huntsville/guestbook-engry-print.aspxn=killebrew&pid=151107856.
81. James B. Little to Official Twins Guestbook, 17 May 2011, retrieved 23 July 2012 from http://twinsguestbook.mlblogs.com/2011/05/17/twins-fans-remember-harmon-killebrew/#comments.
82. Kathy to Legacy.com, 20 May 2011, retrieved 28 July 2012 from http://www.legacy.com/guestbook/huntsville/guestbook-entry-print.aspxn=killebrew&pid=151107856; Sam Tuccio to Official Twins Guestbook on 17 May 2011, retrieved 23 July 2012 from http://twinsguestbook.mlblogs.com/2011/05/17twins-fans-remember-harmon-killebrew/#comments.
83. Mike Murphy to Official Twins Guestbook, 13 June 2011, retrieved 23 July 2012 from http://twinsguestbook.mlblogs.com/2011/05/17/twins-fans-remember-harmon-killebrew/#comments.
84. Jeff Arundel, "Harmon Killebrew," *Ride the Tide,* Triad Records, 1995, compact disc.
85. Ibid.

Bibliography

Arundel, Jeff. "Harmon Killebrew." *Ride the Tide*. Triad Records, 1995. Compact disc.
Aschenburner, Steve. *The Good, the Bad, and the Ugly Minnesota Twins: Heart-Pounding, Jaw-Dropping, and Gut-Wrenching Moments from Minnesota Twins History.* Chicago: Triumph Books, 2008. Nook Edition.
Aschenburner, Steve. *Harmon Killebrew: Ultimate Slugger.* Chicago: Triumph Books, 2011. Nook Edition.
Barker, Vance. "The Minnesota Twins Public Memorial Service for Harmon Killebrew." *Minneapolis Events Examiner*, 27 May 2011. Retrieved 17 August 2012 from http://www.examiner.com/events-in-minneapolis/the-minnesota-twins-public-memorial-service-for-harmon-killebrew-1.
Blount, Rachel. "By Arriving in a Sea of No. 3s, Fans Show Killebrew Was No. 1." *Minneapolis Star-Tribune*, 24 May 2011. Retrieved 12 August 2012 from http://www.startribune.com/blount-by-arriving-in-a-sea-of-no3s-fans-show-killebrew-was-no-2/122482274/.

Bollinger, Rhett. "Killebrew Lauded as a Class Act by Ex-Teammates." *Minnesota Twins Daily Clips: Wednesday*, 18 May 2011. Retrieved 24 January 2021 from http://www.pressbox.athletics.com.

Campbell, Dave. "Passing of a Legend: 'Pride of Payette' Killebrew Succumbs to Cancer." *Payette Argus-Observer*, 18 May 2011. Retrieved 24 January 2020 from http://www.argusobserver.com.

Date, Steve. "Never Flashy, Harmon Killebrew Was the Perfect Role Model for a Minnesota 8-Year-Old." *MINNPOST*, 18 May 2011. Retrieved 24 January 2020 from http://www.minnpost.com.

Grider, Sylvia. "Spontaneous Shrines: A Modern Response to Tragedy and Disaster." *New Directions in Folklore* (2001), 1–8. Retrieved 24 January 2020 from http://www.scholarworks.iu.edu.

Hurrie, Larry. "Payette's Gentle Giant: Remembering the Man They Called 'The Killer.'" *Payette Argus-Observer*, 26 May 2011. Retrieved 24 January 2020 from http://www.argusobserver.com.

Neal, La Velle. "Killebrew was 'Paul Bunyan with a Uniform On.'" *Minneapolis Star-Tribune*, 18 May 2011. Retrieved 18 August 2012 from http://www.startribune.com/sports/twins/122004519.html?page=all&page=3&c=y#continue.

Pershing, Linda and Nichelle Y. Bellinger, "From Sorrow to Activism: A Father's Memorial to His Son Alexander Arredondo, Killed in the US Occupation of Iraq." *Journal of American Folklore* 123 (2010): 1–26.

Remembering Harmon. Fox Sports North, 26 May 2011.

Santino, Jack. "Performative Commemoratives, the Personal and the Public: Spontaneous Shrines, Emergent Ritual, and the Field of Folklore." *Journal of American Folklore* 117 (2004): 363–72.

Thursby, Keith. "Harmon Killebrew Dies at 74; Hall of Famer Was One of Baseball's Premier Home-Run Hitters." *Los Angeles Times*, 18 May 2011. Retrieved 17 August 2012 from https://www.latimes.com/archives/la-xpm-2011-may-18-la-me-harmon-killebrew-20110518-story.html.

"Top 10 Sluggers of the 1960s." 1960s Baseball. Retrieved 24 January 2020 from http://www.1960sbaseball.com.

CHAPTER 9

After Life

Laying Flower Memes on my Mother's Grave and the Recollective Realm of Life after Death

Olivia Guntarik and Claudia Bellote

My mother died from a rare condition many years ago and exactly a year to the day before my first child was born. It seemed fitting to name my daughter in her honor. As a further gesture of respect and acknowledgment, it also made sense to gather the best photographs I had of her and present the images as a shrine of remembrance at her funeral. It surprised me how many people attended. People of all ages, from far and wide, from many cultures. Students from the school she taught at held a vigil and read poems. For months afterward our house was filled with cards and letters carrying messages of love, hope, and consolation. We needed those messages as they helped us cope; we needed them to carry on with our lives in the core of our grief. We needed them to help us acknowledge our loss and to remember her.

Postcards from the Edge

The above reflection was written by one of the authors (Guntarik), and in it she contemplates her personal journey of grief through the loss of her mother. By documenting this journey, and juxtaposing these reflections against other practices of digital remembrance, we have learned that the cultural and historical aspects of loss can often be hard to capture in online forms. Online memorials do not always accommodate these aspects of grief, such as how different cultures and religions can influence the kinds of responses, behaviors, and rituals we have around death. Our experience creating a digital memorial provided opportunities for us to engage with some of these cultural nuances while revealing differences about the place and meaning of death in human life for the living.

Figure 9.1. *A shrine for the author's deceased mother. Photo by Olivia Guntarik.*

We began our journey into grieving practices in a predictable place—a cemetery, though this was not your average cemetery. There were no tombs, crucifixes, or cursive inscriptions carefully engraved in stone. There was no tramping required through lonely gravesites, nor was there a need to tiptoe through a forlorn environment of weeping mourners. There were no funerals to attend. No one in clothes of mourning. No flowers on the graves. This was a digital cemetery. We were grief tourists navigating the online world of digitized mourning, making connections between the birth of technologies in the past and the media revolutions of the present and imagining a different kind of future with the dead. We were also finding ways to bring the past into the future in order to make sense of the present. For indeed, how might we understand the future without an adequate exploration of the past?

Throughout history, inventions of new technologies have paved the way for new modes of mourning and ritual practices. The camera in the

Victorian era led mourners to take photographs with the dead, something that became common practice. Technology has evolved with the rise of social media, the camera phone, and selfie culture. New practices of grieving have come to the fore, presenting strange and exciting opportunities for analysis and discovery.

Indeed, the practice of viewing a deceased person's profile in social media is opening the way to new studies in grief tourism. As we ourselves navigated these online mourning sites, we began to develop a better sense of our own roles as grief tourists, in many ways becoming complicit in the creation of a particular kind of social reality. As tourists seeking to discover more about this emerging phenomenon of digitized mourning, we visited multiple postmortem profiles and read through endless messages of sympathy and grief that people posted to these sites. What we found astounding was that many of the users had not known the deceased or their family and friends, yet these users left repeated messages. And even more unexpected, some of these messages were not always sympathetic (as we will later discuss).

"Grief tourism" is often used interchangeably with the term "dark tourism," and it has been applied to tourists traveling to places associated with suffering, death, and dying. Grief tourist sites include the Killing Fields of Cambodia, Chernobyl in the Ukraine, and any site related to the Holocaust, such as Auschwitz or other concentration camps in Europe. Journalist Angela Riechers describes, perhaps quite harshly, how this kind of tourism involves "busloads of gawkers roar[ing] up and shed[ding] a few tears before moving on to the next stop on the day's itinerary. The visit allows them to feel they've witnessed history."[1]

Tourists visit grief sites for many reasons, among them to instigate a particular emotional affect, to tap into a certain desire for a sacred experience, and/or to reflect on sites of trauma generally.[2] Grief tourism allows strangers to mourn over deceased people who they have no relation to, and this mourning can play out in a multitude of ways across the physical and virtual worlds. Digitized mourning has come under the nomenclature of grief tourism, which can be understood as a new way for people to grieve; indeed, it might be seen as an *extension* to offline grieving. In digitized forms of mourning, tourists visit online rather than physical sites of suffering, and this is the key difference. The digital sites allow mourners to grieve and share memories of the deceased, sometimes privately in closed circles and at other times in public communal ways. Though people travel to mourning sites from the relative comfort of their home using their online connections, the idea is that they are still participating vicariously in a form of grief tourism.

Despite the multiple modes that grief tourism takes, digital grief tourists are often considered disingenuous and deserving targets of online trolls (people who incite conflict by posting inflammatory or controversial commentary). "'I didn't know you but I'm very sorry you're dead' is a flashing neon declaration of trollability. 'This isn't grief,' Paulie [a troll] once argued. 'This is boredom and a pathological need for attention masquerading as grief.'"[3] Our own position as grief tourists was never to cross the line by provoking people's emotions. We never left messages on the sites we visited and usually left each site (if we had to register as users) without stirring any curiosity among other users. In this way, we traversed through multiple sites of mourning as anonymous and invisible users in search of grievers, reading through their commentary simply to understand how and why they were using these sites.

In our travels, we stumbled across many new digital innovations. Users had developed infinite creative digital techniques to commemorate the dead and to rekindle memories about their deceased loved ones, as well as to attract other users to their site. There were interactive message boards and opportunities to present excerpts from old letters written by the deceased to which people could respond. There were postmortem apps that allowed "heirs" to receive "messages" (written before the sender's death) from their deceased loved one. There were apps with gamified features that allowed the ghosts of the dead to "haunt" people's phones. The apps included notification features, reminding users to gather for important anniversaries, or alerting them to lay flower memes or send postcards to the deceased as a form of direct communion.

All this got us thinking about public and private forms of grieving. We saw that the act of mourning could develop into a near religious cult–like activity: people searching out other mourners to make connections through their memories of the deceased. Celebrity mourning, in particular, reached a fever pitch in the immediate postmortem period of a celebrity's death, and it was evident that fans were not only finding ways to connect with other fans during this time but also publicly sharing their grief and their favorite memories of the late celebrity. In the more family-centered spaces of grieving, mourners were able to create closed circles that allowed them to share only to their private password-protected networks. We also often noted a shift between the role of mourners as they moved between being cared for by other mourners and then offering caregiving themselves in the form of words of comfort.

In our observations, we often felt like voyeurs and distant witnesses of other people's suffering. Yet as grief tourists, we were also inspired by these sites and the messages of hope they carried in their commentary. It made sense for one of the authors (Guntarik) to write postcards of her own to reflect on her own loss. This provided a way for her to renew a connection with the past.

Figure 9.2. *Photographs and a postcard written by the author to her mother. Photo by Olivia Guntarik.*

Mourning in the Other Realm

Social media is ridden with complexity and contradiction.[4] This is a digital realm that we see as recollective in its capacity to invoke people's sense of recall, memory, and nostalgia for the lost. In this space, digital commentary about life and death chime with other people's responses in forms that have allowed us to fossick, like collectors and retrievers of other people's memories, through a dizzying web of content.

A Google search for mourning websites highlights the limitless forms that grief adopts. Expressions of grief materialize as memes, selfies, hashtags, status updates, and interactive commentary about the dead. This sharing of grief through media content allows people to express their grief to a wider community, illustrating in clear visual forms the ways that mourning has become public and shared. The shared grieving provides an added communal layer to the mourning process by complementing traditional experiences of bereavement.[5] Grieving can be both communal and cultural. For instance, Aboriginal Australians have used social media to express "sorry business"—cultural practice and protocols associated with death—providing ways for Indigenous people to connect with one another through their identified communities.[6]

Digitized mourning is emerging as a powerful force on social networks, prompting many to suggest it is a new way to grieve. These public displays have become more socially acceptable and have led grievers to renew their relationships with the deceased.[7] The ability to revisit online profiles of the deceased allows mourners to "renegotiate" their relationship with that person.[8] This is important for mourners who may not have had a positive relationship with an individual prior to that person's death. Furthermore, the chance to immediately and directly respond to a griever online allows those in the griever's social network to maintain a sensitive distance while extending their sympathy in a nonintrusive manner. Many studies noted young people's attraction to and versatility with social media, how adolescents can often use mourning websites to create a connection with other mourners through opportunities to address the dead directly.[9] They can reminisce about shared past experiences using their peer vernacular, provide life updates, and explore their emotional response and coping mechanisms.[10]

Online commentary can be sporadic and spontaneous. A comment from one user posting feelings of depression reads, "The tears are my way of escaping the hurt that is baring my eyes … NO ONE CARES, and it's a scary place to be, ABSOLUTELY ALONE ~ in a world unknown and Dark."[11] Another posts feelings of anger: "I hate the fact that u did this to yourself. I hate it that u didn't tell anyone. But there's nothing I can do. I can be mad all I want."[12] Messages of acceptance get tangled up in this emotional rollercoaster of shared grief, providing further opportunities for mourners to remember: "adam your father and i miss ya so much. but it gives us some comfort in are [sic] hearts to know so many people care … you will never be forgotten."[13]

Messages to the dead acquire vivid life-affirming qualities where personal details about the mourner's life are shared as though the deceased were still alive. Some messages initially begin with the mourner's sense of helplessness and grief. These feelings soon evolve into acceptance of the death and later into full-scale personal accounts about the mourner's life. Posts like these are seen to contribute to the identity of the deceased even in the post-death timeframe. They "reinforce the deceased user's place in a social network while gradually adding identity content to this persistent space."[14]

The differences between adolescent and adult responses to death are significant as adolescents may go through "random, yet recurrent episodes of grief—feeling intense emotions for a brief period and then returning to a sense of normalcy that is disrupted when some event or experience triggers emotions related to loss."[15] While adult grief, in general, can follow a more predictable path that centers on denial, anger, bargaining, depression, and acceptance,[16] teenagers who are still developing cognitively are using different coping methods to deal with death. Teens can struggle with a range of social issues in the bereavement process: "the predictability of events, their self-image, their sense of belonging, sense of fairness or justice, and sense of mastery or control of their environments and experiences."[17] We observed these struggles in explicit and varied ways in our study with the challenges young people face in expressing their grief online, and in seeing the popularity of "grieving games" smartphone apps for coping with bereavement, specifically aimed at the youth market.[18]

In navigating these diverse forms of online bereavement, we arrived at new understandings about how grief can impact each and every one of us in different ways. We found that digitized forms of mourning could provide an outlet to deal with grief, yet their sociocultural implications for existing and ongoing forms of grieving were far from adequately explored. We turn now to digital mourning sites and youth culture to reflect on the ways young people cope with death and ask what role digital sites more generally hold in our lives as long-term sites of remembrance, and as examples of self-care and caregiving.

> Dear Mother: This is a private site that I wish not to share with others. It helps me to connect with you for the moment if only to see you again through your photographs. It helps me to remember the person who you were to me, who you still are to me. A mother. A teacher of language and culture. I can use this site as a keepsake and memento that is private and only accessible by me. I can collate your photographs here. I only have one video of you where you are speaking … my dearest treasure. I know of other videos where you are teaching your students how to dance, how to speak language, how to present themselves to the world. I have a photograph of you holding a flag with a loudspeaker in your hand, which I will include here. This reminds me of other photographs I need to find and store in this keepsake dedicated to you. This is a private site that I wish not to share with others (not yet …).

Self-Care and Selfie Culture

> A snapshot. A camera phone. Later, she would not come to recognize her own image. In her fog of grief, she had found herself with her father at the funeral home. She had posed in front of the body. A body that was being prepared for burial. A body dressed in the fine clothes that she had selected for the occasion. A body that she couldn't bear to look at, to even train her eyes up to the face. And yet, how she wanted to treasure that moment. Without a second thought, she whipped out her mobile phone, took a selfie with the coffin as backdrop, shared it to Snapchat, and tweeted #broken. This was a reference to her favorite poem, a word in a song she loved doing the rounds on the airwaves, a way to express how she felt without having to say a thing. Her friends reposted and shared the message.

They sent sympathy memes, a direct message: "call me," "let's talk," "I'm here for you." Their response minimized her sense of rawness. It was the only response she could bear because what she felt in those days was beyond words.

The picture that emerges here is a graphic one. The fallout may provoke shock, horror, cries of disgust. Respect the dead. How dare she! How insensitive and inappropriate. But who is speaking here, and who is to say what is the best way to eulogize the dead?

Selfies may not be part of the new norm of grieving, but they have become a part of contemporary mourning practice. When journalist Jason Feifer created a Tumblr piece titled "Selfies at Funerals," he did not expect to find so many funeral selfies lurking online. Yet many of these types of selfies appeared across Facebook, Instagram, and Twitter simply by searching for the hashtags "selfie" and "funeral." When his Tumblr blog went viral, many respondents bemoaned, "What happened to our humanity, as if social media has emptied everything, even death, of meaning and gravitas."[19]

While selfies offer ways to remediate rituals of mourning, the backlash against them raises questions about how to grieve and by what means. Critics have tended to focus on youth culture as an easy target in leveling their accusations toward "a whole generation of disrespectful, whiney, irresponsible teenagers" and decrying that this generation has been "conned into thinking obsessive, endless, mindless (moronic) photographing of oneself is akin to living."[20] The selfie is seen as a display of narcissism and attention-seeking behavior at its grandest, and not a legitimate or appropriate way to mourn. It is seen as lacking respect, indeed an insult to the dead.

Yet history shows us that this kind of photographic practice was not uncommon in the nineteenth century. In the Victorian era, photographs were regularly taken of and with the deceased; the photographs were seen as keepsakes and special mementos to the family of the deceased.[21] Similarly, death masks were crafted by taking a cast directly from the corpse and retained as a reminder of events in material form. Black armbands as mourning clothes were worn for months and sometimes years afterward.[22] These historical examples represent social and cultural practices of expressing grief. They symbolize the various ways that people have mourned publicly over time.

In other words, the photograph can be understood as an *artifact* of death and a *signifier* of ongoing ritual practice. The photograph represents a visible symbol of grief, not far removed from the taking and sharing of a selfie, also depicting grief. The funeral selfie is a contemporary keepsake and reminder of the dead. The digital camera as the new technology replaces the technology of the analog camera, but the act of taking the photograph retains significance as an expression of grief. This act permits what Cumiskey and Hjorth refer to as the ability for mourners to create levels of "psychological distance," highlighting the complexities of human emotions.[23]

In this way, the selfie symbolizes a contemporary form of cultural practice, providing insights into human experiences of everyday life in the present. The materiality of the selfie is ephemeral in nature because of its instantaneous and digital affordances, partly the reason why its value has been misjudged. It makes sense then to view the funeral selfie as analogous to the Victorian-era photograph, irrespective of where the "self" may be located in the photograph. And if we were to consider the selfie or photographs associated with death as signifiers of grief, then might not all artifacts of death provide faithful depictions of mortality? What we are suggesting is that the significance of images as reflections of cultural and historical expressions of and responses to grief have not been adequately theorized. This is unsurprising given that analysis of digital mourning sites represents a new field of research in the digital humanities.

Selfies call attention to particular events and family and communal experiences in the human life cycle. As a precise representation of time, the selfie can be read against this sociohistorical grain. From the earliest forms of taking photographs with (or painting images of) the dead, the funeral selfie can be interpreted as an explicit social practice, which in turn is contextualized through a person's social networks. In this way, the selfie highlights both presence and absence. We are more likely to "see" and understand the grieving selfie if we are part of the griever's social network or friendship circle. We are less likely to engage with the mourner's grief if we are not part of their close community of friends and extended family. In this way, a person's grief can be both accessible to us and inaccessible.

The photograph, the image, and the self all communicate an archive of cultural practices associated with death and mourning. The funeral selfie acts as a memento to the dead and a connection to an individual's history with the dead that can instantly be digitally shared. As a representation of time and place, such images offer ways to understand a particular social and temporal condition. They afford insights into time-old rituals, and, consistent with ways of viewing the photograph as a site of social practice,[24] the photograph can alert us to hidden patterns that may not otherwise be perceived. These patterns may foreground moments of change and continuity, narrative experiences, and insights on social history and mourning practices.

The presentation of "self" and expressions of the grieving selfie in the present can be seen as a cultural response to death. The meanings attached to the social and temporal dimensions that surround the self can be traced through the mourner's social media content, their words, images, and social networking activity. The time and location settings, enabled on the selfie taker's mobile phone, permits those in their network to see exactly where and when the image was captured. The selfie represents a narrative, personal data, an emotion, a particular being in time, shareable instantaneously through the algorithms of digital connection. As an embodiment of those social networks, the selfie marks a persona, a position, and an emotional and intellectual state. Those in the network can respond immediately; they tag and share the selfie with their networks, creating an important feedback loop and recirculating and remediating content. Most importantly, those in the network and support circle can ask the selfie taker, "R U OK?" The selfie expresses an immediate invitation for caregiving and humanity.

Selfie culture has attracted scorn and bitterness. Yet selfies articulate a particular expressive mode of being or identities in performance; they challenge "the sheer nerve of telling someone who has just lost a loved one that they are 'self-absorbed twits' for not playing the part of mourner correctly."[25] The taking of a funeral selfie might be viewed as a means of reassurance when faced with the reality of death. The teenagers who were shamed online for taking selfies at funerals were finding a means to cope and mourn in their own way. Their grief outlet was their communication device, a handheld phone, a larger social network, a connection to a particular moment, group of people, and place.

Funeral selfies have become part of a new and emerging social practice, and they are understood as being associated with grieving "practices that are the natural outgrowths of contemporary life for many."[26] While funeral selfies fuel debates about their legitimacy as grief artifacts, they also reflect the tensions across online and offline sites of mourning. The clash between the public and private and between the past and present is evident here. These new practices are being embraced by those who are often geographically distanced from their families and those who are part of a youth culture already familiar with using social media. Such digital spaces offer direct communion with the dead, the potential to provide immediate care or to express modes of self-care through online technologies. Moreover, digital mourning sites allow communities to maintain their cultural traditions through a channel that extends existing cultural practices. By sharing their grief, social media users are able to openly express their loss with their wider networks and process their emotions in a public forum.

This is a forum where people are given license to imagine themselves in parallel realities. These parallel realities comprise multiple networks and a multipresence of time, community, and connection. Particular formations of community emerge that bind individuals to certain ways of thinking and behaving, and to specific social norms and behavioral expectations. Some formations represent the benevolence of communities. Other communities are territorial or invasive in nature, highlighting the more destructive features of the digital realm as a space of violence, abuse, and terror. In this multivalent environment, communities intersect and clash. What we see through these social practices surrounding the dead is an endless cycle of messages and memories filled with hope and goodwill. It is also a universe where ideas and egos come head to head in ways that highlight the digital realm as a place of contradiction and danger, one that shines light on the social conditions associated with death. This is a space where rules around the dead are broken; people act in isolation, and social mores are destroyed.

The Realm of Fantasy and Performance

Grievers are not the only users of digital mourning sites. Online trolls attracted to the macabre also find these sites a tantalizing fantasy space. Many of these sites are vulnerable to hateful attacks, with trolls targeting memorial and RIP pages for their own gain. And when mourners are trolled, they respond and return the attacks with equally angry and bitter remarks, effectively "taking the bait."

Sites dedicated to victims of violent deaths have become a drawcard for trolls. Mourners of these sites are "victimized a second time by people making particularly nasty comments about them, especially when their death had been reported by the media."[27] Teenager Chelsea King's various memorial sites were hijacked in this manner. King was murdered in 2010 near her home in California, and as soon as she was reported missing, Facebook pages were set up in efforts to locate her. This included a website that her family set up called "Chelsea's Light," while many more unofficial sites were also established. When news of her death was announced, these sites quickly turned into memorial sites, such as "1,000,000,000 [sic] Million STRONG to Remember Chelsea King," "In Loving Memory of Chelsea King," and "Chelsea King: RIP." These memorial pages were created by people who did not know Chelsea but acted as "interactive newspaper obituaries" and "virtual funeral parlors," enabling people to share news and to keep abreast of the latest developments surrounding her death.[28]

Trolls acted swiftly to sabotage these sites. They posted nasty, gratuitous, and hateful content to King's dedication sites, and soon enough these online spaces became digital battlegrounds. "This is sick what some have wrote" and "you're really lucky i don't know who you are … i didn't know Chelsea but she deserves some respect … i hope one day i will meet you and slap the shit out of you." Users reacted to comments with shock, outrage, and anger: "I am so disgusted at your comment. She was some one's [*sic*] child," "you are a huge asshole," and "ur horrible and disrespectful!!!! I feel sorry for you!!!!!! i wish you go to hell soon!"[29]

For users of similar sites established to commemorate close family members, they knew that the attacks on mourners would be unrelenting. A comment aimed at the mother of a deceased fourteen-year-old girl included an image of a horse and cart pulling her daughter's coffin with the words "Happy Mother's Day," while another image appeared with the caption "Help me, Mummy. It's hot in hell."[30] On a memorial page dedicated to their only child who had drowned at age fifteen, the parents were subjected to images of drowning people with captions such as "LOL u drowned you fail at being a fish."[31]

Australia has become a hotspot for high-profile instances of trolling. When murder victims Trinity Bates and Elliot Fletcher were targeted, trolls posted pornography and offensive comments to both children's Facebook RIP pages. One of the trolls, Bradley Paul Thomas, was later identified and pleaded guilty to "distributing child exploitation material, using the internet to menace, harass or cause offence and possessing child exploitation material."[32] He was sentenced to three years in prison, making Australia the first nation to take punitive measures against trolls.[33] The death of Eurydice Dixon in Melbourne in 2018 gave trolls another opportunity to resort to menacing behavior online. Many mourners on Facebook noted that she deserved to be remembered for how she lived her life, not how she lost it. However, trolls were quick to dampen this sentiment by stating that she deserved to be murdered and that she was responsible for her own death for walking home alone at night. Additionally, Dixon's physical memorial was also defaced, with organizers describing the act as a "real-world version of the same mentality."[34]

Trolls prevail in the online world partly because the structures of social networking sites function in their favor. Facebook "positions the user as the subject of every sentence he or she utters, indeed as the centre of his particular—and therefore the—social universe."[35] This self-involvement allows trolls to target users where it hurts—their sense of self—because Facebook is solipsistic by design. Trolls reject the idea of this sense of a Facebook self, an "ongoing process of emotional repudiation,"[36] which is why many of them refer to themselves in the third person. This is so they can minimize the damage and hurt they have caused online, as it is not the "real" them posting horrific images and comments but someone else, an alter ego. Trolls take on the tone of legitimate users who willingly share, post on, or create memorial pages. Site users who are deemed to be using them for authentic means become the targets of their abuse. Trolls seek out these users and, once they are able to identify their emotional investment, "force their victims to confront precisely those things that motivate the popularity of memorial pages—fear of helplessness, fear of losing a loved one, fear of human parts."[37]

Trolls are masters of drama, feasting on the fears of others. They dance around mourners in order to provoke a response. They become peddlers of fake news in the form of carefully crafted and made-to-look-authentic RIP pages where they cunningly lure the naïve. They allow membership to grow before they "flip" the page "from something innocuous ('RIP [insert name of dead white teenager]') to something outrageous ('Click Like if You Think [dead white teenager] Deserved to Be Taught a Lesson')."[38] The Facebook pages set up for missing American teenager Jalesa Reynolds were mostly used for trolls to bait "self-righteous white people who were scandalized by the suggestion that they cared more about a dead white girl than a dead black girl."[39] Trolls are seen as senseless, callous monsters who represent "privilege gone berserk."[40] The digital realm facilitates such behavior; it promotes and amplifies the drama of the dance, as the drama becomes their own dance with death.

The drama weaves a heady and complex blend of agendas and emotions. It is performed on a stage and a scale that can be likened to what Walter Benjamin has said of certain Depression-era images of Paris, referring to them as the "scenes of a crime."[41] These "scenes" showcase the social morphology surrounding death and their associated ritual practices. We become spectators of destruction and disarray through our participation in and consumption of these scenes. As the drama unfolds, trolls sit center stage as the all-powerful assailants, plotting the downfall of their victims. Their sole intention is to "disrupt and upset as many people as possible, using whatever linguistic or behavioral tools ... available."[42] Anonymity feeds the behavior of trolls, who relish the power and foreboding their words exert, as they continue to bait the mortally wounded through the drama of death. In this way, trolls acquire prestige among other trolls by bringing down their victims.

The real and digital rub up against one another in forms that throw up the contradictions in the encounter between the real and the imagined, between hope and loss, the tensions between the different users, consumers, and producers of these sites. What may be less apparent is that the multiple players in these scenes of death are no different to the multiple players that exist in the offline world. The digital culture is a part of a real-world scene, highlighting what Žižek has referred to as the "dialectical materialism" between two realities.[43] The real and the virtual are one and the same, meaning that all our experiences might be viewed as virtual. Our use of digital technologies becomes an extension of our real lives and experiences. As people look to the virtual to fulfill their needs in grief, the digital realm momentarily absolves their loss and provides them with a sense of security. For Kasza this is a false illusion, because "when the 'virtual reality or real virtuality' created by new technologies becomes the (only) response to our (unfulfilled) needs and dreams, affecting the very essence of 'who we are or who we want to be,' it often evokes the less mature, anti-social impulses or aspects of ourselves, that so far have been kept in control by the accepted standards: cultural, social or political."[44] Trolls are part of the extreme in digital culture; they remind us that the digital space is one of both social order and disorder.

Digital technologies offer a means through which to explore and talk about death, whether that is to reconcile the past, to seek comfort through shared and communal grieving, or to participate in more sinister activities motivated by ill will. Death and the dead are both revered and reviled in this digital realm. The technology acts as a mediator, in effect becoming the medium between the living and the dead. Humans, as consumers of the media content the technology produces and reproduces, become the mediators between mortality and the machine. And in "mediating" the line between life and death, we come closer not only to the idea of what it means to die but also what it means to live. Our role as mediators of social practices surrounding the dead blurs the boundaries between the digital, the spiritual, and the real, and between the imagined and the material. The artifactual and cultural materialities associated with death find their ultimate expression in this realm. The realm is an extension of public responses to death, a continuum of ritual practices associated with the dead. For many, it is also an expression of a deep desire for an afterlife, a hope and longing that we may someday see our dead loved ones once again.

Conclusion

Digital sites of mourning are tumultuous, strange places where all kinds of characters live and lurk. There are those who are real mourners, grieving genuinely, and there are others who are seen to be grieving for superficial, selfish, or spiteful motives. There are the early adopters of new media, changing and challenging the ways we grieve online, and there are those who are using these sites for cultural practices: history gathering, digital archiving, finding missing loved ones, and grief tourism. Then there are trolls who live in the dankest corners of the Web, ready to attack anyone at any time for the sake of entertainment and or to elicit a response. When these characters meet, mayhem and disarray follows, and with it an emotional war of words and images is unleashed, flooding onto the digital screen with no apparent end.

History has shown us that grief and mourning were only previously observable at funerals and other physical sites devoted solely to the deceased person's memory. The shifting of these practices to online modes necessitates new ways of engaging with digital spaces and exposing the contradictions within our social, cultural, and economic systems. Death selfies may be a shocking, unusual, or unorthodox way to express grief, revealing the moral repulsion held by those unable to shake the idea that commemoration of the dead can only occur through traditional means. Yet social media highlights the emergence of everyday social experiences, which have now merged with digital practices around death as new forms of mourning—communal, personal, and performative. These online displays of grief show no signs of abating, and they continue to play out in the public eye for a wider audience to see, celebrate, contribute to, participate in, share, observe, comment on, and even destroy at the click of a button.

The private spaces of death and mourning are often invisible and less accessible. Yet we know that in these spaces, multiple images move easily across time and place, sitting in an in-between space where they momentarily hover, expand, and vanish. They clash with a narrative of selfie culture that may not mean anything to anyone except those to whom that selfie was shared, tangling with personal grief for a mother long gone, and contrasting with historical knowledge both accessible and inaccessible, present and absent. What was most acute to us was the ways in which these historical images point to a time when the dead were revered and respected, as memories of the deceased continued to play a role for the living—teaching us how to act, how to live, and how to be in communion with living entities. The extreme and violent practices of trolls and their online abusive behavior draws attention to this transformation and changing standards through the passage of time.

Death across the digital and the real allies with what Taussig has called the "bodily unconscious"[45]: body (sensing) and eye (seeing) merge to become that which the eye observes (being). Life and death, like past and present, and death and the digital afterlife, ensnare one another in one continuum, and so we come closer to knowing death through its opposite or through another's death. We have no personal concept of death; it is always something "other," and something that happens to others. It is part of the unknown, perhaps better left to the esoteric. Seen as a destination, the atheists will claim that we go into the ground and that is it. Seen in the light of hope, Christians will declare that we go to heaven, that there is an afterlife. With hope comes faith; infinite possibilities reveal themselves about the spiritual, the life that continues after our death. A belief system to adhere to, a value system to peddle a social ontology. All this relates. None of this takes away the simple fact that we must all sooner or later meet the same fate.

The digital afterlife is a screen upon which we can project our future, desire, uncertainty, all that which we cannot know.[46] This is a speculative space, one that bestows a flash of precognitions on our own impending death. And so, this is how the afterlife offers counsel, allows us to keep memories of the dead alive, permits us to make sense of death so we ourselves can know what it is to live and to go on living despite experiencing death in our lives. A memory becomes a contemplation about our own mortality. A memory becomes a commemoration to individuals dearly loved and lost. A memory can express forms of enduring care for the living; it can also be sabotaged, reduced to the most nihilistic encounter. We hear in these speculations the fleeting echoes of redemption. We come to recognize that what dies and what is continuously dying are our own memories, always to be replaced, reconciled, and reimagined. The digital afterlife, like the notion of the afterlife itself, is a fantasy state, a relationship with the dead that will continue to change so long as we are alive to the act of remembering, even as the memories themselves die away.

Dear Mother: I dedicate this site to commemorate your life and legacy. I offer a way to remember you and reminisce about our time together. It may sound strange for other people who may have not known you to read this. It doesn't matter to me. All that matters is that this is a commemoration site, a space to dedicate my memories to you, a place that helps me feel closer to you, a place to recollect. We only have these recollections. I know that you are here with me. Your voice. Your image. Your being. Your spirit. Your life. This is what we will celebrate. This is what we will carry in our hearts. This is what we will remember in your memory, our promise. We will lay flowers at your grave.

Olivia Guntarik works in the digital humanities and writes fictocriticism. She is an associate professor in the School of Media and Communication at RMIT University.

Claudia Bellote completed her honors on digital mourning sites at RMIT University in 2018. She has recently returned to Melbourne after living in Edinburgh and visiting memorial sites around Scotland.

Notes

1. Angela Riechers, "My Mourning Junkie: Wailing at the Facebook Wall," paper presented at Workshop on Memento Mori: Technology Design for the End of Life (Austin, 2012).
2. See Anna Martini and Dorina Maria Buda, "Dark Tourism and Affect: Framing Places of Death and Disaster," *Current Issues in Tourism* (2018): 1–14, 10.1080/13683500.2018.1518972; Nick Osbaldiston and Theresa Petray, "The Role of Horror and Dread in the Sacred Experience," *Tourist Studies* 11, no. 2 (2011): 175–190, https://doi.org/10.1177/1468797611424955; Maria Tumarkin, *Traumascapes: The Power and Fate of Places Transformed by Tragedy* (Melbourne: Melbourne University Publishing, 2005).

3. Whitney Phillips, "LOLing at Tragedy: Facebook Trolls, Memorial Pages and Resistance to Grief Online," *First Monday* 16, no. 12 (2011): n.p., retrieved 3 November 2018 from https://firstmonday.org/article/view/3168/3115.
4. See Brian Carroll and Katie Landry, "Logging On and Letting Out: Using Online Social Networks to Grieve and to Mourn," *Bulletin of Science, Technology & Society* 30, no. 5 (2010): 341–49; Amanda Williams and Michael Merten, "Adolescents' Online Social Networking Following the Death of a Peer," *Journal of Adolescent Research* 24, no. 1 (2009): 67–90; Jimmy Sanderson and Pauline Hope Cheong, "Tweeting Prayers and Communicating Grief over Michael Jackson Online," *Bulletin of Science, Technology & Society* 30, no. 5 (2012): 328–40.
5. Kelly R. Rossetto, Pamela J. Lannutti, and Elena C. Strauman, "Death on Facebook: Examining the Roles of Social Media Communication for the Bereaved," *Journal of Social and Personal Relationships* 32, no. 7 (2012): 974–94.
6. Bronwyn Carlson and Ryan Frazer, "It's Like Going to a Cemetery and Lighting a Candle: Aboriginal Australians, Sorry Business and Social Media," *AlterNative: An International Journal of Indigenous Peoples* 11, no. 3 (2015): 211–24.
7. Jed R. Brubaker and Janet Vertesi, "Death and the Social Network," in *Proc. CHI Workshop on Death and the Digital* (Toronto, 2010).
8. Carroll and Landry, "Logging On," 341–49.
9. See Williams and Merten, "Adolescents' Online Social Networking," 67–90; Brubaker and Vertesi, "Death and the Social Network"; Martin Gibbs, Marcus Carter, Bjom Nansen, and Tamara Kohn, "Selfies at Funerals: Remediating Rituals of Mourning," *Selected Papers of Internet Research 15.0* (23–25 October 2014); Carroll and Landry, "Logging On," 341–49.
10. Joan N. McNeil, Benjamin Silliman, and Judson J. Swihart, "Helping Adolescents Cope with the Death of a Peer: A High School Case Study," *Journal of Adolescent Research* 6, no. 1 (1991): 132–45.
11. Williams and Merten, "Adolescents' Online Social Networking," 80.
12. Ibid.
13. Carroll and Landry, "Logging On," 345.
14. Brubaker and Vertesi, "Death and the Social Network."
15. Williams and Merten, "Adolescents' Online Social Networking," 70.
16. Elisabeth Kübler-Ross, *On Death and Dying* (New York: Macmillan, 1969).
17. McNeil, Silliman, and Swihart, "Helping Adolescents," 132–45.
18. Springwise, "Smartphone App Helps Bereaved Young People Cope with Death," n.d., 2017, retrieved 3 November 2018 from https://www.springwise.com/smartphone-game-helps-bereaved-young-people-cope-death/.
19. Gibbs et al., "Selfies at Funerals."
20. Ibid.
21. Kathryn Beattie, *Aspects of Acceptance and Denial in Painted Posthumous Portraits and Postmortem Photographs of Nineteenth-Century Children* (Montreal: Concordia University, ProQuest Dissertations Publishing, 2006).
22. Carroll and Landry, "Logging On," 341–49.
23. Kathleen M. Cumiskey and Larissa Hjorth, *Haunting Hands_: Mobile Media Practices and Loss* (New York: Oxford University Press, 2017), 31.
24. See Susan Sontag, *On Photography* (New York: Macmillan, 2001); Marianne Hirsch, "The Generation of Postmemory," *Poetics Today* 29, no. 1 (2008): 103–28; Judith Butler, "Torture and the Ethics of Photography," *Environment and Planning D: Society and Space* 25, no. 6 (2007): 951–66.
25. Gibbs et al., "Selfies at Funerals," 2.
26. Ibid., 3.
27. Rebecca Kern, Abbe E. Forman, and Gisela Gil-Egui, "R.I.P.: Remain in Perpetuity. Facebook Memorial Pages," *Telematics and Informatics* 30 (2012): 6.
28. Phillips, "LOLing at Tragedy."
29. Ibid.

30. Tanith Carey, "Help Me, Mummy. It's Hot in Hell: A Special Investigation into the Distress of Grieving Families Caused by the Sick Internet Craze of Trolling," *Daily Mail*, 24 September 2011, retrieved 3 November 2018 from https://www.dailymail.co.uk/news/article-2041193/Internet-trolling-Investigation-distress-grieving-families-caused-trolls.html.
31. Gregory Pratt, "Cruel Online Posts Known as RIP Trolling Add to Tinley Park Family's Grief," *Chicago Tribune*, 12 August 2013, retrieved 3 November 2018 from http://www.chicagotribune.com/suburbs/ct-xpm-2013-08-12-ct-met-rip-trolling-20130812-story.html.
32. Amelia Bentley, "Facebook Vandal Jailed," *Sydney Morning Herald*, 25 March 2011, retrieved 3 November 2018 from https://www.smh.com.au/technology/facebook-vandal-jailed-20110325-1c9mq.html.
33. Williams and Merten, "Adolescents' Online Social Networking."
34. Angela Lavoipierre, "Eurydice Dixon: Facebook Trolls Leave 'Vile' Comments on Melbourne Vigil Event Page," ABC, 19 June 2018, retrieved 3 November 2018 from http://www.abc.net.au/news/2018-06-19/eurydice-dixons-mourners-trolled-on-vigil-facebook-event-page/9883924.
35. Whitney Phillips, *This Is Why We Can't Have Nice Things: Mapping the Relationship between Online Trolling and Mainstream Culture* (Cambridge, MA: MIT Press, IEEE Xplore MIT Press eBooks Library, 2015).
36. Ibid.
37. Ibid.
38. Ibid.
39. Ibid.
40. Ibid.
41. Walter Benjamin, "The Work of Art in the Age of Mechanical Reproduction," in *Illuminations*, ed. Hannah Arendt (New York: Shocken Books, 1969), 226.
42. Phillips, *This Is Why*.
43. Slavoj Žižek, *The Parallax View (Short Circuits)* (Cambridge, MA: MIT Press, 2006).
44. Joanna Kasza, "Post Modern Identity: 'In Between' Real and Virtual," *World Scientific News* 78 (2017): 41–57.
45. Michael Taussig, *What Color Is the Sacred?* (Chicago: University of Chicago Press, 2010).
46. Nicola Wright, "Death and the Internet: The Implications of the Digital Afterlife," *First Monday* 19, no. 6 (2 June 2014), retrieved 3 November 2018 from https://firstmonday.org/ojs/index.php/fm/article/view/4998/4088; doi: http://dx.doi.org/10.5210/fm.v19i6.4998.

Bibliography

Barker, Graham. "The Ritual Estate and Aboriginal Polity." *Mankind* 10, no. 4 (1976): 225–39.

Beattie, Kathryn. *Aspects of Acceptance and Denial in Painted Posthumous Portraits and Postmortem Photographs of Nineteenth-Century Children*. Montreal: Concordia University, ProQuest Dissertations Publishing, 2006.

Benjamin, Walter. "The Work of Art in the Age of Mechanical Reproduction." In *Illuminations*, edited by Hannah Arendt, 217–251. New York: Shocken Books, 1969.

Bentley, Amelia. "Facebook Vandal Jailed." *Sydney Morning Herald*, 25 March 2011. Retrieved 3 November 2018 from https://www.smh.com.au/technology/facebook-vandal-jailed-20110325-1c9mq.html.

Berndt, Ronald Murray. *Australian Aboriginal Religion*. Leiden: Brill Archive, 1974.

Brubaker, Jed, and Janet Vertesi. "Death and the Social Network," in Proc. CHI Workshop on Death and the Digital. Toronto, 2010.

Butler, Judith, "Torture and the Ethics of Photography." *Environment and Planning D: Society and Space* 25, no. 6 (2007): 951–66.

Byard, Roger W., and Wayne C. Chivell, "The Interaction of Death, Sorcery and Coronial/Forensic Practices within Traditional Indigenous Communities." *Journal of Clinical Forensic Medicine* 12, no. 5 (2005): 242–44.

Carey, Tanith. "Help Me, Mummy. It's Hot in Hell: A Special Investigation into the Distress of Grieving Families Caused by the Sick Internet Craze of Trolling." *Daily Mail*, 24 September 2011. Retrieved 3 November 2018 from https://www.dailymail.co.uk/news/article-2041193/Internet-trolling-Investigation-distress-grieving-families-caused-trolls.html

Carlson, Bronwyn, and Ryan Frazer. "It's Like Going to a Cemetery and Lighting a Candle: Aboriginal Australians, Sorry Business and Social Media." *AlterNative: An International Journal of Indigenous Peoples* 11, no. 3 (2015): 211–24.

Carroll, Brian and Katie Landry. "Logging On and Letting Out: Using Online Social Networks to Grieve and to Mourn." *Bulletin of Science, Technology & Society* 30, no. 5, (2010): 341–49.

Cumiskey, Kathleen M., and Larissa Hjorth. *Haunting Hands: Mobile Media Practices and Loss*. New York: Oxford University Press, 2017.

Dodson, Patrick L., Jacinta K. Elston, and Brian F. McCoy, "Leaving Culture at the Door: Aboriginal Perspectives on Christian Belief and Practice." *Pacifica* 19, no. 3 (October 2006): 249–62. doi:10.1177/1030570X0601900304.

Gibbs, Martin, Marcus Carter, Bjom Nansen, and Tamara Kohn. "Selfies at Funerals:Remediating Rituals of Mourning." *Selected Papers of Internet Research 15.0.* (23–25 October 2014).

Glaskin, Katie, "Death and the Person: Reflections on Mortuary Rituals, Transformation and Ontology in an Aboriginal Society." *Paideuma* 52 (2006): 107–26. Retrieved 3 November 2018 from http://www.jstor.org.ezproxy.lib.rmit.edu.au/stable/40341918.

Hirsch, Marianne, "The Generation of Postmemory." *Poetics Today* 29, no. 1 (2008): 103–28.

Kasza, Joanna, "Post Modern Identity: 'In Between' Real and Virtual." *World Scientific News* 78 (2017): 41–57.

Kern, Rebecca, Abbe E. Forman, and Gisela Gil-Egui. "R.I.P.: Remain in Perpetuity. Facebook Memorial Pages." *Telematics and Informatics* 30 (2012): 2–10.

Kübler-Ross, Elisabeth. *On Death and Dying*. New York: Macmillan, 1969.

Lavoipierre, Angela. "Eurydice Dixon: Facebook Trolls Leave 'Vile' Comments on Melbourne Vigil Event Page." ABC, 19 June 2018. Retrieved 3 November 2018 from http://www.abc.net.au/news/2018-06-19/eurydice-dixons-mourners-trolled-on-vigil-facebook-event-page/9883924.

Martini, Anna, and Dorina Maria Buda. "Dark Tourism and Affect: Framing Places of Death and Disaster." *Current Issues in Tourism* (2018): 1–14. 10.1080/13683500.2018.1518972.

McNeil, Joan N., Benjamin Silliman, and Judson J. Swihart. "Helping Adolescents Cope with the Death of a Peer: A High School Case Study." *Journal of Adolescent Research* 6, no. 1 (1991): 132–45.

Metcalf, Peter, and Richard Huntington. *Celebrations of Death: The Anthropology of Mortuary Ritual*. Cambridge: Cambridge University Press, 1991.

Osbaldiston, Nick, and Theresa Petray. "The Role of Horror and Dread in the Sacred Experience." *Tourist Studies* 11, no 2 (2011): 175–90. https://doi.org/10.1177/1468797611424955.

Phillips, Whitney. *This Is Why We Can't Have Nice Things: Mapping the Relationship between Online Trolling and Mainstream Culture*. Cambridge, MA: MIT Press, IEEE Xplore MIT Press eBooks Library, 2015.

———. "LOLing at Tragedy: Facebook Trolls, Memorial Pages and Resistance to Grief Online." *First Monday* 16, no. 12 (2011): n.p. Retrieved 3 November 18 from https://firstmonday.org/article/view/3168/3115.

Pratt, Gregory. "Cruel Online Posts Known as RIP Trolling Add to Tinley Park Family's Grief." *Chicago Tribune*, 12 August 2013. Retrieved 3 November 2018 from http://www.chicagotribune.com/suburbs/ct-xpm-2013-08-12-ct-met-rip-trolling-20130812-story.html.

Riechers, Angela. "My Mourning Junkie: Wailing at the Facebook Wall." Paper presented at Workshop on Memento Mori: Technology Design for the End of Life. Austin, 2012.

Rossetto, Kelly, Pamela Lannutti, and Elena Strauman. "Death on Facebook: Examining the Roles of Social Media Communication for the Bereaved." *Journal of Social and Personal Relationships* 32, no. 7 (2012): 974–94.

Sanderson, Jimmy, and Pauline Hope Cheong. "Tweeting Prayers and Communicating Grief over Michael Jackson Online." *Bulletin of Science, Technology & Society* 30, no. 5 (2012): 328–40.

Sontag, Susan. *On Photography*. New York: Macmillan, 2001.

Springwise. "Smartphone App Helps Bereaved Young People Cope with Death." N.d., 2017. Retrieved 3 November 2018 from https://www.springwise.com/smartphone-game-helps-bereaved-young-people-cope-death/.

Taussig, Michael. *What Color Is the Sacred?* Chicago: University of Chicago Press, 2010.

Tumarkin, Maria. *Traumascapes: The Power and Fate of Places Transformed by Tragedy*. Melbourne: Melbourne University Publishing, 2005.

Williams, Amanda, and Michael Merten. "Adolescents' Online Social Networking Following the Death of a Peer." *Journal of Adolescent Research* 24, no. 1 (2009): 67–90.

Wright, Nicola, "Death and the Internet: The Implications of the Afterlife." *First Monday* 19, no. 6 (2 June 2014). Retrieved 3 November 2018 from https://firstmonday.org/ojs/index.php/fm/article/view/4998/4088; doi: http://dx.doi.org/10.5210/fm.v19i6.4998.

Žižek, Slavoj. *The Parallax View (Short Circuits)*. Cambridge, MA: MIT Press, 2006.

CHAPTER 10

A Monumental Problem

Memorializing the Jonestown Dead

Rebecca Moore

Whenever I am asked why I study Peoples Temple, I am always a bit embarrassed to say "for both personal and professional reasons." I must first disclose my own connections to the mass murder/suicide at Jonestown and then explain how those led me into the field of religious studies. The fact that my two sisters and nephew died in Jonestown in 1978 inevitably leads some to say, with condescension, that my work must be very therapeutic. In addition, academics may question my objectivity, since I began from an apologetic stance before mastering the methodology and vocabulary of formal scholarship. My knowledge of Peoples Temple has grown over the past four decades since my family members died in Jonestown, so I have had to revise my initial thinking and admit in public forums and published monographs that I was wrong in my preliminary conclusions.

Thus, I find Renato Rosaldo's critique of traditional forms of scholarship and academic writing—especially in the field of anthropology—extremely liberating.[1] His observation that "by invoking personal experience as an analytical category one risks easy dismissal" resonates strongly in my own career.[2] The expansion of the number of narratives depicting life in Peoples Temple resembles the "garage sale" metaphor Rosaldo utilizes to describe the transformation of classic forms of ethnography.[3] After Jonestown, the only opinions presented were those of critical ex-members; it took decades for other survivors, observers, and scholars to voice alternative views. Nevertheless, mainstream narratives of good and evil, leaders and followers, victims and victimizers took deep root and were evident as recently as 2018, the year of the fortieth anniversary of the tragedy, despite the more nuanced perspectives that were available. Among the many competing narratives, one was literally set in stone to memorialize the Jonestown dead. Some background information is needed to set the stage for the drama that ensued to make this happen.

On 18 November 1978, more than nine hundred members of an agricultural commune died by ingesting cyanide-laced fruit punch. These deaths occurred shortly after a group of young men from the project assassinated Leo J. Ryan, a member of Congress, and three journalists at a nearby jungle airstrip. Residents of Jonestown belonged to Peoples Temple, a new religious movement based in California that espoused racial equality and social justice. At least 70 percent of those who died were African American, with almost half of the total being African American women. With the exception of eight Guyanese children, all were US citizens.

Because the deaths occurred on foreign soil, because the death toll was so high, and because the heat and humidity of the Guyana jungle was accelerating decomposition of the remains, the bodies were quickly repatriated to the United States without proper medico-legal investigation to determine how exactly they died. The dead were shipped to the military mortuary at Dover Air Force Base in Delaware, thousands of miles away from their homes in California. The unidentified and unclaimed bodies were kept in Dover for six months until an interfaith group in San Francisco found the financial means to transport and bury more than four hundred bodies at Evergreen Cemetery in Oakland, California. For decades, a simple granite marker identified the location. Meanwhile, the pastor of a nondenominational church in Los Angeles continuously raised money for a large memorial. Two seven-foot-long engraved stone panels were unveiled at the thirtieth anniversary observance of the deaths, and more were planned to create a thirty-six-foot wall once the pastor secured additional funding. Efforts to erect a monument by a rival group, however, led to the successful installation in 2011 of four three-by-six-foot granite plaques listing the names of all who died that day. Lawsuits followed, along with recriminations and criticism over the inclusion of the name of the group's infamous leader, Jim Jones, on the plaques.

My husband, Fielding McGehee, and I played supporting roles throughout these controversies. Because we were not Temple members but rather bereaved relatives, insiders "who were there" saw us as outsiders. My academic writing also pushed us into the etic category, as observers never entirely part of the group.[4] Our involvement in the memorialization process, however, drew us to the emic side, where we were clearly partisan.

Like Rosaldo, we had a unique social location by virtue of our suffering a loss and being able to write about a "grief observed." The anthropologist's examination of his own emotions upon the death of his wife helped him comprehend the rage felt by the Ilongot headhunters he had been studying and gain insight into what had once been incomprehensible. Rosaldo's cool, scholarly, etic approach was transformed into a hot, emotional, emic perspective. He finally grasped what drove the bereaved

Ilongot people of the Philippines to target a victim, behead him, and cast away the head—an act that freed them of the fury over their loss. This subjective experience gave Rosaldo unique insights that anyone might understand intellectually but that only the bereaved can feel emotionally. I can relate on a private level to his experiences of the death of his wife and his brother, especially when he describes his parents' emotions over the loss of their son. I did not fully understand my parents' grief in 1978 until our own daughter died at age fifteen in 1995.

These experiences changed not only Rosaldo's life but also his outlook on the entire field of anthropology. While I value his insights, especially his critique of the historical emphasis on ritual rather than on emotion or bereavement—"force" is the word he frequently uses—I am also a bit leery of relying too much upon small subjective experiences for developing large theories concerning culture. Rosaldo himself notes this anxiety when he cautions against deriving a universal theory from somebody else's personal knowledge.[5] Furthermore, an essentialist approach can emerge after harrowing events in which *only* direct participants are granted authority, credibility, or authenticity to speak. As the Argentine sociologist Elizabeth Jelin writes of traumatic incidents, "For many, personal suffering (especially when it was experienced directly in 'your own body' or by blood-connected relatives) can turn to be the basic determinant of legitimacy and truth."[6] Jelin warns that limiting authority to those who suffered directly may allow them to "slip into a monopolistic claim on the meaning and content of the memory and the truth."[7]

A challenge to the monopoly of the personal-subjective—the essentialist stance—became visible in the clash over how the Jonestown dead were to be appropriately memorialized. The "community of the bereaved," to use Rosaldo's terminology,[8] did not agree on the question of who had the moral right to speak for the dead, and this lack of consensus played a large a role in the dispute. An unexpected twist made one faction more sympathetic to those who died than the other faction. The philosopher Avishai Margalit's examination of the "thick" relations between family members helps to explain the behavior of the bereaved Jonestown community.

Utilizing the insights of Rosaldo, Margalit, and others, this chapter closely examines the process that led to the installation of a monument memorializing the Jonestown dead—a process that took thirty-three years. It begins by looking at the treatment of the bodies in what religion historian David Chidester calls "rituals of exclusion."[9] It then discusses the processes that led to the decision to set a necrology—a list of the dead—in stone. While participants agreed to such a register in principle, tensions emerged over which narrative would be told: were perpetrators to be listed with the innocents? Anger erupted between two rival groups that sought to erect a memorial, with hard feelings resulting once the four plaques were in place. Consideration of the relevant ethical issues follows, with a discussion of racial aspects involved in the controversy. This analysis makes it clear that incorporating personal insights into professional assessments of bereavement processes enriches our understanding of human culture—which is exactly the point Renato Rosaldo wishes to make.

Rituals of Exclusion

Those who died in Jonestown fell far from home—geographically, socially, and politically. They had emigrated from the United States in the 1970s to the only South American country in which English was spoken, the Cooperative Republic of Guyana. They had abandoned friends, family, and belongings in the expectation that their utopian experiment would succeed. Those who arrived were predominantly African American, exiled from what they felt was a nation in which racism was hopelessly embedded within its very structure. They believed that communal sharing—what they called "apostolic socialism"—was the only way in which inequality might be overcome. Thus, when the utopia came to a shocking and gruesome end, the dead received little sympathy. Their remote location in the dense jungle interior of the Northwest District of Guyana made them relatively inaccessible. The corpses decayed rapidly in the intense heat and humidity.

Two medical doctors assigned by the US government to report on the scene recommended that the bodies be buried on-site, given the state of advanced decomposition.[10] The government of Guyana quickly quashed this suggestion, so members of the US Army Graves Registration team were dispatched to recover the dead. This meant identifying the bodies before bagging them and shipping them, first via helicopter to Guyana's capital city and then in large transport planes back to the United States. By the time their work ended, the team was using snow shovels to scoop up the liquefied remains. The final figures for the dead were ultimately based on a literal head count, since skulls and other body parts often became detached from torsos.

The dreadful condition of the remains prompted what David Chidester called the "thingification" of the Jonestown dead—a survival mechanism for those who had to disinfect, prepare, and embalm the bodies before identification could be attempted back in the United States. Relying upon Mary Douglas's important work on purity and danger,[11] Chidester noted three primary, overlapping fears that the people in Delaware had about potential contagion. The first anxiety concerned public health and the possibility that the physical bodies might contaminate the ground itself

Figure 10.1. *Monument placed at Evergreen Cemetery by the Emergency Relief Committee in 1979. Photo by Laura Johnston Kohl, courtesy The Jonestown Institute.*

should they be buried in Delaware. The second apprehension centered on the possibility that Delaware might become a magnet for other cults, or even serve as a shrine to Jonestown. Finally, Chidester identified a worry over the spiritual vulnerability the living might have in the face of the evil dead. Thus, hygienic, social, and spiritual dangers threatened the purity of the people of Delaware.[12] "The Jonestown dead defied fundamental classifications regarding what it is to be a human being in American society," Chidester concluded. "Therefore the bodies were not 'ours'; they were not part of 'us'; they were not to be included in the ritual recognition according to fully human dead in the American cult of the dead."[13]

A first step toward remedying the situation was taken by outsiders. Composed of Protestant, Catholic, and Jewish religious leaders in San Francisco, the Guyana Emergency Relief Committee (ERC) sought to bring the unclaimed and unidentified bodies back home. Because Peoples Temple had declared bankruptcy and gone into receivership, the ERC had to acquire funding from the courts for this project. The easy part was getting money for transport and interment; the hard part was finding a cemetery that would accept the bodies. After several false starts with cemeteries in the San Francisco Bay Area, the ERC persuaded Evergreen Cemetery to inter the dead. Located in a predominantly middle-class African American neighborhood in Oakland, California, Evergreen was, and remains today, an ideal final resting place. Hundreds of coffins were stacked on top of each other and placed in an excavated hillside with a magnificent view of San Francisco Bay.

Key to the ERC's planning process was the rejection of cremation for disposition because it was inconsistent with Black funerary traditions. Chidester compared the ERC's actions to the rites of passage outlined by Arnold van Gennep.[14] The committee advocated a process by which the dead would be detached from the living through the transition of an earth burial and would be reincorporated into the memory of a restored community.[15] In contrast, the city of Dover, Delaware, reversed van Gennep's formula by excluding the dead from the community in refusing to bury them nearby and rushing to remove the bodies from the state as quickly as possible.

As someone whose three-and-a-half-year-old nephew is buried at Evergreen Cemetery, I cannot help but appreciate Rosaldo's discussion of parody in anthropological discourse when I read Chidester's account of rituals of exclusion and inclusion.[16] Chidester seems to exemplify Rosaldo's point exactly about the classic focus on ritual at the expense of bereavement. Nevertheless, there is value in providing technical rather than evocative language to describe certain situations. To develop Chidester's argument, I later wrote about how the exclusion of the stigmatized dead of Jonestown led to the disenfranchisement of grief suffered by those who personally knew them.[17] When bereaved relatives and Jonestown survivors read about disenfranchised grief, they suddenly had a vocabulary to describe exactly what they had experienced—or so they told me.

Chidester's analysis misses the force felt by aggrieved relatives when they witnessed the disrespectful handling of the bodies. Like many other family members, I remain shocked over the failure of the US government to properly investigate what actually happened in Jonestown.[18] The ignominious deaths, coupled with the unceremonious treatment of those who died, certainly ignited the desire to somehow restore their humanity through an appropriate memorial.

Memorial Mania

Erika Doss, a professor of American studies, has identified a growing trend in modern society: the erection of temporary shrines and permanent memorials:

If wildly divergent in subject and style—few of today's memorials hold to the classicizing sentiments of earlier generations—these commemorative sites collectively represent what I call "memorial mania": the contemporary obsession with issues of memory and history and an urgent, excessive desire to express, or claim, those issues in visibly public contexts.[19]

A significant feature of many public monuments is the inclusion of names of the deceased—though the word "necrology" does not appear at all in her 2008 volume and only a single time in a second book on the subject.[20] Yet "names are *de rigueur*" in American commemorative culture; they "are familiar, comforting, and recognizable signs of real people, literal evidence of humanity."[21]

Relatives of the Jonestown dead needed this "literal evidence of humanity" of their loved ones. From the outset, the media dehumanized the dead by focusing on the bodies, in what religion historian Jonathan Z. Smith called the pornography of Jonestown: "The daily revisions of the body count, the details on the condition of the corpses ... lurid details of beatings, sexual humiliation, and public acts of perversion."[22] Few people apart from family and friends knew Peoples Temple members as human beings. Coupled with the removal of the bodies to Delaware and the lack of identification of almost four hundred individuals, the listing of names was a step toward restoring their humanity. Historian Daniel Sherman observed that the names of the deceased stood for absent bodies—or for bodies without names—in the World War I memorials erected in France.[23] Such monuments transferred emotion usually directed toward the body to the inscribed name, which symbolized concretely the body.[24] All of the proposals for a Jonestown monument included some sort of necrology in which, consciously or unconsciously, the names symbolized the unidentified and those interred elsewhere.

In the absence of personal grave markers, or even individual gravesites, for the Jonestown dead, the names became a paramount concern. In effect, they restored the humanity of the corpses, shown facedown in the mud again and again in the media. But, as Doss notes, naming becomes "a subject of considerable controversy as questions of who counts (victims *and* perpetrators?), who counts where and when ... and who counts the most ... are hashed out during the design process and even later."[25] This turned out to be the case for the Jonestown monument.

A Tale of Two Monuments

Memorial services were held at San Francisco churches in 1979 to mark the first anniversary of the deaths. Los Angeles pastor, now bishop,

Jynona Norwood began holding services each year at Evergreen Cemetery. Assisted by her uncle, Fred Lewis—whose wife and seven children died in Jonestown—Norwood was granted widespread legitimacy by virtue of the fact that she claimed twenty-seven relatives who died in the tragedy, including her mother. These annual services provided the opportunity for a variety of people to come together to remember the event: relatives, public officials, strangers. But less than a handful of survivors or former members of the Temple attended the annual observances. Many did not know of the service, some had become hostile to organized religion, and some remained too traumatized to participate.

Within a decade, Bishop Norwood began a fundraising campaign to erect a monument that would list the names of those who died. A committee composed of Norwood, my father John V Moore, Jackie Speier (who was severely wounded in the attack on Congressman Ryan), Grace Stoen Jones (who fought Jim Jones over custody of her son), and others cooperated in the fundraising project. Although the committee raised several thousand dollars, it fell apart in 1985 over issues of control and authority.

Bishop Norwood clearly became what Elizabeth Jelin identifies as a "memory entrepreneur," that is, an individual "who seek[s] social recognition and political legitimacy of *one* (their own) interpretation or narrative of the past."[26] Norwood's services, which had started out by honoring and remembering those who died, became political events, complete with endorsements and appearances by public officials. The victims were neglected, and the perpetrators—chiefly Jim Jones—were emphasized.

Meanwhile, survivors and former members began to "come out of the Peoples Temple closet," in the words of one survivor, and started attending Bishop Norwood's annual service. The twenty-fifth anniversary in 2003 marked a turning point. Many traveled from around the country and, in addition to attending Norwood's morning event, they held a private remembrance ceremony in the afternoon, apart from the media. Although the private memorials grew in size, they never really rivaled the publicity-oriented morning services.

After three decades of continuous fundraising for a monument, Bishop Norwood unveiled two large monoliths on the thirtieth anniversary, with about one hundred names engraved on each. They were brought into the cemetery on sizeable trailers but were not installed. The 2008 service also precipitated the decision of most former Temple members to abandon Norwood's service in favor of their own afternoon event. Her emphasis on the evil of Jim Jones had displaced the task of remembering the deceased.

Rival sets of memory entrepreneurs emerged as a result. It would be fair to say that my husband and I already functioned as such with our development of Alternative Considerations of Jonestown and Peoples Temple, a website dedicated to gathering and publishing as much primary source information as possible.[27] Our goal then, and today, was to humanize the dead by remembering their lives and not only their deaths. Our entrepreneurial purpose had been, and remains, to preserve and present as many different narratives as possible. Yet, in a surprise to us, the most important element of the site became the listing of "Who Died?" which features photographs, biographical information, and remembrances of each individual who died in Jonestown.[28] The popularity of this component demonstrated the ongoing desire for some type of memorialization, virtually if not concretely.

Another memory entrepreneur was Lela Howard, who established the Mary Pearl Willis Foundation in honor of her aunt who died in Jonestown.[29] Howard offered a free service to relatives who wanted to locate the gravesites of other Jonestown victims. The subtext of her effort to identify the burial grounds of the dead was to restore dignity to African Americans. She was the first to successfully organize a public reading of all the names of those who died on 18 November 1978, including that of Jim Jones: this event did not occur until the thirtieth anniversary in 2008.

Anticult groups functioned as memory entrepreneurs as well. For example, the Cult Awareness Network used the deaths in Jonestown as a morality tale to warn the public against the danger of cults. Anticultists compared all new religious movements to Peoples Temple.[30]

In short, a number of memory entrepreneurs were engaged in employing "Jonestown" and all that the event signified for various purposes. Many of these and other entrepreneurs could claim equal or even superior moral authority to that of Bishop Norwood. These included residents of Jonestown who escaped the deaths merely by being elsewhere that day, individuals who lost members of their immediate family, and individuals who had been part of Peoples Temple.

An ad hoc group, the Jonestown Memorial Fund (JMF or Jonestown Memorial), eventually secured the money to complete the task of raising a monument. Composed of Jim Jones Jr. (the adopted son of Jim Jones, who lost more than twenty relatives in Jonestown), John Cobb (who lost thirteen relatives), and Fielding McGehee (who lost three relatives), the committee met with officials at Evergreen Cemetery in the summer of 2010. They signed a contract with the cemetery later that year to deliver four plaques that would be set flat on the ground—rather than upright—to conform to the fragility of the hillside. Within three weeks, the JMF raised the $15,000 needed from more than 120 different donors.

Figure 10.2. *The four plaques comprising the monument devoted to those who died 18 November 1978, dedicated at Evergreen Cemetery in May 2011. Photo by Mercurywoodrose, courtesy Wikimedia Creative Commons.*

Evergreen Cemetery donated $25,000 worth of labor and materials to extensively restore the hillside and to outline the area with a circular stone wall topped by a wrought iron railing. A dedication service was held Memorial Day weekend, 29 May 2011. In less than one year, the JMF finished what Bishop Norwood had promised for more than three decades.

The three members of the JMF did not anticipate the furor that would ensue when they decided to include the name of Jim Jones among the 918 listed on the plaques. Because they saw the monument as denoting a historical event, they believed that it was imperative to name everyone who died that day.[31] Moreover, they felt that if they attempted to separate the innocent from the guilty, they would have to exclude any number of perpetrators: the killers of Congressman Ryan and the journalists, the medical staff who mixed and injected the poison, the Jonestown leadership group who planned the event, the parents who killed their children. According to this logic, only the murdered children were truly innocent and could be registered.

Figure 10.3. *Flowers laid upon the new plaque, 2011. Photo by Laura Johnston Kohl, courtesy The Jonestown Institute.*

The Ethics of Memorialization

Common wisdom holds that morality tends to be personal while ethics refers to collective notions of right and wrong. Yet Avishai Margalit finds ethics embedded in the "thick" relations between family members and tribal communities; morality, more general and more generic, is applied to universal situations, that is, occasions in which personal connections are "thin." Morality, in his usage, "ought to guide our behavior toward those to whom we are related just by virtue of their being fellow human beings, and by virtue of no other attribute."[32] Ethics, in contrast, is a form of caring that can be directed only at those "with whom we have historical relations, and not just a brief encounter."[33] Thus, we have different obligations to human beings: "in morality, human respect; in ethics, caring and loyalty."[34] How does this distinction work in the case of memorializing the Jonestown dead?

Emphasizing her personal losses, Jynona Norwood sought to prohibit the agents who caused the loss from being listed on any proposed monuments, finding them unworthy of remembrance. This would seem to fall within Margalit's category of ethics, in which thick relations determine one's actions. Although segregation between the worthy and the unworthy became clear in Bishop Norwood's rhetoric over the years, it was strikingly evident at the fortieth anniversary celebration. At that time, she displayed three large (three-by-eight-foot) plywood panels she called a "movable wall." The names and photographs of selected deceased were mounted on these panels. Two panels bore the heading "Innocent Children," and the third was labeled "Heroes Memorial." (It was not clear why these adults were identified as heroes.) Before her service at Evergreen Cemetery begins each year, Bishop Norwood covers the memorial plaques that have been set into the ground with a green tarp so as to blot out Jim Jones's name. Reiterating her claim that including Jones's name is akin to listing Adolf Hitler on a Holocaust memorial, Bishop Norwood seems to place family and loyalty above any other consideration. Moreover, she continues to exhibit the anger and rage over the deaths that Rosaldo describes so vividly regarding his own wife's demise.

Yet Bishop Norwood's annual services rarely feature other relatives or survivors from Peoples Temple or Jonestown. Rather, they always showcase public officials as guest speakers. Printed programs publish testimonial letters from city, state, and national officials. The comedian Dick Gregory, for example, spoke at her service in 2010. The program from 2018 reprinted a Certificate of Honor from the mayor of San Francisco, a Certificate of Special Congressional Recognition from Congresswoman Barbara Lee, and a letter from Congresswoman Nancy Pelosi; Martin Luther King III was the keynote speaker. Despite the "thinness" of their association with the dead, this group explicitly chose sides, exhibiting the loyalty characteristic of Margalit's ethical behavior.

The Jonestown Memorial services, on the other hand, are led by survivors, and they attract former Temple members rather than the general public. As a result, this group functions, in effect, like a family. Although anyone can attend the informal services, few do. At the fortieth anniversary, for example, only a single Associated Press reporter was present in the afternoon; the TV trucks departed after Bishop Norwood's morning service. Following the 18 November afternoon observance, all who attended were invited to gather for a no-host dinner at a nearby restaurant. On only two occasions has the survivor group printed a program:

at the 2011 dedication of the plaques (in order to list all who died and all who contributed to the cost of the plaques) and on the fortieth anniversary. Speakers at this last event had all been members of the Temple, with the exception of the children of survivors.

Perhaps most remarkable is the fact that the speakers at the afternoon service in 2018 represented different factions of Temple membership when it existed. Three had left the group in the early 1970s; one of these had been part of the "Eight Revolutionaries" who harshly criticized practices in the Temple.[35] Three had been on the Jonestown basketball team, who escaped the deaths by playing in Georgetown the weekend of the tragedy. Two others happened to be in the capital city as well. All undoubtedly would have died had they been in Jonestown on 18 November.

Ironically, those who support the inclusive necrology adopted Margalit's "moral" stance of universalism, despite the thickness of their relationships and their widely different perspectives. While they do not necessarily approve of the inclusion of Jim Jones or others who can be considered perpetrators, they nevertheless embrace all of the dead by virtue of their shared humanity.

What seems paradoxical in these two approaches is that the ostensibly family-focused Norwood group represents official, nonrelational interests, while the universalist group represents primarily former Temple members. It is the "universalists" who were primarily family members and the "exclusionists" who were primarily unrelated actors. This seems to be the opposite of what Margalit predicts.

The philosopher offers one possible explanation for this seeming anomaly: proximity. He examines the parable of the Good Samaritan in the New Testament (Luke 10:30–37) and observes that it is physical proximity rather than friendship or association that makes the wounded man on the road evoke compassion in the heart of his ethnic enemy, the Samaritan.[36] The Samaritan responded to a moral duty but not an ethical one, which belonged to the injured man's countrymen who passed him by. "People who suffer close to us elicit more care and compassion than those who are remote."[37] Similarly, the survivors of Jonestown knew many of the people whose names appeared on the plaques, whereas the officials at Bishop Norwood's services did not. It seems as though those most intimately affected by the losses would bear the most hostility toward the perpetrators. The opposite was the case. The deceased had been real to them—had literally been neighbors and thus merited the compassion of being named. Although not all approved of including Jim Jones's name on the plaques, they nevertheless could accept its appearance as part of the larger project of commemorating all who died on that date in history.

The Factor of Race

The majority of the Jonestown dead were African American. A two-day conference of Black church leaders convened in 1979 saw the deaths as part of a long history of oppression and violence perpetrated by whites against Black people.[38] Scholarly works made African American involvement in the Temple a focal point of discussion.[39] Popular narratives of Jonestown, however, neglected or excluded distinctly Black perspectives, even though two of the earliest accounts presented the eyewitness testimony of African Americans.[40] Several things happened to bring Black consciousness to the forefront.

At the risk of appearing immodest, I believe that the *Alternative Considerations* website provided a venue for many different perspectives, including those of African Americans. In addition, the publication of demographic charts and graphs on the website revealed the devastating losses suffered by the Black community in San Francisco.[41] The willingness of African American survivors to step forward and provide interviews to the media, especially in the twenty-first century, also reconfigured the Jonestown story.

One strand of the new narrative concentrated on victimization and exploitation. Although this had long been a constitutive part of Jonestown analyses—with members exploited for money, labor, sex, and more—adding the element of race dramatically altered the reception of this theme.[42] Another strand highlighted the agency exhibited by African Americans in the Temple. Feminist author and memory entrepreneur Sikivu Hutchinson explicitly raised the issue of race when she asked, "Where are the black feminist readings on and scholarship about Peoples Temple and Jonestown?"[43] Her novel *White Nights, Black Paradise* addressed some of the issues involved in the erasure of African American women from the Jonestown story by presenting a diverse assortment of strong, Black female characters.[44]

These and other narratives contributed to the feeling among some in various Black communities that including Jim Jones's name on any memorial disrespected the victims and indicated if not a racist attitude, then a lack of racial sensitivity. The deaths of so many African Americans required some sort of political statement of opposition, and excluding Jones's name seemed to serve this purpose. Nevertheless, a number of African Americans wrote letters to Evergreen Cemetery in support of mounting the plaques with Jones's name, while a number of whites wrote in protest.

Separate but important considerations contributing to the fissures that existed between partisans of the different memorials were those of Black religious and funerary traditions. Bishop Norwood's memorial services

Figure 10.4. *The monument at Evergreen Cemetery was completely refurbished for the fortieth anniversary of Jonestown, 2018. Photo by Laura Johnston Kohl, courtesy The Jonestown Institute.*

strongly reflected the African American church in appearance and content. Gospel songs, prayers, "amens" from the audience, and the frequent invocation of God made it clear that this was a religious, rather than secular, commemoration. A visitor to the memorial service in 2018 described it as "evangelically focused and exclusive." She continued: "The entire service was very much like a Pentecostal Black church with strong, rousing sermonizing, singing, and dancing."[45]

This approach is at odds with the sentiments of many survivors. The religious elements of Peoples Temple all but disappeared in Guyana. Individual members may well have retained deep Christian faith, but overall survivors did not wear their religion, or irreligion, on their sleeves. Some became committed Christians, others devout atheists. An absence of overt religious symbols and language characterized the survivors' memorial services, although some individuals did in fact pray or use religious language when talking about loved ones.

Black funerary traditions may also have contributed to the disconnect between the two groups wanting to memorialize the dead. As noted above, the Guyana Emergency Relief Committee insisted on burial, rather than cremation, as part of Black church traditions. In her analysis of African American funeral rituals, English professor Karla FC Holloway described the dramatic, and even theatrical, emotionalism her informants reported of Black funerals. She observed more touching, kissing, and involvement with the body than at white funerals.[46] When Bishop Norwood displayed the monoliths at her service in 2008, a number of African Americans

Figure 10.5. *A pillow monument commemorating the 2011 dedication of the new monument was installed for the fortieth anniversary observance, 2018. Photo by Laura Johnston Kohl, courtesy The Jonestown Institute.*

not only laid flowers upon them, they also hugged or touched the stones themselves. Photographs show some weeping in the background. As Rosaldo notes, "People express their grief in culturally specific ways,"[47] thus the overtly emotional displays at the Norwood services contrast with the quiet, introverted memorials held by survivors; this disparity may well be due to race and the cultural expectations of behavior at funerals and memorial services.

Enlarging the Field of Discourse

Jelin assesses the difficulties in memorializing the past, especially when it has been traumatic, as in the cases of the experiences under brutal dictatorships in South America in the twentieth century. What are the standards? Who is the authority? And more to the point, "Who embodies *true* memory"?[48] Disagreement over erecting a monument for those who died in Jonestown was unavoidable, given the disputed nature of the deaths and the various interests at play. As a partisan in the quarrel, I believe that listing everyone, rather than excluding some, was the right thing to do. I did not want to see anyone's anger (my own included) engraved in stone.

Excluding Jim Jones's name would have meant accepting a comfortable narrative that grossly simplifies a very complex tale. His presence would have been larger, not smaller, by his omission. Now he is no greater than any other individual who was part of Peoples Temple.

Jelin introduces two terms for the word "us" from the indigenous Guarani language used daily by people in Paraguay. One, *ore*, "marks the boundary separating the speaker and his or her community from the 'other,' the one who listens and observes." The other, *ñande*, "is an inclusive 'us' that invites the interlocutor to be part of the community."[49] The wish to embrace only the Jonestown innocent is understandable, but that seems to me to comprise a small "us" rather than an expansive one. Although it is unquestionably easier to be expansive from a position of privilege than one of disprivilege, I think it is worth the effort to widen the circle whenever possible; to make "us" into *ñande*.

This consideration of "us"—insiders and outsiders, ethnographers and subjects—gets to the heart of Rosaldo's attempt to remake analysis in the social sciences. If we consider ritual, along with narratives, practices, and habits, as a busy intersection, we do find "a space for distinct trajectories to traverse."[50] The complexity of real life demands such openness. At the same time, the specific reality of bereavement and grief challenges that approach. Rosaldo recognizes this when he criticizes the way that "most ethnographic descriptions of death stand at a peculiar distance from the obviously intense emotions expressed, and they turn what for the bereaved are unique and devastating losses into routine happenings."[51]

Traffic at the intersection of Jonestown memorialization is very busy indeed, and far from routine. In 2018, a reconstituted Jonestown Memorial Fund raised money to completely refurbish the site for the fortieth anniversary. Attractively colored pressed concrete replaced ragged dirt and grass, while the plaques themselves were lined with white rock; the names engraved in stone were highlighted to make them more readable. A pillow marker was installed that noted the May 2011 dedication of the memorial, and a small QR symbol was placed on it to direct visitors with smart devices to a website that featured photos of all who died in Jonestown.[52] In 2019, a complete listing of where all the dead are buried was posted to the *Alternative Considerations* website, since fewer than half the fatalities are interred at Evergreen Cemetery.[53]

Renato Rosaldo's observations have broadened the field of anthropology to include scholars like myself. Because of my unique social position as both an insider and an outsider, I have had to negotiate and, at times, forge a new pathway through traditional disciplinary boundaries. Yet incorporating personal insights into scholarly assessments of bereavement processes has helped my efforts to enlarge public understanding of the events of Jonestown—just as Rosaldo enriched our understanding of

Ilongot rituals by relating them to the experience of his wife's tragic death. It is a tricky line to walk in both worlds, the emic and the etic, but it is definitely worth the attempt.

Rebecca Moore is emerita professor of religious studies at San Diego State University. She is currently reviews editor for *Nova Religio: The Journal of Alternative and Emergent Religions*, published by University of California Press. Her most recent book is *Beyond Brainwashing: Perspectives on Cultic Violence* (Cambridge University Press, 2018).

Notes

1. Renato Rosaldo, *Culture and Truth: The Remaking of Social Analysis* (Boston: Beacon Press, 1993).
2. Ibid., 11.
3. Ibid., 44.
4. Rebecca Moore, "Taking Sides: On the (Im)possibility of Participant-Observation," in *The Insider/Outsider Debate: New Perspectives in the Study of Religion*, ed. George D. Chryssides and Stephen E. Gregg (Sheffield: Equinox, 2019), 151–70.
5. Rosaldo, *Culture and Truth*, 15.
6. Elizabeth Jelin, *State Repression and the Labors of Memory* (Minneapolis: University of Minnesota Press, 2002), 44.
7. Ibid.
8. Rosaldo, *Culture and Truth*, 29.
9. David Chidester, "Rituals of Exclusion and the Jonestown Dead," *Journal of the American Academy of Religion* 56, no. 4 (Winter 1988): 681–702.
10. "What Pathologists Investigated the Deaths That Occurred in Jonestown, Georgetown, and Port Kaituma?" Alternative Considerations of Jonestown and Peoples Temple (2018), retrieved 16 January 2021 from https://jonestown.sdsu.edu/?page_id=85214.
11. Mary Douglas, *Purity and Danger: An Analysis of Concept of Pollution and Taboo* (London: Routledge, 1966).
12. Chidester, "Rituals of Exclusion," 687–91.
13. Ibid., 691.
14. Arnold van Gennep, *The Rites of Passage*, trans. Monika B. Vizedom and Gabrielle L. Caffee (London: Routledge, 1960 [1908]).
15. Chidester, "Rituals of Exclusion," 693–94.
16. Rosaldo, *Culture and Truth*, 46–48.
17. Rebecca Moore, "The Stigmatized Deaths in Jonestown: Finding a Locus for Grief," *Death Studies* 35, no. 1 (2011): 42–58.
18. Rebecca Moore, "Last Rights," Alternative Considerations of Jonestown and Peoples Temple (1988), retrieved 16 January 2021 from https://jonestown.sdsu.edu/?page_id=16585.
19. Erika Doss, *Emotional Life of Contemporary Public Memorials: Towards a Theory of Temporary Memorials* (Amsterdam: Amsterdam University Press, 2008), 7.
20. Erika Doss, *Memorial Mania: Public Feeling in America* (Chicago: University of Chicago Press, 2010), 216.
21. Ibid., 152.
22. Jonathan Z. Smith, *Imagining Religion: From Babylon to Jonestown* (Chicago: University of Chicago Press, 1982), 109.

23. Daniel Sherman, "Bodies and Names: The Emergence of Commemoration in Interwar France," *American Historical Review* 103, no. 2 (April 1998): 447.
24. Ibid., 456.
25. Doss, *Memorial Mania*, 152.
26. Jelin, *State Repression*, 33–34, italics in original.
27. Alternative Considerations of Jonestown and Peoples Temple, Special Collections at San Diego State University, retrieved 16 January 2021 from https://jonestown.sdsu.edu/.
28. "Who Died?" Alternative Considerations of Jonestown and Peoples Temple, Special Collections at San Diego State University, retrieved 16 January 2021 from https://jonestown.sdsu.edu/?page_id=33.
29. Lela Howard, "Jonestown Relative Announces New Foundation," *the jonestown report* 9 (2007), retrieved 16 January 2021 from https://jonestown.sdsu.edu/?page_id=33168.
30. Rebecca Moore, "Godwin's Law and Jones' Corollary: The Problem of Using Extremes to Make Predictions," *Nova Religio* 22, no. 3 (November 2018): 145–54.
31. Fielding McGehee, "Jim Jones' Name on the Marker: A Discussion of the Committee's Decision," *the jonestown report* 13 (October 2011), retrieved 16 January 2021 from https://jonestown.sdsu.edu/?page_id=29418.
32. Margalit, *The Ethics of Memory* (Cambridge, MA: Harvard University Press, 2002), 37.
33. Ibid., 44.
34. Ibid., 73.
35. "Eight Revolutionaries," Alternative Considerations of Jonestown and Peoples Temple (2015 [1973]), retrieved 16 January 2021 from https://jonestown.sdsu.edu/?page_id=14075.
36. Margalit, *The Ethics of Memory*, 42.
37. Ibid., 43.
38. David Chidester, *Salvation and Suicide: An Interpretation of Jim Jones, the Peoples Temple, and Jonestown* (Bloomington: University of Indiana Press, 1988), 42–43.
39. C. Eric Lincoln and Lawrence Mamiya, "Daddy Jones and Father Divine: The Cult as Political Religion," in *Peoples Temple and Black Religion in America*, ed. Rebecca Moore, Anthony B. Pinn, and Mary R. Sawyer (Bloomington: University of Indiana Press, 2004 [1980]), 28–46; Rebecca Moore, Anthony B. Pinn, and Mary R. Sawyer, eds., *Peoples Temple and Black Religion in America* (Bloomington: University of Indiana Press, 2004).
40. Ethan Feinsod, *Awake in a Nightmare: Jonestown, the Only Eyewitness Account* (New York: W. W. Norton, 1981); Kenneth Wooden, *The Children of Jonestown* (New York: McGraw-Hill, 1981).
41. "Demographics at a Glance," Alternative Considerations of Jonestown and Peoples Temple (2017), retrieved 16 January 2021 from https://jonestown.sdsu.edu/?page_id=70785.
42. See, for example, Lear K. Matthews and George K. Danns, *Communities and Development in Guyana: A Neglected Dimension in Nation Building* (Georgetown, Guyana: University of Guyana, 1980); reprinted as "The Jonestown Plantation" in *A New Look at Jonestown: Dimensions from a Guyanese Perspective*, ed. Eusi Kwyana (Los Angeles: Carib House, 2016), 82–95.
43. Sikivu Hutchinson, "No More White Saviors: Jonestown and Peoples Temple in the Black Feminist Imagination," *the jtr bulletin* (2014), retrieved 16 January 2021 from https://jonestown.sdsu.edu/?page_id=61499.
44. Sikivu Hutchinson, *White Nights, Black Paradise* (Los Angeles: Infidel Press, 2015).
45. Joy Valentini, email communication, 3 January 2019.
46. Karla FC Holloway, *Passed On: African American Mourning Stories* (Durham, NC: Duke University Press, 2002), 154–55.
47. Rosaldo, *Culture and Truth*, 58.
48. Jelin, *State Repression*, 43, italics in original.
49. Ibid., 43.
50. Rosaldo, *Culture and Truth*, 17.

51. Ibid., 57.
52. "Jonestown Memorial," retrieved 20 May 2020 from https://jonestownmemorial.com/.
53. "Where Are the Jonestown Dead Buried?" Alternative Considerations of Jonestown and Peoples Temple, retrieved 16 January 2021 from https://jonestown.sdsu.edu/?page_id=87578.

Bibliography

Alternative Considerations of Jonestown and Peoples Temple. https://jonestown.sdsu.edu/.

Chidester, David. "Rituals of Exclusion and the Jonestown Dead." *Journal of the American Academy of Religion* 56, no. 4 (Winter 1988): 681–702.

———. *Salvation and Suicide: An Interpretation of Jim Jones, the Peoples Temple, and Jonestown*. Bloomington: University of Indiana Press, 1988.

"Demographics at a Glance." Alternative Considerations of Jonestown and Peoples Temple. 2017. Retrieved 16 January 2021 from https://jonestown.sdsu.edu/?page_id=70785.

Doss, Erika. *Emotional Life of Contemporary Public Memorials: Towards a Theory of Temporary Memorials*. Amsterdam: Amsterdam University Press, 2008.

———. *Memorial Mania: Public Feeling in America*. Chicago: University of Chicago Press, 2010.

Douglas, Mary. *Purity and Danger: An Analysis of Concept of Pollution and Taboo*. London: Routledge, 1966.

"Eight Revolutionaries." Alternative Considerations of Jonestown and Peoples Temple. 2015 [1973]. Retrieved 16 January 2021 from https://jonestown.sdsu.edu/?page_id=14075.

Feinsod, Ethan. *Awake in a Nightmare: Jonestown, the Only Eyewitness Account*. New York: W. W. Norton, 1981.

Holloway, Karla FC. *Passed On: African American Mourning Stories*. Durham, NC: Duke University Press, 2002.

Howard, Lela. "Jonestown Relative Announces New Foundation." *the jonestown report* 9 (2007). Retrieved 16 January 2021 from https://jonestown.sdsu.edu/?page_id=33168.

Hutchinson, Sikivu. "No More White Saviors: Jonestown and Peoples Temple in the Black Feminist Imagination." *the jtr bulletin* (2014). Retrieved 16 January 2021 from https://jonestown.sdsu.edu/?page_id=61499.

———. *White Nights, Black Paradise*. Los Angeles: Infidel Press, 2015.

Jelin, Elizabeth. *State Repression and the Labors of Memory*. Minneapolis: University of Minnesota Press, 2002.

Lincoln, C. Eric, and Lawrence Mamiya. "Daddy Jones and Father Divine: The Cult as Political Religion." In *Peoples Temple and Black Religion in America*, edited by Rebecca Moore, Anthony B. Pinn, and Mary R. Sawyer, 28–46. Bloomington: University of Indiana Press, 2004 [1980].

Margalit, Avishai. *The Ethics of Memory*. Cambridge, MA: Harvard University Press, 2002.

Matthews, Lear K., and George K. Danns. *Communities and Development in Guyana: A Neglected Dimension in Nation Building*. Georgetown, Guyana: University of Guyana, 1980. Reprinted as "The Jonestown Plantation," in *A New Look at*

Jonestown: Dimensions from a Guyanese Perspective, edited by Eusi Kwyana, 82–95. Los Angeles: Carib House, 2016.

McGehee, Fielding. "Jim Jones' Name on the Marker: A Discussion of the Committee's Decision." *the jonestown report* 13 (October 2011). Retrieved 16 January 2021 from https://jonestown.sdsu.edu/?page_id=29418.

Moore, Rebecca. "Godwin's Law and Jones' Corollary: The Problem of Using Extremes to Make Predictions." *Nova Religio* 22, no. 3 (November 2018): 145–54

———. "Last Rights." Alternative Considerations of Jonestown and Peoples Temple. 1988. Retrieved 16 January 2021 from https://jonestown.sdsu.edu/?page_id=16585.

———. "The Stigmatized Deaths in Jonestown: Finding a Locus for Grief." *Death Studies* 35, no. 1 (2011): 42–58.

———. "Taking Sides: On the (Im)possibility of Participant-Observation." In *The Insider/Outsider Debate: New Perspectives in the Study of Religion*, edited by George D. Chryssides and Stephen E. Gregg, 151–70. Sheffield: Equinox, 2019.

Moore, Rebecca, Anthony B. Pinn, and Mary R. Sawyer, eds. *Peoples Temple and Black Religion in America*. Bloomington: University of Indiana Press, 2004.

Rosaldo, Renato. *Culture and Truth: The Remaking of Social Analysis*. Boston: Beacon Press, 1993.

Sherman, Daniel. "Bodies and Names: The Emergence of Commemoration in Interwar France." *American Historical Review* 103, no. 2 (April 1998): 443–66.

Smith, Jonathan Z. *Imagining Religion: From Babylon to Jonestown*. Chicago: University of Chicago Press, 1982.

Valentini, Joy. Email communication. 3 January 2019.

Van Gennep, Arnold. *The Rites of Passage*. Translated by Monika B. Vizedom and Gabrielle L. Caffee. London: Routledge, 1960 [1908].

"What Pathologists Investigated the Deaths That Occurred in Jonestown, Georgetown, and Port Kaituma?" Alternative Considerations of Jonestown and Peoples Temple. 2018. Retrieved 16 January 2021 from https://jonestown.sdsu.edu/?page_id=85214.

"Where Are the Jonestown Dead Buried?" Alternative Considerations of Jonestown and Peoples Temple. 2020. Retrieved 16 January 2021 from https://jonestown.sdsu.edu/?page_id=87578.

"Who Died?" Alternative Considerations of Jonestown and Peoples Temple. 2020. Retrieved 16 January 2021 from https://jonestown.sdsu.edu/?page_id=33.

Wooden, Kenneth. *The Children of Jonestown*. New York: McGraw-Hill, 1981.

Figure 11.1. Left: *Author wears Willie's official R.I.P. t-shirt and symbolically takes him with her to Hangzhou, China.* Right: *Willie's official R.I.P. t-shirt. Photos by Kami Fletcher and Valeria Brunson.*

CHAPTER 11

Long Live Chill

Exploring Grief, Mourning, and Ritual within African American R.I.P. T-shirt Culture

Kami Fletcher

In my hometown of Pine Bluff, Arkansas, on 8 November 2017, my sister Aleta (nicknamed Snooky) received an early morning knock on the door alerting her that Willie "Chill" Oglesby Jr., her twenty-eight-year-old only child, had been murdered. At the morgue she had gone numb as she realized this was the death of her direct family line—Braelyn, Willie's only child, had tragically passed away seven years earlier at the tender age of three.

Living and working thousands of miles away from my hometown, I simply could not make travel arrangements to get to Snooky fast enough. Instead, I called, and amid tears and grief, I talked to her every day, leading up to my flight home for Willie's last rites. During this time, she coped by planning the wake and funeral because it positioned her as a mother instead of a mourner—she continued to care and look after Willie, or as she put it, "making sure her boy looked good." She called me two days before my flight, and in running down her funeral to-do list, told me she decided to include R.I.P. t-shirts as part of Willie's last rites, and that my shirt would be waiting upon my arrival. R.I.P. t-shirts, t-shirts created to commemorate a decedent's life, function as ritualized mourning wear and are perhaps the most visible tradition in the country. Widespread within African American mourning culture, the ritual allowed Snooky to publicly memorialize Willie, making his death matter. According to Snooky, Willie was "loved in all fifty states and some countries," and the R.I.P. t-shirt was a very public way of conveying this message. It celebrated and memorialized his layered life—his role as unforgettable son, playful father, beloved nephew, favorite cousin, and "a real one" to all who ever knew him. Emblazoned on the front was Willie wearing a blue half-zip Ralph Lauren Polo sweater and matching blue Ralph Lauren Polo baseball-style cap with the block phrase "We Love & Miss You ... /CHILL/August 17, 1989 – November 8, 2017" underneath. Snooky memorialized Willie as he always looked in life—dressed in designer clothing, literally fresh to death.

She went on to tell me that she designated the shirts to be worn on the day of his wake. Snooky commissioned forty-four R.I.P. t-shirts so that we could "show Willie love." All in uniformed attire, we—Snooky's immediate family, aunts and uncles, cousins, and close family friends—were a force of love and remembering. Willie may have died alone on that dark street early in the morning, but Snooky made sure that it was his life, populated by people who love him, that would be his legacy.

Why We Wear R.I.P. T-shirts

While very much inside this ritual, I wondered why I was wearing this R.I.P. t-shirt. As someone who studies death, I found this particularly intriguing because I was actively experiencing what I had spent years researching. I wanted to know why we were all participating, and I asked my family and friends the following questions: (1) Why do you wear Willie's R.I.P. t-shirt, and how does wearing it make you feel? (2) How often do you wear it, and why? Answers revealed that they accepted the ritualized mourning wear as important to examining the grief, memory, and mourning within our community. They believed it to be about honor and respect. For example, cousin Styles believed the R.I.P. t-shirt had a dual purpose—as a ritual, it honors the fact that Willie's spirit will forever live on, and in wearing the mourning attire, he paid respects to Willie's life and character. Styles put it this way: "I wore it because I feel like I have him here as I am also laying him to rest [because] it represents the presence of spirit." Cousin Jonte connected the importance of the ritual to Africa, saying, "R.I.P. t-shirts are no different from when our people were jumping the broom ... most people could never realize the mental bondage our people had to endure just so we could stand today." Jonte first identified the memorial practice as an Africanism (cultural carryover from Africa) and then connected the importance of this practice to overcoming the trauma of systemic oppression underlying the African American experience. Jonte clearly showed that this mourning practice had the power to heal and allow us to remember, but we also are able to heal *because* we remember.

Talking with various family members as both an insider and outsider, I wanted to know if the insistence that R.I.P. t-shirts were normal made the roots of this ritual deeper than a cultural fad—the way it was considered in the wider community. Observations were also used to draw conclusions and connect to larger ideas about the nature of R.I.P. t-shirts and African American mourning culture. Centering on written and verbal exchanges, direct and indirect encounters with bereaved family and friends, as well as secondary literature for context, I examined the role of grief, memory, and mourning within our African American community. First, I distinguished the kind of R.I.P. t-shirts used in my family (and families like ours) from the supposedly original form of the custom in gang-related deaths. What I call the "official R.I.P. t-shirt" is commissioned by the next of kin to be worn as a uniform during a portion of the funeral services. "Unofficial R.I.P. t-shirts" were all differently designed because they were created from different persons using their personal memories with the decedent. Both were used to display mourning and memorial, and both were worn well after the active grieving/mourning period. Second, I examined the historical origins of the R.I.P. t-shirt, teasing apart its roots in gang-related deaths and 1980s/1990s street graffiti mourning culture and expression. In suggesting that families of fallen gang members adopted the mourning custom or that the youth adopted it when celebrities such as Tupac Shakur and Biggie Smalls were murdered, or both, I illustrate how the custom expanded beyond gang culture to become widely used in urban areas. Third, I traced the R.I.P. t-shirts from ritual to ordinary/everyday wear (clothing owned by the dead given significance by the living) to comprehend use and purpose to mourning and memorial. Fourth, I illustrated how, as a multipurposed ritual garment, the R.I.P. t-shirt is worn in celebratory style and positioned as what I label a "walking memorial."

Therefore, this chapter is as much an exploration into African American grief as it is an exploration into the meaning of the R.I.P. t-shirt to African American mourning customs and death material culture. A goal was to understand the function of the t-shirt at the intersection of mourning, popular culture, and grief. In doing so, I contextualize the mourning ritual within the broader African American funerary tradition. Ultimately, I hope to show how Black women, men, and young people, like my kin, drew solace, comfort, and refuge from the R.I.P. t-shirt, and even utilized it as a call to action.

The Power of R.I.P. T-Shirts to Black Grief and Mourning

There is power in R.I.P. t-shirts because for Black people it is an important part of the support system, memory-making, and experience-sharing after death. There has been little to no research on (1) understanding the significance of the shirt in this way, beyond economics, and (2) its impact on Black mourning.[1] Current frameworks have limitations for understanding R.I.P. t-shirts but still provide useful concepts to help analyze and interpret their meaning. Social anthropologists Elizabeth Hallam and Jenny Hokey provide three concepts, each uncovered by charting how broader cultural perceptions have shaped memorial and material culture: (1) "memory-making"—memories are static, imprints of the creator, and therefore allow mourners to control memories while simultaneously keeping them safe; (2) "sites of memory"; and (3) "cultural meanings ascribed to space."[2] I use their framework to show how memory through distinctive pictures placed on the R.I.P. t-shirt can structure and shape remembering, arguing that there is a distinction between them—"official R.I.P. t-shirts" and "unofficial R.I.P. t-shirts." First, I wanted to point out that one type of shirt was not more important or legitimate than the other, and second, I wanted to understand that the official one was about the public vision of the decedent and the unofficial one was about the personal vision of the decedent. Therefore, the official R.I.P. t-shirt was the vision of Willie put forth by his mother and shared with the collective kinship structure. Official R.I.P. t-shirts are next-of-kin-created mourning wear that is mass-produced, while unofficial R.I.P. t-shirts are created by individual family/friends and made from personal memories (see figures 11.2 and 11.3). Each type of mourning wear invokes a different emotion because of the pictures and words used and/or the meaning behind the design. Snooky told me it took her no time to select from about twenty photographs the picture she would use for the official R.I.P. t-shirt, because looking at the photo, one in which Willie displays a serious look, was like looking right at him—his expression in the photo was one she had just seen hours before he died, and it was an expression that all who knew him would easily recognize. She also told me she made the conscious choice to put "We Love & Miss You" underneath his picture to "allow our family to show Willie love" and not just her. In other words, the official R.I.P. t-shirt was a purposeful collective act of mourning where Snooky chose words that described Willie not just to her but to all who would wear (and see) the mourning attire.

By contrast, her unofficial R.I.P. t-shirt has text that reads "I love you 2-2"—the sweet and tender response that two-year old Willie would say to her every time she told him she loved him: he would say "I love you" and she would respond "I love you too" to which Willie would respond "I love you 2-2," matching the number he thought his mother had just said. Using the language of the R.I.P. t-shirt, Snooky made this private phrase public in an attempt to make her grief legible and acceptable, an action argued by scholar Rhaisa Williams. Williams argued that Black maternal grief is commonly dismissed due to the historical and stereotypical tropes of motherhood that render Black mothers as breeders and detached mammies who are uncaring, unkind, and uncommitted to their own.[3] Illustrating a sentimental exchange from Willie's childhood—pur-

Figure 11.2. *Willie's family, by blood or bond, wearing the official R.I.P. t-shirt.* Left to right: *close friend Jarren; cousin Candice; cousin Valeria. Photos by Jarren Jefferson, Candice Taylor, and Valeria Brunson.*

posely written underneath his adult picture to covey that this conversation was not just repeated well into his adult life but was also something that bonded them—pushed back against such tropes while claiming public space to grieve and mourn. From this context, both an official and an unofficial R.I.P. t-shirt is an intense act of memory-making underlain with African American social and cultural values that can produce agency and activism helping Black people mark their dead in ways that ensure they are not forgotten, marginalized, or, perhaps most of all, misrepresented.

Broader cultural perceptions may label the mourning wear as deviant subculture, helping not only to explain the confusion and disregard expressed by the dominant culture but also why some African Americans choose not to participate in the ritual and/or oppose it. They are labeled deviant because (1) R.I.P. t-shirts are in strict opposition to American death-denying culture, and (2) they are rooted in American urban gang/street culture. Starting at the turn of the twentieth century, Americans no longer died at home to be funeralized by family. Instead, more and more Americans died in hospitals. Coupled with the fact that the vast majority of cemeteries were located outside city limits and Americans actively lived longer, death was pushed out of life to the point where scholars saw it as an American denial of death. The R.I.P. t-shirt challenged this idea not only by serving as ordinary/everyday wear, clothing owned by the dead given significance by the living, but by also being connected to gang culture where members openly antic-

Figure 11.3. *Examples of unofficial R.I.P. t-shirts for Willie.* Clockwise from left: Snooky, Willie's mother, at her place of work. Cousin Jonathan pictured before going out for weekend fun. Cousin Arianna, during the days before the funeral, wearing the hooded sweatshirt that she had commissioned as an unofficial R.I.P. t-shirt. An unofficial R.I.P. t-shirt with heaven's golden streets, lots of money cascading in the background, and an altered picture of Willie with angel wings alongside the woman who commissioned the shirt. Photos by Aleta "Snooky" Fletcher, Jonathan Thompson, and Arianna Winters.

ipate death. Case in point: one of two scholarly studies of R.I.P. t-shirts to date described it as "rhetoric of fatal violence."[4] The study focuses on Baltimore, where the homicide rate is ten times the national average, arguing that the shirts are found within the Black Baltimore community to make the death matter by serving as informal archives, community obituaries, and even death notices.[5]

As a matter of record and account, R.I.P. t-shirts also function as tangible condolence. Utilized this way, the shirts become powerful for persons who cannot be physically present when the bereaved gather to mourn and heal. When our cousin Candice was unable to travel to Arkansas for Willie's last rites, she made sure she was mailed an official R.I.P. t-shirt, which she wore in solidarity and unity with the family. Upon receiving her shirt she took to social media and wrote "wasn't able to make it to see you one last time but I took you to church with me this morning with my heart filled with joy." This post functioned as a caption to the center photo in figure 11.2 in order to publicly express her wishes to engage in communal mourning with her kin and view his body at the wake and funeral (open-casket wakes and funerals are standard African American funerary custom). As tangible condolence, similar to sympathy cards, R.I.P. t-shirts allow mourners to don the clothing at a distance, post pictures, and literally send their sympathies. When a daughter of my cousin Duke's girlfriend found out about Willie's passing, she immediately commissioned the making of an unofficial R.I.P. shirt for Duke. Through the shirt, we will memorialize our loved one who has passed on.

Soon after the RIP t-shirt was worn during death rituals, it became part of the wardrobe of the living to be worn anywhere the wearer deemed fit. In this way, it doubled as ritual wear and ordinary/everyday wear, clothing owned by the deceased given significance through death. Ordinary/everyday wear is the material culture left behind that holds memories and allows for one more interaction with the dead. Candice turned her R.I.P. t-shirt into not only ordinary/everyday wear but also a walking memorial, a purposeful transporting of the life and death memories from one location to the next. The day after Willie's funeral, Candice wore her shirt to church to honor the memory of his life. To all she encountered, she shared Willie's memory, reminding them of his life and memorializing Willie in a very public way. As walking memorials, the shirts serve as an important source not just for telling but also for publicizing the decedent's story.

As walking memorials, R.I.P. t-shirts increased the longevity of the deceased. The shirts allowed mourners to transport the memorial wherever they went, keeping their loved one relevant and present regardless of place. In *Virtual Afterlives: Grieving the Dead in the Twenty-First Century*, the aforementioned second of two scholarly works on R.I.P. t-shirts, Candi Cann highlighted their importance in examining the "role of place in remembering the dead"—identifying mourners and mourning—and establishing solidarity and collective memorial in grief. Along with car decals and tattoos, part of a phenomenon she calls "moving the dead," R.I.P. t-shirts are important in mapping out mourning space in the realm of the living. "The t-shirt memorial," starts Cann, "allow[s] death to come into everyday discourse." For the African American community where death is not taboo but very much part of life, R.I.P. t-shirts serve as a way to challenge the death-denial culture by using literal bodies of the living to remap mourning onto the landscape of the living. R.I.P. t-shirts confront larger society about its role in African American death.

The use of clothing in collective ritualistic mourning is a powerful tool for bonding and healing. Honest self-reflection revealed that once I was handed Willie's R.I.P. t-shirt, I felt emotionally assaulted by it because I was confronted with his unbearable absence while in his unforgettable presence. However, upon seeing cousin Kendra wearing hers at the wake, I was able to see the shirts as a bonding element to healing. I did not realize it at the time, but my tight embrace with Kendra left her black lipliner imprinted on my right shirtsleeve. After taking off the shirt, I saw it and felt immense joy along with that extended family support Snooky had intended in her commissioning the mourning wear and organizing the ritual. Our close relationship was able to offset the hostility I initially felt when confronted with Willie's death via the R.I.P. t-shirts. I surprisingly felt comfort when I saw Kendra also wearing the shirt. So, when she came up behind me and put her hand on my shoulder, I turned around and hugged her so fiercely that she left her indelible mark, illustrating what material textiles scholar Peter Stallybrass would describe as the power and possession of clothes.[6] Clothes, particularly mourning wear, have the power to hold memory and possess the wearer. Since the wake, when I wear or even look at the shirt and see Willie, reminding me that he has passed on, I also see Kendra's kiss and know that she is right by my side, helping me to heal. Writer and textiles scholar Pennina Barnett reminds us that cloth and clothing such as R.I.P. t-shirts hold time differently, retaining imprints over a continuous period.[7] As ephemeral as we think t-shirts are, even possibly the most ordinary of items, Barnett insists that clothing such as t-shirts are "intimate, immediate, skin-close."[8] And because clothes are as common to us as the body that wears them, it takes the experience of death to highlight the importance of a clothing item like the R.I.P. t-shirt—showing how in its creation and display when worn in mourning it can be used to bond and heal.

R.I.P. t-shirts allow room for healing by metaphorically filling the void of the loved one's absence, serving as a second skin to keep deceased loved ones close and even allowing mourners to fill out the imprint left with their own image. "It's like holding on to a part of them that you just don't

Figure 11.4. *Wearing an R.I.P. t-shirt dedicated to his friend Neech, Yorrel Hughes poses with his daughter. Photo by Yorrel Hughes.*

want to let go, I guess," offered Yorrel Hughes, a Facebook friend. The R.I.P. t-shirt is tangible and allows mourners, like Yorrel, to literally hug, touch, be near, and, as he says, "hold on" to a loved one who has long been dead and buried. When asking him how he felt about wearing the shirt, he said he was "hurt, confused, wanted revenge, torn as if a part of me died too." As an African American male socialized to suppress emotion and not express vulnerability, especially in sadness and pain, Yorrel can wear the R.I.P. t-shirt and give himself an acceptable outlet to fully show his emotion and deep sorrow. This becomes particularly true when, as he added, "sometimes you wear it just to wear it." Yorrel, at thirty-five years old, has worn countless R.I.P. t-shirts, and uses them as spaces to work out his confusion and hurt or just to acknowledge his broken and bereaved self. Scholars of death material culture agree that ordinary/everyday mourning wear allows mourners to also reassemble the decedent's life and create an afterlife. For Yorrel, his continued wear of these shirts is this afterlife—one where his friends and loved ones will never be forgotten and one where he is very active in creating and sustaining their memorialization.

R.I.P. T-Shirts as African American Mourning Culture

Official R.I.P. t-shirts come from the decedent's family, whether blood or bond, and are used to signify mourning and memorial. My family and I are participants in what licensed funeral director and death doula Michelle Acciavatti calls "family-led art and ceremony." In the last century, families in Victorian culture used hair from decedents in beautifully artistic ways to celebrate and mourn. Victorians would place the dead in "natural poses" to create last images via postmortem photography. R.I.P. t-shirts are created with a living picture of the decedent. This living picture is the centerpiece of which the art is made and celebrated. For example, as shown in figure 11.3, cousin Jonathan created an abstract design on a burgundy two-button polo worn for professional dress-up wear rather than on a plain white tee. Using the dark rich burgundy to serve as Willie's flesh tones, Willie's likeness was airbrushed in white to accentuate his glasses, shirt, and expression. Another difference from Victorian culture is that in R.I.P. t-shirt African American mourning culture, the mood is not somber and gloomy but festive, because only happy memories are used to create the official and unofficial R.I.P. t-shirts. This was clearly seen when cousin Shanicqua used a screenshot from a FaceTime call she had with Willie as the picture for her unofficial R.I.P. t-shirt. Shanicqua revealed to me that she and Willie talked every day, and it was their playful telephone interaction that led her to use this photograph in order to create her mourning wear.

As family-led art, an R.I.P. t-shirt is a collaborative effort between the living and the dead that not only helps the two maintain a relationship but is at the core of memory-making and culturally ascribed sites of memory. In written exchanges, Willie's close friend Jarren explained to me that he often wore the official R.I.P. t-shirt. He also disclosed that the left picture in figure 11.2 was a three-layered collaborative memory Jarren wrote,

> It was actually a screenshot of a video [where I was] listening to two of my favorite rappers on a song, and Chill has always been one of my favorite rappers so I decided to "collaborate" the three in a sense by recording the video of the shirt while the song was playing.

One way to unpack the memorial Jarren created was to understand that the official R.I.P. t-shirt was positioned as a memory of Willie's personality, values, and spirit. As Jarren played a rap song by one of his favorite rappers, a song that he and Willie would rap along to, the three collaborated to create this site of memory. And music is often memorialized alongside the decedent, represented by song lyrics. Purposeful and collaborative, R.I.P. t-shirts as African American mourning culture illustrate their uniqueness to build a public memorial through the personal and selected memories. Jarren added that Willie's obituary currently remains in the glove compartment of his vehicle. Here, his use of death material culture shows how R.I.P. t-shirts are not only accessible as sites of memory but also deliberately made public, like obituaries, to be disseminated, shared, and transferred—walking memorials. Official and unofficial R.I.P. t-shirts are created from multiple and layered memories made through an imaginative process, one created from the wearer's direct experiences with the decedent and shaped by intense emotion, resulting in walking memorials, purposely transferrable and thereby accessible.

As family-led art, R.I.P. t-shirts allow the bereaved to control the memories/memorials and keep them safe. They serve as important sites of memory, particularly at the repast, the plentiful feast that immediately follows the funeral/homegoing and body disposal. Starting in the 2000s, it became common for mourners to don official and unofficial R.I.P. t-shirts while feasting and fellowshipping at the repast. The wearing of R.I.P. t-shirts is a reminder to celebrate life in the midst of a death. Happy memories abound, starting with the one on the shirt. According to my sorority sister, Cozetta, wearing the R.I.P. t-shirt at the repast can transform the occasion into a party. "The repast was held at a community hall," starts Cozetta. "It was definitely more of a celebratory atmosphere—a party—an attempt to 'be happy' and enjoy the memories of his life." The fact that the repast was held at the community center and not the church fellowship hall or the funeral parlor exemplifies the shift from mourning to celebration. In addition, her statement that the repast, inclusive to wearing the R.I.P. t-shirts, is the attempt at happiness also illustrates a purposeful shift to a happy celebration. Even more, the R.I.P. t-shirt, then, can be the catalyst for a shift from mourning the absence to remembering the presence and the happy memories shared. Jason Shorter, the beloved cousin of Cozetta, was killed by a drunk driver in 2017. The mourning surrounding his death was deep and sorrowful, which is why, as illustrated in figure 11.5, the repast gave the Shorter family strength through nourishment as well as through fellowship to take a step toward life after death. The repast was a true celebration where the Shorters saw Jason not in a casket but on each other's shirts, close to their hearts.

R.I.P. t-shirts illustrate the celebratory nature that comes with creating events where the purpose is to speak about and share in the life of the deceased to invoke smiles and laughter. Due to this, the shirts are often worn in association with *living* events, events where life is celebrated. In this way, postmortem birthdays are celebrated where attendees don R.I.P. t-shirts or newly created postmortem birthday shirts. In figure 11.5, Cozetta and her family celebrate Jason's first postmortem birthday by

Figure 11.5. *The Shorter family memorializing the passing and celebrating the life of Jason Shorter. The top picture is at the repast—Jason Shorter's mother (in the middle), father (in the white baseball cap), and Jason's cousins. The bottom picture is Jason's first postmortem birthday celebration, complete with birthday cake (as pictured). Photos by Cozetta Phillips.*

Figure 11.6. *Posing for a picture after bowling, Willie's family celebrates his first postmortem birthday. The day included a balloon release at the cemetery, bowling, and a celebration at a dance hall with a DJ and live music. Family members are shown presenting a hand sign to sign the letter "L," meaning "Long Live Chill." This is an expression used to invoke Willie's memory and never forget his life. Photo by Aleta "Snooky" Fletcher.*

wearing his R.I.P. t-shirt and even having birthday cake and a celebratory birthday meal.

Cousin Kendra wore Willie's R.I.P. t-shirt to his first postmortem birthday party. His mother Snooky commissioned the birthday shirts and organized an entire day of events, starting with a balloon release at the cemetery, followed by bowling, and ending at a dance hall with a DJ and live music. Songs were played in Willie's honor, including original raps from his burgeoning rap career with Fam Squad.[9] Partygoers even toasted Willie and surely remembered times when he frequented the dance hall—perhaps recounting his usual rounds, where he would sit, and how he would party. Postmortem birthdays are memorials to the dead but also celebrations using the actions of the living, and so they are meant to remember the good times and also to give a "second life" to the deceased. Journalist Jasmine Sanders wrote about how Quentin Harris uses his brother Julian's deathversary (the anniversary of the death) to keep him alive. Julian was murdered in 2010, and Harris says of the celebrations, "It feels like I'm giving him a second life. ... Like he'll never really be gone, as long as I can help it."[10] Harris makes a single memorial shirt, a new one every year, for the annual celebration honoring Julian. Due to the fact

Figure 11.7. *Cousin Jakihia clutches the R.I.P. hoodie for her little brother E. J., who passed away in 2007 at only four months old. Cousin Shanicqua (third from the left wearing ripped, knee-less denim blue jeans) dons an unofficial R.I.P. t-shirt for Willie. Her R.I.P. t-shirt features the two of them FaceTiming. The high-resolution picture resulted in the shirt costing fifty dollars. This picture was taken at Jakihia's aunt Carroll's (in the middle wearing the white long-sleeved blouse) fiftieth birthday party. Photo by Shanicqua Wise.*

that (1) Harris was incarcerated and unable to make the funeral and (2) Julian's young children were too young to remember their father, Harris feels like these celebrations are more than just events of remembrance—they're a way for Julian to live again for his children.

R.I.P. t-shirts are central during events like repasts and postmortem birthdays, events for and about the living. In this way, the life of the decedent is celebrated, and they are never forgotten. I observed the wearing of R.I.P. t-shirts created many years prior. For example, during Willie's active mourning period, our cousin Carroll celebrated her fiftieth birthday. As illustrated in figure 11.7, attendees such as cousin Shanicqua donned unofficial R.I.P. t-shirts dedicated to Willie. Further still, cousin Jakihia clutches an R.I.P. hoodie memorializing her little brother E. J. who passed away ten years earlier at the tender age of four months old.

Violent/Gang Deaths and the Origins of R.I.P. T-shirts as African American Mourning Wear

By the 1980s and 1990s, graffiti art culture had emerged as an important part of predominantly Black urban gangs. With canned spray paint, gang members tagged and thereby claimed built landscape—city blocks, sections of neighborhoods, and even certain houses and apartment buildings. These same cans of spray paint were used to create what became urban mourning wear in the form of airbrushed t-shirt art. The fat signature letters were part and parcel of the graffiti art that signified gang life and inevitably gang-related death.[11] HBO's critically acclaimed *Gang War: Bangin' in Little Rock*, released in 1994, showed the connection between graffitied gang territory and mourning rituals. When fifteen-year-old Moses Crawford and fourteen-year-old Cleon Perkins were murdered, one of their fellow gang members was interviewed against the backdrop of a graffiti-covered wall expressing anger, sadness, and confusion. In the next scene the same gang member, still against the same graffitied wall, poured beer—libations, offerings to the dead in memory of the dead—on specific words near the bottom of the graffitied wall. The words "Pouring Beer: Gang ritual for mourning" appeared while he was engaged in this ritual. What is important here are two things: Crawford and Perkins were being publicly acknowledged as ancestors to be honored and remembered, and graffiti was specifically used in the ritual to honor and remember the dead. Scholars such as Michael McNally and Teresa Washington have written about libation in gang culture and mourning rituals, its real and imagined function as Africanism, but they have stopped short of directly or even indirectly identifying graffiti and thereby spray paint as part of expressive gang mourning culture.[12] As an expressive gang-mourning cultural signifier, spray paint has brought ephemeral honor to public memorial—marking the life and remembering the spirit.

Spray paint helped gang members create their identity in life and death. Examining the sixty-eight pieces of gang paraphernalia included in David Koon and Kaya Herron's "Bangin' in the '90s: An Oral History of the Little Rock Gang Wars" shined a very important light on the ways in which gang members used variations of the popular airbrush art form to design clothing expressing gang life and death.[13] Creatively designed t-shirts displayed the gang's name, geographical area, and individual member's gang name. For example, one t-shirt was designed with the number twenty-one drawn to resemble dripping blood, representing the twenty-first street gang and signifying the gang's perceived ruthlessness. Another t-shirt featured a drawing of a male wearing multiple gold and diamond necklaces, gun holster at his side. Around him in calligraphy-styled cursive writing was the text "West End Soldiers." Yet another t-shirt was dedicated to a fallen gang member—a large image of an open and empty casket was drawn on the back of the t-shirt with the words "HighlandPark/Rest in Peace Baby Doll." A single rose was outlined on the casket's lid. Within this expressive art form, gang members carved out life and called attention to the death in their communities. These early iterations of R.I.P. t-shirts suggested that the shirt was used to grieve and remember slain members but not necessarily to create a memorial for general public engagement. These early iterations of R.I.P. t-shirts expressed their confusion and pain and became a way for them to cry.

R.I.P. t-shirts were interspersed with gang life in many ways, showing how death was part of it, not separate, for its members. Members utilized the very art that helped them illustrate life and how they should live it (i.e. by being tough, carrying guns, and wearing expensive jewelry). Gang-related death, on the other hand, was illustrated by an emptiness, with empty coffins and generic rest in peace language. In this early stage of the R.I.P. t-shirt, perhaps the emptiness signaled raw grief and mourning instead of memorialization and the preservation of memories. As seen in the case of Crawford and Perkins, gang brothers poured libations on graffitied walls for fallen members, engaging with a public memorial meant for those *inside* their community. Their community loved them, honored them, and made sure they were never forgotten.

Through expressive graffiti and airbrush art, gang members were able to grapple with the onslaught of peer death that perhaps they themselves did not fully understand while simultaneously using the art to call direct attention to their grief and signal that they were actively mourning. These were kids, teenagers, and young men, all under the age of twenty-four, who were dying from a culture of gun violence undergirded by the poverty, failing schools, and joblessness disproportionate in their communities. Between 1990 and 1993 the homicide rate doubled for Black males aged fifteen to nineteen.[14] How does anyone, let alone children and youth, make sense of these deaths? But the collective Black American experience with death has historically been what cultural scholar Karla Holloway described as "mournful collectives … in disconcerting circumstances," meaning that systematic racism underlies African American death.

A culture that was faced with unprecedented violence learned to express its young self through expressive R.I.P. t-shirts, which were accessible and expressive in ways that these young people seemingly could never be. The confusion they felt around this onslaught of death in their lives was illustrated when the *Gang War: Bangin' in Little Rock* filmmakers highlighted fifteen-year-old Robert Tenpenny Jr's suicide. Unclear whether he was a fully initiated gang member like his two older brothers, Tenpenny's mother told filmmakers that shortly before taking his own life, he told her, "Mama, I am so tired of it [gangbanging]. ... I don't know what to do. ... It just don't make no sense." While she talked and her words lingered, the documentary showed two young female teens walking down the street from Tenpenny's home, with one wearing a t-shirt reading "In Memory of Robert." Both awkwardly smiled as they threw gang signs, looking back to see if the camera was still rolling. Perhaps Tenpenny was right; he and his young peers just did not know what to do. They were immersed in a gang life that normalized violent gang-related death but had little to say for processing this death—the volume, the continuous mourning. Ultimately, the R.I.P. t-shirt became a way for these youth to grieve.

R.I.P. t-shirts, arguably rooted in gang mourning culture, transformed to become part of the wider burgeoning hip-hop culture of the 1980s and 1990s. When actor and West Coast rapper Tupac Shakur was murdered in 1996 and East Coast rapper Notorious B.I.G. was murdered six months later in March 1997, R.I.P. t-shirts dedicated to their lives and mourning their deaths could be seen nationwide. By the 1990s, R.I.P. t-shirts, now visible via Hip-hop culture, were not only to memorialize fallen gang members but for any African Americans who wanted to memorialize a loved one. What must be remembered is that fallen gang members were missed and mourned by non-gang-affiliated blood relatives and friends who too adorned the R.I.P. t-shirts in remembrance. Due to racial profiling and an association of the shirts with direct gang affiliation, there was the possibility that many young Black people who actively engaged in the R.I.P. t-shirt ritual were mistaken as gang members themselves, thereby continuing the idea that the ritual was only practiced among gang members. This borrowing of the R.I.P. t-shirt did not just stop at the youth; friends and family, like my kin, also created a way to actively grieve, announce a state of mourning, and memorialize their loved ones in a way that was accessible and understandable to them.

R.I.P. T-Shirts as Political Statements and Social Messages

Cousin Duke told me how deeply troubled he was by the fact that Willie died right when he was financially prospering, and he linked his wearing of R.I.P. t-shirts to visually showing the senseless crime occurring in the Black community. "You took him and now I want the world to see." Disclosing to me that he has worn too many of the shirts to count, Duke uses his R.I.P. t-shirt as a platform to speak to the world about street violence in his community that disproportionately affects Black youth.[15] Duke saw Willie's death in the context of concentrated violence in his

Black neighborhood. According to an April 2017 newspaper article, there was an uptick in homicides in Pine Bluff the year Willie was murdered—a total of twenty-two persons slain in a city with a population just shy of forty-three thousand. Trisha Rhodes, criminal justice professor at the University of Arkansas at Pine Bluff, pointed out that these homicides did not occur across Pine Bluff but were concentrated in small areas of the city that had what she labeled "recurrent crime problems." Continuous crime is a result of poor and failing school districts, high unemployment, and nonexistent municipal resources in city areas that are predominantly Black.

Crime and a call for law and order have led to the mass incarceration and false imprisonment of thousands of African Americans. This modern-day criminalization was the subject of Michelle Alexander's award-winning book, *The New Jim Crow: Mass Incarceration in the Age of Colorblindness*. Alexander explained how a call for cracking down on crime spawned a host of oppressive laws, such as the 1994 Violent Crime Control Act passed by former Arkansas governor turned US president, Bill Clinton. Nationally, the number of African Americans sent to state and federal prisons in the 1980s and 1990s increased to a high of 53 percent.[16] In Arkansas alone from 1988 to 1992, the arrests of murder suspects between the ages of eighteen and twenty-four rose by 93 percent; it increased by 256 percent for those under the age of eighteen.[17] In the 1980s and 1990s, African Americans represented 13 percent of the national population but 30 to 40 percent of the prison population.

The public protest against these laws came by way of t-shirt culture. In the 2000s, shirts with the slogan "Free [insert name]" could be seen, a clear demand for falsely accused loved ones to be exonerated. Black people's politics in the form of resisting oppressive laws have long found themselves on t-shirts.[18] Systemic inequalities undergird current social movements like Black Lives Matter, #SayHerName and Defund the Police, in which protesters wear shirts of slain African Americans like Breonna Taylor, Trayvon Martin, George Floyd, Sandra Bland, and many others. The spirit of the protests center on police killings of unarmed Black people, systemic oppression in the criminal justice system, among others, but it is the R.I.P t-shirts that function as a political statement, a unifying voice, and a rallying cry for social change.

R.I.P. t-shirts reject the dominant narrative that young African Americans killed from street violence were alone and unattached. Willie and Jason had family and friends who loved them, supported them, and never let them forget it. The stereotype is that these young African Americans were just thrown away to the streets, left to suffer and die due to their own mischief and misgivings. The shirt is a constant reminder that not only was this person loved and seen as welcomed by immediate and extended family but also that the death was committed within the larger context of the oppressed Black American experience. In this regard, R.I.P. t-shirts reclaim ownership of the decedent because a mainstream white society has labeled him/her thuggish and unsaintly. Therefore, the R.I.P. t-shirts feature pictures of fond memories, reinterpreting the narrative so that it points to these African Americans as good people deserving of a good death.

In the face of street violence tied directly to failing school systems and lack of job opportunities, R.I.P. t-shirts became a way to subvert this stereotypical narrative of so-called black-on-black crime by celebrating the three-dimensional life lived. This was accomplished by including religious sayings and affectionate terms and attaching accoutrements like angel wings to the image of the person. An example can be found in the t-shirts designed for Cozetta's cousin Jason, who was killed by drunk driver, not from street violence—still, at the age of only thirty-eight his life was cut short by death. His angel wings signify his ascent to heaven, and the "2019" along the right side as well as the "SB4LIFE" ground him securely in a family who loves him. The "2019" is their grandparents' address, and SB stands for "Shorter boy"—the family name. Jason was claimed and wanted, and he will be forever remembered with love.

R.I.P. t-shirts show the larger society that African Americans are securely grounded in families and that family members not only love the decedents but also value them. Willie and Jason held special places among their respective families, and they cannot be replaced. For example, Willie's value and specialness is clearly illustrated by cousin Arianna in her explanation of why she commissioned the making of the unofficial shirt pictured in figure 11.3. She said:

> I got it [R.I.P. t-shirt] made with the stars on it because Willie always shines so bright. There never was a dull moment around him, and even when I wasn't in Arkansas, we were always calling and talking on the phone with each other and texting. I will still be smiling from miles away. And I put the words in purple because I feel like he was always so pure like this heart is so pure. And he always spoke truth and was always honest with everything he said and kept his word on everything he did.

Willie was not just some unknown Black male slain in the streets—unloved and unmissed. He was someone Arianna talked to regularly, even though they were thousands of miles apart. She could confide in him. He would lift her spirits and also tell her the truth when she needed to hear it. Through her unofficial R.I.P. t-shirt, she conveyed her direct and specific relationship with Willie.

Conclusion: Further Research

R.I.P. t-shirts serve multiple purposes within the realm of Black public mourning. First, as ritualized mourning wear, the shirts unify wearers in grief while signaling to the public that they are in mourning. Through this creative way, African American mourning culture allows the bereaved to create living memorials where they frequently interact with the deceased. As illustrated in figure 11.1, I was able to take Willie to China. While alive, Willie had never been out of the country before, but through this new afterlife he experienced global travel and a summer of international experiential learning. To that point, both the official and unofficial R.I.P. t-shirts provide mourners with direct and personal avenues to memorialize the decedent so the loved one will not be forgotten. Beyond ritualized mourning wear, R.I.P. t-shirts serve as mourning spaces to help the bereaved, years and years after active mourning, deal with the loss. R.I.P. t-shirts create avenues for healing by memorializing the life of the decedent, placed within the kinship network and larger community. Further still, R.I.P. t-shirts allow room for healing by metaphorically filling the void of the loved one's absence, serving as a second skin to keep the loved one close, and even allowing mourners to fill out the imprint the deceased left with the mourner's own image. R.I.P. t-shirts are part of the expressive culture so present in African American mourning that allows the truth of African American life to be spoken.

As an exploration into grief, mourning, and ritual, this chapter only scratches the surface of analyzing and critically engaging with R.I.P. t-shirt and African American mourning customs. Three immediate areas where scholarship is needed include: (1) young people's role in R.I.P. t-shirt mourning wear; (2) dissenting voices and critical commentary; and (3) R.I.P. t-shirts and connections, direct/indirect or real/imaged, to African death cultural norms, both past and present. Scholarship that looks at the ways in which the youth are dying and how the t-shirt is used to bring awareness and/or give them a voice can be insightful. Putting a generational lens and historical backdrop to youth culture, death, and mourning will allow the R.I.P. t-shirt to be unpacked and comprehended even more. The R.I.P. t-shirt may illustrate how African American mourning culture has become younger and has thereby evolved in the modern twentieth- and twenty-first-century eras.

In addition, carefully contextualizing and respectfully including dissenting voices from within and outside the culture and community may provide a fuller understanding of the R.I.P. t-shirt. It may be important to understand why some question the act of wearing the likeness of the deceased. Thoughtful discussion with dissenters who view the ritual as coming down on the wrong side of the private versus public nature of

American grieving presents another approach to the ritual that could help break down homogeneity.

Last, research that seeks to uncover African roots of the R.I.P. t-shirt can provide important historical context. R.I.P. t-shirts can be both a source and a practice of identifying African American collective consciousness and determining how this consciousness, knowingly or not, is rooted in our mourning practices.

Dr. Kami Fletcher is an associate professor of American and African American history and co-coordinator of Women's and Gender Studies at Albright College. She is also a founding member and president of the Collective for Radical Death Studies, an international professional organization formed to decolonize death studies and radicalize death practice. Dr. Fletcher is the co-editor of *Till Death Do Us Part: American Ethnic Cemeteries as Borders Uncrossed*, which examines the internal and/or external drives among ethnic, religious, and racial groups to separate their dead (University Press of Mississippi, 2020), and is currently working on *Grave History: Death, Race & Gender in Southern Cemeteries from Antebellum to the Post-Civil Rights Era* (University of Georgia Press, forthcoming), which investigates the racial and gendered dynamics present within the southern places where cemeteries take root. For more on Dr. Fletcher visit her website: www.kamifletcher.weebly.com and/or contact her on Twitter using @kamifletcher36.

Notes

This essay would not be possible without the patience and permission of my sister, Aleta "Snooky" Fletcher. I also want to extend my appreciation to my Jenkins family for their tolerance of my questions and their honest answers during this difficult time—may this essay serve as balm for our grief. Last, I extend deep gratitude to my colleagues who read numerous drafts, namely Joy Giguere and Donald Joralemon.

1. To date, the author has only found two full-length scholarly analyses of R.I.P. t-shirts as mourning wear: Katie Kavanaugh O'Neil, "Embodying the Dead: Function and Meaning in RIP T-shirts," in "Mobtown Memories: Towards a People's History of Violence in Baltimore" PhD diss., University of Pittsburgh, 2017, http://d-scholarship.pitt.edu/33033/; Candi Cann, *Virtual Afterlives: Grieving the Dead in the Twenty-First Century* (Louisville: University Press of Kentucky, 2014), 96–104. Journalist Rachel Siegel highlights the enterprising nature of R.I.P. t-shirts, invoking discussion on how the t-shirt business is profiting off grief and loss. She states in her article, "Some scholars trace the shirts' origins to the late 1980s and early 1990s." Readers are left to guess at the identity of "some scholars" even though she sites Katie Kavanaugh's work on R.I.P. t-shirts in Baltimore as well as the popularity of the practice among those mourning the death of Tupac Shakur and Notorious B.I.G. For more, see Rachel Siegel, "Where Gun Violence Abounds, Honoring Loved Ones with 'Rest in Peace' Shirts," *Washington Post,* 10 August 2019. Journalist Jenn

Shreve traces the popular cultural rise of the R.I.P. t-shirt, questioning how an ordinary t-shirt can and did become an important symbol of public mourning. Shreve asks and then answers, "So how did this trend begin? West Coast gangsters are believed to have started the memorial-tee trend in the early '90s as a way to remember slain gang members, most notably among them being rapper Tupac Shakur." Shreve not only suggests that R.I.P. t-shirt ritual is rooted in gang culture but also that it is specific to California and that Tupac was a notable gangster who was memorialized via the t-shirt. For more, see Jenn Shreve "A Fitting Memorial: The Growing Popularity of the Memorial T-shirt," Slate, 26 August 2003, retrieved from https://slate.com/news-and-politics/2003/08/memorial-t-shirts.html. In addition, Tupac represented the West Coast by show of the infamous West Coast hand sign, but by his own accounts he was not affiliated with a street gang. See Chuck Philips, "From the Archives: Tupac Shakur: 'I Am Not a Gangster,'" *Los Angeles Times*, 25 October 1995, retrieved 1 November 2018 from https://www.latimes.com/local/la-me-tupac-qa-story.html. For more examples connecting R.I.P. t-shirts to urban street culture, see Laurence Ralph, "What Wounds Enable: The Politics of Disability and Violence in Chicago," in *Beginning with Disability: A Primer*, edited by Lennard J. Davis (New York: Routledge, 2017), 142–64; Lucas Morgan, "The Memorial T-Shirts of Inner-City America," Seven Ponds blog, 22 October 2019, retrieved 1 November 2018 from https://blog.sevenponds.com/cultural-perspectives/the-memorial-t-shirts-of-inner-city-america; Meredith May, "R.I.P. Shirts Become an Urban Tradition/Mementos Honoring the Dead Now a Religious Ritual, Complete with Their Own Rules of Observance," *San Francisco Gate* 24 October 2004, retrieved 1 November 2018 from https://www.sfgate.com/bayarea/article/R-I-P-shirts-become-an-urban-tradition-2679156.php.
2. Elizabeth Hallam and Jenny Hockey, *Death, Memory and Material Culture* (Oxford: Berg Publishers, 2001).
3. Rhaisa Kameela Williams, "Toward a Theorization of Black Maternal Grief as Analytic," *Journal of the Association of Black Anthropologists* 24, no. 1 (2016): 17–30.
4. Katie Kavanaugh O'Neil, "Mobtown Memories: Towards a People's History of Violence in Baltimore," PhD diss., University of Pittsburgh, 2017, Retrieved 1 November 2018 from http://d-scholarship.pitt.edu/33033/.
5. Ibid.
6. Peter Stallybrass, "Worn Worlds: Clothes, Mourning, and the Life of Things," *Yale Review* 81, no. 2 (1993): 35–50.
7. Pennina Barnett, "Cloth, Memory and Loss," in *Art Textiles of the World: Great Britain*, vol. 2, ed. Jennifer Harris (Manchester: Whitworth Art Gallery, 2015), 24–31.
8. Ibid.
9. Fam Squad is the rap group composed of Willie and his cousins Jonathan, Corey, and Timothy and their close friend Jarren. For more, see their Facebook page: https://www.facebook.com/famsquadhhh.
10. Jasmine Sanders, "Memorial T-Shirts Create a Little Justice, a Tiny Peace," *New York Times*, 14 November 2017, retrieved 1 October 2018 from https://www.nytimes.com/2017/11/14/style/memorial-t-shirts.html.
11. Harald Myer-Delius, "The Airbrushed T-Shirt: A History of Hip-Hop and Mourning," 11 February 2016, retrieved 1 October 2018 from https://blog.printsome.com/airbrushed-t-shirt/.
12. For examples, see Teresa Washington, *Manifestations of Masculine Magnificence: Divinity in Africana Life, Lyrics, and Literature* (United States: Oya's Tornado, 2014); Michael McNally, *Ojibwe Singers: Hymns, Grief, and a Native Culture in Motion* (St. Paul: Minnesota Historical Society Press, 2009).
13. David Koon and Kaya Herron, "Bangin' in the '90s: An Oral History," *Arkansas Times*, 16 July 2015, retrieved 1 November 2018 from https://arktimes.com/news/cover-stories/2015/07/16/bangin-in-the-90s-an-oral-history.
14. Ibid.

15. Dale Ellis, "Pine Bluff Police Tackle Killings as City Looks to Rebuild," *Arkansas Democrat Gazette*, 10 April 2017, retrieved 1 November 2018 from https://www.arkansasonline.com/news/2019/apr/10/pb-police-tackle-killings-as-city-looks/.
16. Human Rights Watch, "Punishment and Prejudice: Racial Disparities in the War on Drugs," vol. 2, no. 2G (2000), retrieved 1 November 2018 from https://www.hrw.org/legacy/reports/2000/usa/Rcedrg00-01.htm#P163_27221.
17. Koon and Herron, "Bangin' in the '90s."
18. Cynthia Greenlee, "How Statement T-Shirts Unite Black History, Culture, and Fashion," *Elle*, 2 March 2018, retrieved 1 November 2018 from https://www.elle.com/fashion/a18921564/black-history-culture-statement-t-shirt/.

Bibliography

Barnett, Pennina. "Cloth, Memory and Loss." In *Art Textiles of the World: Great Britain*, vol. 2, edited by Jennifer Harris, 24–31. Manchester: Whitworth Art Gallery, 2015.

Bonnell, Daniel. *Shadow Lessons: The Unexpected Journey of an Inner City Art Teacher*. Eugene, OR: Resource Publications, 2012.

Britt, Donna, and Amber Stegall. "'RIP' Shirts Have Changed How People Mourn in South Louisiana." WAFB, 10 July 2014. Retrieved 12 August 2019 from https://www.wafb.com/story/25991707/rip-shirts-have-changed-how-people-mourn-in-south-louisiana/.

Cann, Candi K. *Virtual Afterlives: Grieving the Dead in the Twenty-First Century*. Lexington: University Press of Kentucky, 2014.

Ellis, Dale. "Pine Bluff Police Tackle Killings as City Looks to Rebuild." *Arkansas Democrat Gazette*, 10 April 2017. Retrieved 1 November 2018 from https://www.arkansasonline.com/news/2019/apr/10/pb-police-tackle-killings-as-city-looks/.

Ford-Smith, Honor. "Gone but Not Forgotten: Memorial Murals, Vigils, and the Politics of Popular Commemoration in Jamaica." In *At the Limits of Justice: Women of Colour on Terror*, edited by Suvendrini Perera and Sherene Razack, 263–88. Toronto: University of Toronto Press, 2014.

Goggin, Maureen Daly, and Beth Fowkes Tobin. *Women and the Material Culture of Death*. New York: Ashgate Publishing, 2013.

Graves-Brown, Paul, et al. *The Oxford Handbook of the Archaeology of the Contemporary World*. Oxford: Oxford University Press, 2013.

Greenlee, Cynthia. "How Statement T-Shirts Unite Black History, Culture, and Fashion." *Elle*, 2 March 2018. Retrieved 1 November 2018 from https://www.elle.com/fashion/a18921564/black-history-culture-statement-t-shirt/.

Hallam, Elizabeth, and Jenny Hockey. *Death, Memory and Material Culture*. Oxford: Berg Publishers, 2001.

Henry, Vincent E. "Crisis Intervention and First Responders to Events Involving Terrorism and Weapons of Mass Destruction." In *Crisis Intervention Handbook: Assessment, Treatment, and Research*, 4th ed., edited by Kenneth Yeager and Albert Roberts, 214–47. Oxford: Oxford University Press, 2015.

Holloway, Karla. *Passed On: African American Mourning Stories, A Memorial*. Durham, NC: Duke University Press, 2003.

Human Rights Watch. "Punishment and Prejudice: Racial Disparities in the War on Drugs." Vol. 2, no. 2G (2000). Retrieved 1 November 2018 from https://www.hrw.org/legacy/reports/2000/usa/Rcedrg00-01.htm#P163_27221.

Koon, David, and Kaya Herron. "Bangin' in the '90s: An Oral History." *Arkansas Times*, 16 July 2015. Retrieved 4 October 2018 from https://arktimes.com/news/cover-stories/2015/07/16/bangin-in-the-90s-an-oral-history.

May, Meredith. "R.I.P. Shirts Become an Urban Tradition/Mementos Honoring the Dead Now a Religious Ritual, Complete with Their Own Rules of Observance." *San Francisco Gate* 24 October 2004. Retrieved 10 November 2018 from https://www.sfgate.com/bayarea/article/R-I-P-shirts-become-an-urban-tradition-2679156.php.

McNally, Michael. *Ojibwe Singers: Hymns, Grief, and a Native Culture in Motion*. St. Paul: Minnesota Historical Society Press, 2009.

Moore, Jennifer Grayer. *Fashion Fads through American History: Fitting Clothes into Context*. Santa Barbara, CA: Greenwood Publishing Group, 2016.

Morgan, Lucas. "The Memorial T-Shirts of Inner-City America." Seven Ponds blog, 22 October 2019. Retrieved 25 September 2018 from https://blog.sevenponds.com/cultural-perspectives/the-memorial-t-shirts-of-inner-city-america.

Myer-Delius, Harold. "The Airbrushed T-Shirt: A History of Hip-Hop and Mourning," 11 February 2016. Retrieved 1 October 2018 from https://blog.printsome.com/airbrushed-t-shirt/.

O'Neill, Katie Kavanaugh. "Mobtown Memories: Towards a People's History of Violence in Baltimore." PhD diss., University of Pittsburgh, 2017. http://d-scholarship.pitt.edu/33033/.

Philips, Chuck. "From the Archives: Tupac Shakur: 'I Am Not a Gangster.'" *Los Angeles Times*, 25 October 1995. Retrieved 1 November 2018 from https://www.latimes.com/local/la-me-tupac-qa-story.html.

Ralph, Laurence. "What Wounds Enable: The Politics of Disability and Violence in Chicago." In *Beginning with Disability: A Primer*, edited by Lennard J. Davis, 142–64. New York: Routledge, 2017.

Rothstein, Ethan. "Gun Violence Victims Honored with T-Shirt Memorial." *Arlington Now*, 16 September 2014. Retrieved 1 November 2018 from https://www.arlnow.com/2014/09/16/gun-violence-victims-honored-with-t-shirt-memorial/.

Sacasa, Edwin, and Alain Maridue. *Shirt Kings: Pioneers of Hip Hop Fashion*. Årsta: Dokument Press, 2013.

Sanders, Jasmine. "Memorial T-Shirts Create a Little Justice, a Tiny Peace." *New York Times*, 14 November 2017. Retrieved 1 November 2018 https://www.nytimes.com/2017/11/14/style/memorial-t-shirts.html.

Shreve, Jenn. "A Fitting Memorial: The Growing Popularity of the Memorial T-shirt." *Slate*, 26 August 2003. Retrieved 1 November 2018 from https://slate.com/news-and-politics/2003/08/memorial-t-shirts.html.

Siegel, Rachel. "Where Gun Violence Abounds, Honoring Loved Ones with 'Rest in Peace' Shirts." *Washington Post*, 10 August 2019. Retrieved 1 November 2018 from https://www.washingtonpost.com/business/2019/08/10/mass-shootings-everyday-grief-honoring-loved-ones-with-rest-peace-shirts/?noredirect=on.

Stallybrass, Peter. "Worn Worlds: Clothes, Mourning, and the Life of Things." *Yale Review* 81, no. 2 (1993): 35–50.

Ward, Jason Morgan. "'A Monument to Judge Lynch': Racial Violence, Symbolic Death, and Black Resistance in Jim Crow Mississippi." In *Death and the American South*, edited by Craig Friend and Lorri Glover, 229–49. New York: Cambridge University Press, 2014.

Washington, Teresa. *Manifestations of Masculine Magnificence: Divinity in Africana Life, Lyrics, and Literature*. United States: Oya's Tornado, 2014.

Williams, Rhaisa Kameela. "Toward a Theorization of Black Maternal Grief as Analytic." *Journal of the Association of Black Anthropologists* 24, no. 1 (2016): 17–30.

Conclusion

Kalliopi M Christodoulaki and Aubrey Thamann

In the chapters of this volume, researchers have provided their connections to dying and death and discussed how these connections have impacted their study. We have tried to place our experiences into the text as a means to better understand the beliefs, feelings, and behaviors of the people we are studying and, at times, to challenge our original position. During our research, we discovered that there was interplay in the field between the subjects of our study and ourselves, and we acted as both objective scientists and emotional human beings. A fluidity exists between the researcher and the researched, as we discovered—at times we were student, teacher, observer, observed, kin, stranger, fan, mourner, death tourist, and author. We recognized our role in the descriptions we set forward in this text, and we encourage each reader to synthesize the information covered in this book using interpretations shaped by their experiences, personality, and culture (which happens inevitably), just as our interpretations were shaped by these factors as well.

We wanted to bring emotion into the study of mortuary practices, for as Renato Rosaldo states, "Most ethnographic descriptions of death stand at a peculiar distance from the obviously intense emotions expressed, and they turn what for the bereaved are unique and devastating losses into routine happenings."[1] These are not routine experiences for the bereaved within these chapters, which is something we discovered when repositioning ourselves to see another vantage point. What we found was that the researchers are not unaffected by their experiences. Death made us question our life and, in these studies, our research.

We begin this book with people becoming aware of their mortality when faced with the likelihood of their impending death. They fear death, in part, because of the emotional pain it causes. For it is with death that important relationships are often thought to end.[2] This fear makes individuals search for ways to avoid it, much like the women studied by

Alison Witchard, who underwent surgery, and the immortalists, studied by Jeremy Cohen, who actively focus on ways to extend their life and escape death. In both chapters, people want to stay alive, as they tell the researchers—not for selfish reasons but to maintain social connections. For the women in Witchard's chapter, it is to "be around" for their family. For the immortalists in Cohen's chapter, it is to maintain a connection to the community, a connection required if one is to become immortal. Reflexivity assisted both researchers in appreciating the motivations of their research subjects. Witchard was able to sympathize with those undergoing an invasive procedure in order to be present for one's family, drawing from her experience with her grandmother's death. Cohen better understood the immortalists' desire for unending life while watching his great-uncle die. In both cases, we see an ongoing desire to live, to avoid death, or at the very least to push it as far into the future as one can.

What happens when that future is evident? Carina Nandlal and Kalliopi M Christodoulaki both focus on the importance of caring for loved ones at the end of their life. The impending loss, which manifested in both a physical and mental decline, is clearly personal, and both researchers use the past and the present to focus on the connections that they created with the people they love. Caregiving, while emotionally demanding and socially isolating, gives an opportunity to find ways to cope by sharing activities with the afflicted, reaching out to others for support, and simply spending time with those at the end of their lives. Performance of duties, whether as a caregiver, relative, or community member, helps bring people together during a time when those who are coming to terms with a loss can only focus on their own pain. Both Nandlal and Christodoulaki found that their experiences with caregiving helped them grow emotionally and philosophically. In some ways, death was accepted. It became, as Nandlal writes, "comprehensible." It was during these times as caregivers that positive memories were created to help soften the negative ones. Together both caregiver and terminal patient confronted the inevitability of death.

Fear of death and fear of emotions are again discussed in both Aubrey Thamann's and Ekkehard Coenen's chapters. Funeral directors help the bereaved cope with these fears at private consultations and during funerals, which bring grieving people together to create a community. Duty is also evident in these chapters, just as it was in Nandlal's and Christodoulaki's; Thamann feels tied to family members who have passed away, to perform for them, to honor them. She, as Coenen also discovered, found that funeral directors perform as well. They focus on their duties to the deceased and the bereaved and thus avoid displays of emotion, wanting the funeral process to go smoothly for those present. Here, funeral directors and ethnographers both try to control their emotions to perform well in their professions. After their experiences in the field, Thamann and Coenen have come to understand the funeral director's central role in performing so that others can get through the complexities of death in places where mortuary practices have moved from the family home to the funeral home.

Sarah Nytroe learned how religious rituals can ease experiences with death while interviewing her grandparents about the loss of their son. Catholic rituals that were performed made him part of the Catholic community and provided his parents with practices and beliefs that created a bond to the child they lost. Nytroe found that she could balance her personal connection to those she interviewed with objective scholarly work to create a more nuanced study of Catholic practices so as to better understand how these practices along with ideas of a "good death" provide comfort to those individuals coping with a loss.

While for some the funeral is the end of a public connection to the deceased, for others it is only the beginning. People maintain ties to the dead, receive support from others when they grieve, and search for outlets to express their feelings about the deceased or about death in a variety of ways. They may do this during memorial services (Christodoulaki, Nytroe, Hanson, and Moore) or by using artifacts, actual and virtual, that stand as reminders of the dead (Hanson, Guntarik and Bellote, Moore, and Fletcher). Several chapters discuss memorialization and how it is used to negotiate the deceased's memory and their connection to the bereaved.

Debbie Hanson's study of fans and teammates memorializing baseball legend Harmon Killebrew was a way for her to honor the dead while remembering the past. By memorializing him in this book, she does what those she is studying are doing: highlighting an emotional connection to Killebrew and the Minnesotan social values that he exemplified. It is an account of how a community of fans, including Hanson, came together to connect online and in person through Killebrew in order to discuss an idealized past and the desired social values that are thought to be presently lacking.

Similarly, Olivia Guntarik and Claudia Bellote's study shows that private mourning and public mourning are now being done online. Humans are, as Guntarik and Bellote say, "'mediating' the line between life and death." People write the deceased directly. They create spaces to remember the deceased. Teenagers post funeral selfies. All of these are new mediums of connecting to the departed. These forms of online memorialization allow the researchers to access the good and bad aspects that exist in internet memorials of the deceased. While many find support, others must deal with trolls, who disagree with the way others mourn the dead. Both memorializers and trolls work to maintain or alter the memories of the decedents, showing the researchers that online memorials and memories are constantly shifting.

The complications of different views of mourning and memorialization are also the focus of Rebecca Moore's study of the Jonestown memorials. After all, as Moore asks, who should speak for the dead? What connection to the deceased is more valid? She comes to the conclusion that by embracing multiple perspectives and by challenging the definition of "us," of insider and outsider, while remembering that bereavement is personal, one may better understand the study associated with death. Mourners have different perspectives and different agendas in how they memorialize the dead. People who lost others in Jonestown search for a connection to those who died and to others suffering from a similar loss. There is a faction that wants to humanize the dead, to focus on their life, and another that wants to focus on the atrocities associated with their death.

Kami Fletcher's work shows how the African American community tries to emphasize the life of the deceased. It is an intimate look at the death of young Black American men and the ways they are mourned within their families and communities, with family members and friends deciding how best to represent them on R.I.P. t-shirts. These forms of art and clothing become walking memorials to individuals who are often discounted by the larger society, and show that the deceased mattered and are mourned. Fletcher has experienced these practices as a participant and as a researcher, and she gives us insight into the wearing of R.I.P. t-shirts through both her insider view and her academic perspective.

All the researchers in this edited volume have written stories of dying and death. For some, the story is that of a horror best avoided. For others, there are obligations that must be met. Yet others find it as a means to a metamorphosis. Our connection to dying or death has elucidated what our research subjects were dealing with, and therefore we, as researchers, have come to understand an aspect of our study with more clarity. In some cases, the impact is personal; it has changed us as people. Michael Lambek writes, "Anthropology is a vocation, I tell my undergraduate students when I'm playing the enchanter, in which work and life form a unified whole. Anthropological labour is (relatively) unalienated; fieldwork is a chunk of one's life, not a hole in it, and a part of growing up."[3] Several researchers experienced this while in the field. Professionally, Jeremy Cohen ended up "getting it" when he came to understand the people he was studying and realized that empathy is crucial to good ethnographic work; he was able to empathize with a desire to live when faced with someone close to death. Alison Witchard came to appreciate on a personal level why a woman would go through an invasive procedure in order to live, as her grandmother underwent surgical interventions to help her live just a bit longer. Kalliopi M Christodoulaki was able to understand the people she was studying and their emotions and motivations when she experienced events that forced her to challenge her feelings and beliefs. She decided that, for her, the people to hold closest are those who will be there during those final moments, as she was for her grandmother. Aubrey Thamann felt like "a real anthropologist" during her experiences in the field. She was able to use her role as a researcher and a mourner to understand funeral directors and to process her experiences with the death of those she cared about. Ekkehard Coenen learned the language and posture of detachment crucial to the performance of funeral directors, only to have to translate that language for his readers. He has moved from being a student to a researcher, participating as Thamann did in the funeral process. Olivia Guntarik and Claudia Bellote visited online grief sites and also created a digital memorial to a deceased parent. This shift from observers to participants enabled them to engage with the positives and negatives of the digital afterlife and to understand the fluidity of memories and the ways individuals cope with death.

Death is a loss, but it can also be used to signify the importance of life and the connection we have to others, and eventually—hopefully—it can allow us to make sense out of that loss. Ned H. Cassem writes, "Encounters with death and the dying, although often involving sorrow and tragedy, frequently serve as reminders of the preciousness of life. Reflection on death may often serve to italicize the value of time and life itself."[4] We have tried to participate in that reflection. Throughout this book we have witnessed people coming together during those moments of loss and creating ties to life. Whether it is with family, friends, funeral directors, religious organizations, social networks created online, or in person, people process death often by reaching out to others. We are able to understand dying and death because of what we have been told about both and our experiences with each. It is during the times of loss that we may need to reaffirm what we have learned and to reconnect to life and the living.

We write this chapter in the middle of a global pandemic, and some of the saddest stories we have found are those in which people die away from their loved ones. There are accounts of people being buried in the clothes that they died in, of body bags lining hospital halls or being crammed into refrigerated trucks, of small funerals, and of inadequate good-byes. To die is to be human, but we would like to have something that we can control—if not for us, we tell ourselves, then for the person we will lose or the person we have lost. Some people have pushed death onto others; they will die, not us. Yet others see death looming over them and their loved ones daily. We all have tried to adapt by balancing thoughts of dying and death with those of living and life while we wait to see what the future holds. If we were to offer any insight into all of this, we may simply suggest the Latin phrase *memento mori*.

When we lose our friends let us submit ourselves to the order of the universe as we ourselves will submit to it when it sees fit to dispose of us. Let us accept without despair the decree of Fate which condemns them in the same way that we ourselves will accept it without resistance when it is pronounced against us. The duties of burial are not the final duties of friends. The earth that has been disturbed will settle over your lover's ashes but your soul will retain all his sensibility.[5]

Kalliopi M Christodoulaki is a cultural anthropologist and independent researcher currently working as a limited term lecturer at Purdue University. She received her doctorate in anthropology from Purdue University in 2010, and her dissertation research focused on gender roles, community identity, and value systems on the island of Karpathos in Greece. Her research interests include religious practices, social identity, and cultural change.

Aubrey Thamann is an American studies scholar and anthropologist. She received her doctorate from Purdue University in 2016. Her dissertation was an ethnographic study of funeral directors in Indiana, focusing on the social role they play in offering us the much-needed shared experience of collective grief in the funeral. An interdisciplinary scholar at heart, Thamann has begun research into the fields of fat studies and food studies, specifically exploring where these fields intersect.

Notes

1. Renato Rosaldo, *Culture & Truth: The Remaking of Social Analysis* (Boston: Beacon Press, 1993), 57.
2. This is dependent on the spiritual and cultural beliefs of the individuals involved. In the first two chapters, those studied believe that relationships end upon death.
3. Michael Lambek, "Afterword: Our Subjects/Ourselves: A View from the Back Seat," in *Auto-Ethnographies: The Anthropology of Academic Practices*, ed. Anne Meneley and Donna J. Young (Ontario: Broadview Press, 2005), 237.
4. Ned H. Cassem, "Bereavement as Indispensable for Growth," in *Bereavement: Its Psychosocial Aspects*, ed. Bernard Schoenberg, Irwin Gerber, Alfred Wiener, Austin H. Kutscher, David Peretz, Arthur C. Carr, with editorial assistance of Lillian G. Kutscher (New York: Columbia University Press, 1975), 15.
5. Denis Diderot, *Jacques the Fatalist* (New York: Penguin Books, 1986 [1796]), 60.

Bibliography

Cassem, Ned H. "Bereavement as Indispensable for Growth." In *Bereavement: Its Psychosocial Aspects*, edited by Bernard Schoenberg, Irwin Gerber, Alfred Wiener, Austin H. Kutscher, David Peretz, Arthur C. Carr, with editorial assistance of Lillian G. Kutscher, 9–17. New York: Columbia University Press, 1975.

Diderot, Denis. *Jacques the Fatalist*. Translated by Michael Henry. New York: Penguin Books, 1986 [1796].

Lambek, Michael. "Afterword: Our Subjects/Ourselves: A View from the Back Seat." In *Auto Ethnographies: The Anthropology of Academic Practices*. Edited by Anne Meneley and Donna J. Young, 229–240. Ontario: Broadview Press, 2005.

Rosaldo, Renato. *Culture & Truth: The Remaking of Social Analysis*. Boston: Beacon Press, 1993.

Index

A
Aboriginal Australians, 171
absent bodies, 193
abuse, 177–78
adolescents, 172
African American, 33, 159, 188, 190, 192, 195, 200, 209, 210, 213, 217, 225, 226, 227. *See also* Black people
    church, 201
    collective consciousness, 229
    community, 211, 216, 238
    death, 216, 224
    funeral rituals, 201, 215
    grief, 211
    mourning culture, 8, 209, 211, 218, 223, 228
    social and cultural values, 213
    women, 188, 200
afterlife, 76, 79, 93, 134, 138, 140, 141, 180–82, 217, 228, 239
airbrush, 218
    t-shirt art, 223
    art form, 223–24
"Amazing Grace," 92, 99, 100
anger, 3, 6, 40, 79, 82, 93, 100, 127, 160, 172, 173, 178, 189, 198, 202, 223. *See also* rage
anointing of the sick, 134
anthropologist, 1, 39, 41, 45, 103, 104, 126, 188, 212, 239
anthropology, 1, 5, 15, 30, 42, 113, 187, 189, 203, 238
    of death, 44–45
anti-aging, 32–33
anticult groups, 195

anxiety, 18, 29, 34, 36–37, 40, 41, 45, 91–92, 189, 190
Ariès, Philippe, 94, 113
art, 218–19, 223–24, 238
atheists, 181, 201
Australia, 7, 14, 16, 19, 33, 53, 57, 178
authenticity, 189
autoethnographic, 110

B
Bach, Johann Sebastian, 61–62
Baltimore, 153, 215
    Catechism, 128, 137
bereavement, 2, 5, 7, 18, 59, 83, 109–10, 112–14, 117, 120, 127, 171, 173, 189–90, 192, 203, 238
Black Lives Matter, 226
Black people, 8, 33, 179, 211–13, 223, 225–28, 238. *See also* African American
    church, 201
    community, 200, 215, 225–26
    funerary traditions, 192, 200–1
    youth, 225
blood, 98, 101, 102, 138, 189, 213, 218, 223, 225
bowel cancer. *See under* cancer
breast cancer. *See under* cancer
BRCA mutation, 14–16, 19
Brown, Bernadeane, 32, 34, 37
Brown, Charles, 32, 34
burial, 59, 71, 78–80, 110–11, 113–14, 119–20, 130–31, 133, 139–40, 173, 192, 195, 201, 240
    green, 31

C

California, 33, 177, 188, 192, 230
cancer, 13–26, 34, 35, 96, 105, 160
    bowel, 13, 19
    breast, 6, 14, 16–17, 19–21
    esophageal, 90, 104, 151
    hereditary, 14–15, 18–19, 22, 24
    lung, 131
    ovarian, 6, 14, 17, 26
    pancreatic, 90
    prevention, 14
caregiver, 7, 34, 55, 58–59, 71, 75, 236
caregiving, 6, 53–55, 58, 64, 70, 83, 170, 173, 176, 236
casket, 31, 76, 77, 92, 97, 100, 102, 112, 116, 131, 139, 215, 219, 224
Catholicism, 128, 132, 136, 142
Caucasian, 33, 101. *See also* white
cemetery, 31, 76, 83, 111–18, 139–40, 168, 188, 191–92, 194–96, 198, 200, 203, 221
childhood, 24, 56, 105, 128–29, 157, 162, 212
Christian, 80, 100, 181, 201
clergy, 73, 112, 125, 134
code-switching, 103
commemoration, 7, 154, 181–82, 201
communitas, 90, 95–96, 98, 97, 100, 104, 106
coping, 172–173, 237
corpse, 2, 74, 75, 76, 78, 113, 114, 116, 117, 118, 119, 120, 174, 190, 193
cremation, 4, 113, 192, 201
crime, 93, 116, 225–27
crying, 3, 55, 73, 74, 75, 83, 84, 96, 101, 112, 116
cryonics, 39
cult, 34, 39, 42, 45, 170, 191
Cult Awareness Network, 195
curse, 19, 20, 73, 74
cybershrine, 7–8, 151, 157, 160, 161. *See also* shrine

D

death denial, 31, 36, 38, 40, 44, 45, 94, 173, 213, 216
death management, 53, 55–56
death phobia, 21, 91
death positive, 31, 36, 42–44
deathversary, 221
dehumanize, 193
Delaware, 188, 190–93
dementia, 7, 53–61, 64, 96, 105
depression, 58, 60, 92–93, 105, 172–73
Derrida, Jacques, 21–22, 31
despair, 55, 58, 240
digital afterlife, 181–82, 239
digital cemeteries, 7, 168. *See also* cybershrine
digital culture, 179–180
digital humanities, 175
digital memorial, 167, 239. *See also* cybershrine
digital mourning sites, 173, 175–77, 180
digital remembrance, 167
digital technologies, 169–71, 174, 176, 179–80
disability, 153
disease, 17, 34–35, 53, 61, 133
disgust, 6, 94, 117, 121, 174, 178
distress, 35, 54–55
Douglas, Mary, 190
duty, 70, 72, 77, 84, 199, 236, 240. *See also* obligation; responsibility

E

elder, 54, 56, 75, 77
eldercare, 7
embalming, 89, 94, 97, 100, 101–5, 190
Emergency Relief Committee, 191, 201
Emerson, Ralph Waldo, 94–95
emic, 41, 188, 204
empathy, 7, 30, 37, 41–43, 45, 58, 64, 238
esophageal cancer. *See under* cancer
ethics, 36, 46, 76, 197–98
ethnographic, 2, 5, 14, 36, 40, 41, 42, 89, 91, 98, 109, 126, 203, 235, 238
ethnography, 6, 41, 42, 110, 187
etic, 188, 204
Evergreen Cemetery, 188, 191, 192, 194–96, 198, 200, 201, 203
extreme unction, 131, 134, 138

Index

F
Facebook, 174, 177–79, 217
faith, 60, 105, 125–35, 137–42
fate, 29, 35, 181, 240
fear, 6, 17, 18, 21–23, 35–38, 40, 42–45, 53, 55, 60, 73–74, 78, 82–83, 91–93, 99, 109, 179, 190, 235–36. *See also* terror
fieldwork, 89, 120
Freud, Sigmund, 5, 40
funeral, 3, 4, 69, 76–81, 84, 89–90, 92–94, 96, 98–100, 102–5, 110–14, 118–21, 130, 133, 139, 154, 167–68, 174–76, 180, 201, 209, 211, 214–15, 219, 222, 236–37, 239
funeral director, 1, 4, 7, 31, 89–91, 94–100, 102–6, 110–14, 117–21, 218, 236–37, 239
funeral home, 94, 99, 105, 110, 113–15, 118–21, 131, 139, 173, 219, 237
funeral industry, 4, 7, 31, 99, 109, 111, 114–15, 118, 121
funerary ritual, 2–4, 96, 98–99, 112, 131, 133, 139–40, 201–2

G
gang culture, 211, 213, 223–5, 230
gang members, 211, 223–5, 230
gang-related death, 211, 223–5
Geertz, Clifford, 24, 41
gene mutation, 14–16
Germany, 32, 110, 111
Goffman, Erving, 100, 103
good death, 7, 73, 125, 128, 135, 227, 237
grave, 77, 79, 112, 116, 120, 131, 140, 168, 182, 193, 195
Greece, 9, 69–70, 72–73, 80–81, 85
Greek, 75–76, 80–83
Greek Orthodox, 76
grief tourism, 8, 168, 169, 170, 180
  digital, 169
guilt, 3, 35–36, 55, 72, 93, 100
Guyana, 188, 190, 191, 201

H
haunted, 18, 20, 43, 113
health, 16, 26, 33, 38–40, 42, 53, 55, 58, 60, 74, 92, 135, 137, 190
heaven, 39, 97, 134, 139, 140, 181, 214, 227
Heidegger, Martin, 22, 29, 31, 36
hell, 134, 139, 178
helplessness, 74, 77, 172, 179
hereditary cancer. *See under* cancer
hero, 154, 156, 158, 198
homegoing, 219
honoring, 194, 221
horror, 174, 238
horror films, 90, 91, 116
hospice, 105, 153
hospital, 25, 29, 31, 34, 72–75, 89, 94, 101, 116, 129, 130, 137–40, 153, 213, 239
humanity, 32, 58, 60, 174, 176, 192–3, 199
humanize, 195, 238
humor, 119, 121

I
identity, 7, 9, 22–23, 58, 60, 69–70, 79, 85, 125, 126, 128–30, 137, 172, 223
idol, 158
illness, 6–7, 16, 54–55, 58, 61, 69, 72, 84. *See also* sick
Ilongot, 4–5, 38, 127, 188–89, 204
immortal, 29–45, 236
immortality, 6, 22, 29–45
Indiana, 7, 89
inequality, 190
insider, 41, 42, 188, 203, 210, 238
Instagram, 174
interdisciplinary, 1, 4
intersubjective, 22, 41, 42, 43, 135, 136, 140, 142
isolation, 55, 132, 177

J
Jewish, 191
Jim Crow, 226
jokes, 95, 96, 106, 119
Jones, Jim, 188, 194, 195, 196, 198, 199, 200, 203
Jonestown, 187–204
Jonestown Memorial Fund, 195, 203

K

Karpathos, 69, 77, 80
keepsake, 173, 174
Killebrew, Harmon, 7, 151–162, 237
Knights of Columbus, 100, 107n24, 140
Kübler-Ross, Elizabeth, 95

L

last breath, 75
laughter, 16, 71, 104, 105, 158, 219
layman, 114
legacy, 21, 79, 151, 159–61, 182, 210
Legacy.com, 157–59
legitimacy, 174, 176, 178, 189, 194, 212
Lévinas, Emmanuel, 22, 31
life extension, 6, 29, 32
liminality, 90, 95, 98, 102–3
longevity, 6, 29, 31–34, 37, 42, 45, 215
lung cancer. *See under* cancer
Lutheran, 129, 132

M

marginalized, 109, 213
Mary Pearl Willis Foundation, 195
mass, 59, 100, 129–30, 137, 139, 140
mastectomy, 15, 17, 19
meaning of death, 128, 141, 167
media, 154, 168, 171, 177, 180, 193–94, 200
    social, 169, 171–72, 174–76, 181, 215
medical research, 14, 33, 93
medical technologies, 21
Melbourne, 57, 178
memento, 173–75
memento mori, 239
memorabilia, 160
memorial, 1, 69, 79–81, 105, 111–13, 118, 120, 154–60, 178, 188–94, 198, 200–3, 210–12, 215–18, 219, 221, 223–24, 228, 237–38. *See also* digital memorial
memorialization, 3, 7–8, 23, 157, 187–89, 195, 197, 201–3, 209, 215, 217–18, 220–28, 237–38
memory entrepreneur, 194–95, 200
mentor, 1, 90, 104, 121

methodology, 187
Midwest, 128, 133, 153–54
military, 29, 100, 188
mistranslation, 30, 40–41, 44–45
Mitford, Jessica, 104
modernity, 21
monument, 188–89, 191, 193–96, 198, 201–2
morality, 195, 197
morbid, 29, 31, 43
morgue, 209
mortality, 2, 21, 24, 30, 37–40, 42–44, 59, 64, 91, 126, 133, 175, 180, 182, 235
morticians, 104
mortuary practices, 1, 2, 69, 80–81, 98, 235, 237
mourning period, 76, 211, 222
murder, 111, 177–78, 187, 196, 209, 211, 221, 223, 225–26
music therapy, 59

N

necrology, 189, 193, 199
norm, 34, 36, 70, 174, 176, 228
Norwood, Bishop Jynona, 194–202
nostalgia, 171
nursing home, 53, 94, 132

O

obituary, 177, 215, 219
objectivity, 4, 5, 30, 93, 111, 113–14, 118, 125–28, 135–36, 140–41, 187, 235, 237
obligation, 3, 36, 71, 72, 73, 76, 77, 80, 81, 82, 83, 197, 238. *See also* duty; responsibility
omen, 73
online trolls, 8, 169–70, 177. *See also* trolls
oppression, 63, 200, 210, 226
other, 22, 30, 36, 38, 43, 44, 45, 203
outsider, 30, 39–40, 42, 102, 112, 121, 188, 191, 203, 210, 238
ovarian cancer. *See under* cancer
ovaries, 14–20, 24

P

pancreatic cancer. *See under* cancer

Parkinson's disease, 34
participant observation, 14, 32, 40
pastor, 111, 188, 193
Pentecostal black church, 201
People Unlimited, 32–33, 35, 40, 44–45
performance, 25, 36, 37, 57, 69, 80–83, 98–103, 176, 236, 239
performative, 2, 7, 98, 156, 181
period of mourning. *See* mourning period
personal loss, 90, 127–31, 133, 136, 140–42, 198
personhood, 59, 61
Philippines, 5, 127, 189
philosophy, 6, 32
photograph, 92, 95–96, 99–100, 105, 155–57, 161, 167, 169, 173–75, 195, 198, 202–3, 212, 215, 218. *See also* selfie; postmortem photography
Pine Bluff, Arkansas, 209, 226
plaque, 188, 190, 195–96, 198–200, 203
popular culture, 91, 211
postmortem birthdays, 219–22
postmortem photography, 218
power, 24, 38–39, 53, 56, 58, 73, 102, 158, 179, 210–11, 215–16
prayer, 60, 73–74, 105, 125, 130–31, 133, 140, 152, 201
prejudices, 111, 121
priest, 73, 74, 80, 105, 131, 134, 138–40
profane, 98
Protestant, 191
psychological distance, 175
purgatory, 134, 139–40

Q
QR symbol, 203
qualitative research, 41

R
RAADfest, 6, 29, 32–33, 38–45
racial equality, 188
racial profiling, 225
racial sensitivity, 200
racism, 190, 200, 224
rage, 4, 5, 40, 126, 127, 188, 198. *See also* anger
reflexivity, 1, 5, 41, 89, 236

religion, 35–36, 42, 45, 81, 125, 129, 135, 167, 189, 193–94, 201
remembrance, 80, 167, 173, 194–95, 198, 222, 225
responsibility, 36, 39, 40, 44, 77, 94, 130, 139. *See also* duty; obligation
risk-reducing surgery, 6, 14–20
rite of passage, 90, 98, 102–3
Rosaldo, Renato, 2–5, 30, 38, 89–90, 126–27, 141, 187–92, 198, 202–3, 235
rosary, 105, 129–31, 140, 156

S
sacrament, 131, 133–35, 138, 139
sacred, 79, 169
sadness, 6, 56, 74, 83, 94, 112, 115, 217, 223. *See also* sorrow
salpingo-oophorectomy, 6, 15, 20
San Francisco, 188, 191–93, 198, 200
Schechner, Richard, 102–3
Scheper-Hughes, Nancy, 19
Second Vatican Council, 125–26, 130–31, 133–36, 142
selfie, 169, 171–76, 181, 237
shrine, 7, 151, 156–57, 160–61, 167–68, 191–92. *See also* cybershrine
sick, 20, 35, 71–73, 93, 134–35, 137–38, 142. *See also* illness
sin, 74, 93, 138–39
social cohesion, 3, 4, 89, 95. *See also* social solidarity
social conflict, 95
social drama, 95, 98, 102
social justice, 188
social media. *See under* media
social movement, 226
social network, 172, 175–76, 178, 239
social practice, 175–77, 180
social prestige, 69
social solidarity, 2, 4. *See also* social cohesion
sorrow, 3, 63, 100, 133, 217, 219, 239. *See also* sadness
soul, 73–74, 76–77, 79, 81, 83, 101, 138, 140, 240
South Dakota, 129, 133, 155
spectator, 2, 5, 41, 43, 102, 179
spirit, 80, 138, 182, 210, 218, 223

spiritual, 39, 74, 82, 129, 131, 133–34, 138–40, 180–81, 191
status, 40, 42, 77, 80–83, 95, 103
stillborn, 138–39
stress, 35, 58, 103, 110, 112
Strole, James (Jim), 32, 34, 37
stroke, 70–71, 105
subjectivity, 2, 109, 112, 114–15, 121, 126–27, 135–36, 142, 189
suffering, 2, 13, 17, 22–24, 31, 45, 55, 58–61, 63, 75, 93, 96, 105, 112, 116, 169–70, 188–89, 238
suicide, 3, 34–35, 84, 90, 92–93, 100, 105, 187, 224
surgery, 6, 16–17, 20–22, 129, 236
survivors, 93, 96, 113, 117, 187, 192, 194, 198–202
sympathy, 106, 128, 133, 140, 169, 172, 174, 190, 215

T
taboo, 2, 53, 55, 94, 109, 216
theologians, 125
terror 35, 40, 41, 45, 177. *See also* fear
terror management theory, 90, 93
tragedy, 34, 63, 80, 187, 194, 199, 239
transformation, 37, 62, 102–3, 181, 187
transhumanist, 32–33, 36, 43, 46, 46n7, 47n25
trauma, 56, 113, 169, 189, 194, 202, 210
tribute, 154–55, 157–58, 161
trolling, 178
trolls, 8, 170, 177–81, 237. *See also* online trolls

Tumblr, 174
tumor, 16, 21, 25
Turner, Victor, 90, 98–99
twinsguestbook.com, 157–61
Twitter, 174

U
United States, 14, 32, 93–94, 188, 190
universal, 5, 93, 133, 141, 189, 197
universalism, 199
urn, 112, 115

V
van Gennep, Arnold, 192
vegetative state, 71
Venezuelan, 33, 39
victim, 177–79, 187, 189, 193–95, 200
victimization, 177, 187, 200
Victorian, 169, 174, 175, 218
violence, 177, 200, 215, 224–27

W
wake, 41, 94, 209, 210, 215, 216
walking memorial, 211, 215, 219, 238
well-being, 38, 60, 138
West, 4, 15, 42, 58, 81, 93, 94, 104, 113
white, 159, 179, 200, 201, 227. *See also* Caucasian
World War I memorial, 193
World War II, 129–30, 132

Y
YouTube, 157

www.ingramcontent.com/pod-product-compliance
Lightning Source LLC
Chambersburg PA
CBHW051535020426
42333CB00016B/1941